EDWARD VII'S LAST LOVES

Alice Keppel & Agnes Keyser

RAYMOND LAMONT-BROWN

SUTTON PUBLISHING

First published in the United Kingdom in 1998 by
Sutton Publishing Limited · Phoenix Mill
Thrupp · Stroud · Gloucestershire · GL5 2BU

Paperback edition first published in 2001

British Library Cataloguing in Publication Data
A catalogue record for this book is available from the British Library

ISBN 0 7509 2637 6

Typeset in 11/13pt Bembo Mono.
Typesetting and origination by
Sutton Publishing Limited.
Printed in Great Britain by
J.H. Haynes & Co. Ltd, Sparkford.

CONTENTS

ACKNOWLEDGEMENTS

The author wishes to acknowledge with particular thanks the help given by Major Bruce Shand, Sonia Keppel's literary executor, in supplying answers to family queries. Further thanks go to Major Shand and to Messrs Hamish Hamilton, publishers, for permission to quote from Sonia Keppel's autobiography *Edwardian Daughter* and for the reproduction of pictures therefrom. Gratitude is also expressed to Violet Trefusis's literary executor, John Nova Phillips, for his input on queries about the Keppels.

Regarding Edmonstone family matters the author is indebted to Sir Archibald Edmonstone (great-nephew of Alice Keppel) and Lady Edmonstone and to Lady McGrigor (great-niece) for specific comments to questions on the Edmonstones of Duntreath. Thanks go to Sir Archibald too for permission to reproduce family portraits from his collection.

Each quotation is individually acknowledged as it occurs in the text, but special thanks for permission to quote are extended to the following. To Angela Lambert for line quotes from *1939: The Last Season of Peace*; to the Estate of Vita Sackville-West, via Curtis Brown, for the quotes from her *The Edwardians*; to Weidenfeld & Nicolson for a quote from Dame Rebecca West's *1900*; to Gordon Brook-Shepherd for quotes from his volume *Uncle of Europe*; to Random House UK Ltd for quotes from *The Diary of Virginia Woolf*, Vol. IV; and to Frank Magro, literary executor for Sir Osbert Sitwell, and Macmillan for quotes from *Great Morning*, Vol. III of the autobiography *Left Hand Right Hand*. The author's thanks are recorded to the Estate of Anita Leslie for the quotes from her *The Marlborough House Set*. Mention too is made of the invaluable conversation the author had with Miss Leslie on Alice Keppel and Agnes Keyser.

Advice and comments on Alice and George Keppel's life in Florence have been supplied by the following to whom the author gives very grateful thanks:

Dr Edward Chaney; the Rt Revd Bishop Eric Devenport; Gladys Elliott; the late Joan Haslip; Michael Holmes, HM Consul, Florence; Nancy Pearson; Mark Roberts, Librarian, the British Institute of Florence; the Rt Revd Bishop J.R. Satterthwaite and the Countess of Sutherland.

More grateful thanks go to those listed below for their advice, patience and help at various stages of the book's genesis: Diana, Countess of Albemarle; Mrs E. Collier, Beaconsfield Area Library; David Cliffe, Royal County of Berkshire Reference Library; Viscount Boyd; Gordon Brook-Shepherd; and Graham Snell, Brooks's.

There are no companion volumes on the life and family of Agnes Keyser, and documentation on her is sparse and scattered. Further, Commander I.K. Brooks, house governor of the King Edward VII's Hospital for Officers, noted that 'but few documents recording the history of the Hospital from 1899 to 1952 . . . survived the various moves of the Hospital'. So, in building up the story of Agnes Keyser and her work I am particularly grateful to the following. For data on the history of the hospital, Peter Evans, Marketing Officer of the hospital has provided basic material. On the family I thank Miss Anne Keyser (grand-daughter of Charles Edward Keyser); Peter Keyser (great-great-nephew of Sister Agnes); Frederick N. Hicks of the Stanmore and Harrow Historical Society; Mrs Evelyn Philips (née Keyser); Mrs Muriel Sperling; Mrs Ursula Wadham (great-niece); Mrs E.R. West; Mr E.H. Whittall. General queries have been answered by: Robert Hale, Archivist, Berkshire Record Office; Mrs Helen Pugh, Archives Assistant, British Red Cross; Jo Knell, Cabinet Office; Mr Adrian Fitzgerald; Lady de Bellaigue, Registrar, Royal Archives, Windsor Castle; Christine Hancock, general secretary, Royal College of Nursing;

ACKNOWLEDGEMENTS

Caroline Mulryne, Keeper, St John Ambulance Collections; and Mrs Jill Wellesley.

On the death of King Edward VII, 6 May 1910, a historical tragedy was enacted. In accordance with his will the king's private papers and personal letters were burned by Viscount Knollys, his private secretary and Viscount Esher, Constable of Windsor Castle. All the surviving letters from Alice Keppel to her royal lover were burned as were those of Agnes Keyser. After the death of Violet Trefusis, her literary executor, John Phillips, gave to the Royal Archives at Windsor a few letters from Edward VII to Alice and there are a few extant letters from Agnes Keyser to King George V and Queen Mary. I acknowledge the gracious permission of Her Majesty the Queen to quote material from the Royal Archives. Queen Alexandra's papers were also eradicated by her order on her death, 20 November 1925, by her woman-of-the-bedchamber, Charlotte Knollys.

Genealogical Tables: the Keysers, the Edmonstones and the Keppels

Only genealogical data of main persons relevant to the text are mentioned.

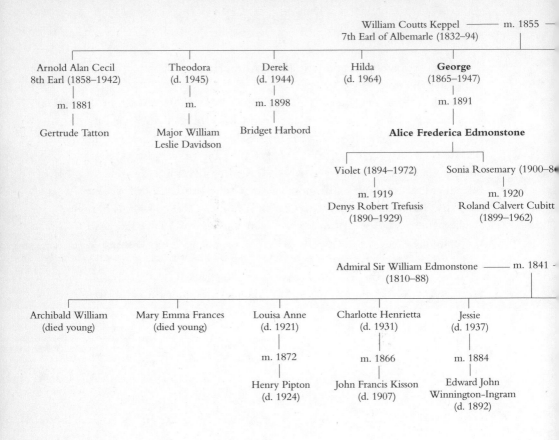

William Coutts Keppel ——— m. 1855 —
7th Earl of Albemarle (1832–94)

Arnold Alan Cecil
8th Earl (1858–1942)
|
m. 1881
|
Gertrude Tatton

Theodora
(d. 1945)
|
m.
|
Major William
Leslie Davidson

Derek
(d. 1944)
|
m. 1898
|
Bridget Harbord

Hilda
(d. 1964)

George
(1865–1947)
|
m. 1891
|
Alice Frederica Edmonstone

Violet (1894–1972)
|
m. 1919
Denys Robert Trefusis
(1890–1929)

Sonia Rosemary (1900–8●
|
m. 1920
Roland Calvert Cubitt
(1899–1962)

Admiral Sir William Edmonstone ——— m. 1841 –
(1810–88)

Archibald William
(died young)

Mary Emma Frances
(died young)

Louisa Anne
(d. 1921)
|
m. 1872
|
Henry Pipton
(d. 1924)

Charlotte Henrietta
(d. 1931)
|
m. 1866
|
John Francis Kisson
(d. 1907)

Jessie
(d. 1937)
|
m. 1884
|
Edward John
Winnington–Ingram
(d. 1892)

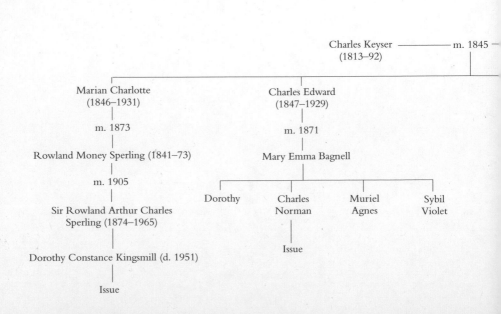

Charles Keyser ——— m. 1845 —
(1813–92)

Marian Charlotte
(1846–1931)
|
m. 1873
|
Rowland Money Sperling (1841–73)
|
m. 1905
|
Sir Rowland Arthur Charles
Sperling (1874–1965)
|
Dorothy Constance Kingsmill (d. 1951)
|
Issue

Charles Edward
(1847–1929)
|
m. 1871
|
Mary Emma Bagnell

Dorothy

Charles
Norman
|
Issue

Muriel
Agnes

Sybil
Violet

The Keppels

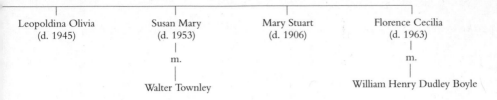

—— Sophia Mary McNab

Leopoldina Olivia	Susan Mary	Mary Stuart	Florence Cecilia
(d. 1945)	(d. 1953)	(d. 1906)	(d. 1963)
	m.		m.
	Walter Townley		William Henry Dudley Boyle

The Edmonstones

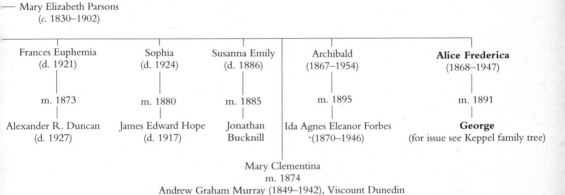

—— Mary Elizabeth Parsons
(c. 1830–1902)

Frances Euphemia	Sophia	Susanna Emily	Archibald	**Alice Frederica**
(d. 1921)	(d. 1924)	(d. 1886)	(1867–1954)	(1868–1947)
m. 1873	m. 1880	m. 1885	m. 1895	m. 1891
Alexander R. Duncan	James Edward Hope	Jonathan	Ida Agnes Eleanor Forbes	**George**
(d. 1927)	(d. 1917)	Bucknill	·(1870–1946)	(for issue see Keppel family tree)

Mary Clementina
m. 1874
Andrew Graham Murray (1849–1942), Viscount Dunedin

The Keysers

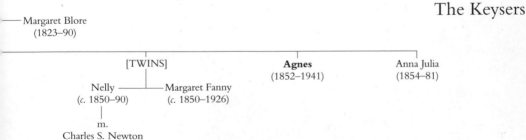

—— Margaret Blore
(1823–90)

	[TWINS]		**Agnes**	Anna Julia
Nelly ——	—— Margaret Fanny		(1852–1941)	(1854–81)
(c. 1850–90)	(c. 1850–1926)			
m.				
Charles S. Newton				

The Separate British Royal Households, 1901

A key checklist for social networkers like Alice Keppel and Agnes Keyser.

HM King Edward VII *Personal* under Gen. Rt. Hon. Sir Dighton Macnaughten Probyn; *Lord Chamberlain's Department* under Edward Hyde Villiers, the Earl of Clarendon (NB: A separate hereditary and domestic court was retained for Scotland); *Lord Steward's Department* under Sidney Herbert, the Earl of Pembroke and Montgomery; *Department of Master of the Horse* under W. Cavendish-Bentinck, Duke of Portland. (NB: The King's Court was further composed of a range of other departments.)

HM Queen Alexandra *Lord Chamberlain*: Charles John Colville, Lord Colville of Culross.

HRH The Prince of Wales *Comptroller & Treasurer*: Lt-Col. Hon. Sir William Carrington.

HRH The Princess of Wales *Private Secretary*: Major-General Sir Stanley de Astel Calvert Clarke.

The King's Sister-in-law
HR & IH Marie of Russia, Duchess Alfred of Saxe-Coburg-Gotha, Duchess of Edinburgh. *Private Secretary*: Baron Megden.

The King's only surviving Brother
HRH Prince Arthur, Duke of Connaught & Strathearn; *Comptroller & Secretary*: Col. Alfred Mordaunt Egerton.

The King's Sister-in-law
HRH Princess Louise of Prussia, Duchess of Connaught & Strathearn; *Secretary*: Andrew Wilson Murray.

The King's Sister-in-law
HRH Princess Helena of Waldeck-Pyrmont, Duchess of Albany; *Comptroller*: Sir Robert Hawthorn Collins.

The King's Brother-in-law
HRH Prince Christian of Schelswig-Holstein; *Joint Comptroller & Treasurer*: Maj. James Euan Baillie Morton; Col. Hon. Charles George Cornwallis Eliot.

The King's Sister
HRH Princess Louise, Duchess of Argyll. *Equerry & Secretary*: Maj. N. Cuthbertson.

The King's Sister
HRH Princess Beatrice, Princess Henry of Battenberg; *Comptroller & Treasurer*: Col. Lord William Cecil.

The King's youngest daughter
HRH Princess Charles of Denmark, Princess Maud; *Comptroller & Private Secretary*: Col. Henry Knollys.

INTRODUCTION
TWO PERFECT LOVES

Agnes Keyser had no time for women. She liked men, sick men, wounded men, impecunious men, men she could dominate and scold and pamper.

> Anita Leslie (1914–87), *The Marlborough House Set* (1972)

One of [Alice Keppel's] secrets of success was that she could be amusing without malice; she never repeated a cruel witticism.

> Sir Harold Nicolson (1886–1968) in conversation

The light breeze gusting along London's North Audley Street had blown away the early morning fog as friends, acquaintances and admirers of Alice, the Hon. Mrs George Keppel chatted, strode away, or caught taxis from the steps of St Mark's Church. All of those who had listened to the memorial service conducted by the Revd K.H. Thorneycroft on that Wednesday, 1 October 1947, could remember well King Edward VII and Alice whom he had loved for the last twelve years of his life alongside his affectionate relationship with Agnes Keyser.[1]

Alice's death notice in *The Times* for 13 September of that year had stirred memories of the long-gone Edwardian Society in which Alice and Agnes had been significant players. For many their memory brought light and colour into Clement Attlee's socialist Britain on that chilly early afternoon. The anonymous obituarist in

The Times had noted that with the death of Alice Keppel an era had finally come to an end. She was hailed as one of the last great hostesses of her generation who efficiently worked within the rules of Society. It was emphasised, too, that her intimate association with the eminent men of her day had given her an unchallenged understanding and knowledge of the behind-the-scenes aspects of great political and international affairs. Sometimes her wit and diplomacy smoothed situations which would have caused her royal lover to explode with the irascibility for which he was famous. Another hand had added more in *The Times* for 20 September. Describing her as being larger than life, and generous to all she met, the obituarist averred she was classless in her dealings with all ranks.[2] The tone underlined what HSH Daisy, Princess of Pless, née Cornwallis-West had said: 'What spirit, wit and resilience the woman has.'[3]

Sir Osbert Sitwell's obituary of Alice Keppel in *The Times* succinctly honoured the woman born into the secure, orderly, structured pre-1914 Society that all attending her memorial service could recall. The Sitwells had enjoyed a close friendship with Alice and her husband George for many years and Osbert Sitwell had written with intimate sincerity saying that she had never been old in spirit, seeking out the young in company and enveloping them with good nature to make them feel at ease. He also dwelt on the deep timbre of her voice and her bold direct look that gave the person she was talking to a feeling of full attention. Wherever she went, said Sitwell, she created a 'special beauty'.

For Osbert Sitwell, and many of his contemporaries, Alice Keppel was the *grande dame* of the Edwardian era. Sitwell was to say more about his socialising with the Keppels in his autobiography:

Another house at which I was a frequent visitor during these and ensuing years was Mrs George Keppel's [16] Grosvenor Street, surely one of the most remarkable houses in London. Its high façade, dignified and unpretentious as only that of a London Georgian mansion can be, very effectively disguised its immense size. Within existed an unusual air of spaciousness and light, an atmosphere of luxury, for Mrs Keppel possessed an instinct for splendour, and not only were the rooms beautiful, with their grey walls, red lacquer cabinets, English eighteenth-century portraits of people in red coats, huge porcelain pagodas, and thick magnificent carpets, but the hostess conducted the running of her house as a work of art in itself. I liked greatly to listen to her talking; if it were possible to lure her away from the bridge-table, she would remove from her mouth for a moment the cigarette which she would be smoking with an air of determination, through a long holder, and turn upon the person to whom she was speaking her large, humorous, kindly, peculiarly discerning eyes. Her conversation was lit by humour, insight and the utmost good-nature: a rare and valuable attribute in one who had never had – or, at any rate, never felt – much patience with fools. Moreover, a vein of fantasy, a power of enchantment would often lift what she was saying, and served to emphasise the exactness of most of her opinions, and her frankness. Her talk had about it a boldness, an absence of all pettiness, that helped to make her a memorable figure in the fashionable world.[4]

Discreet, loyal, humorous, gregarious, hospitable: all are epithets that have been applied to Alice Keppel. Although they were all true in varying relevant circumstances, they have been repeated to the point of caricature, and their middle-class sugariness belies her real role in Edwardian royal Society. Her discretion for instance was only a matter of degree. Before she was 'widowed' as a royal mistress on the death of King Edward VII, Alice Keppel was nothing less than a high-profile character; she was the monarch's *maîtresse en titre* and everyone knew it; even crowds that gathered to see the king attend London's theatreland shouted out as he came and went: 'Where's Alice?' She was even to be referred to in the *Survey of London* series as 'confidante of King Edward VII'.

Her discretion seemed to be lacking, too, when it came to visits to the homes of the great and good with the king; there she was always to be found standing or sitting near her lover in the official photographs for the picture papers of the day. And her 'pushy presence', some were to say, was such a constant irritation to Queen Alexandra that it drove her to eschew her husband's company.

Yet Alice Keppel was also a member of what Gordon Brook-Shepherd, Diplomatic Correspondent and Assistant Editor of the *Sunday Telegraph* and author of the seminal work on Edward VII, *Uncle of Europe* (1975), called 'the most extraordinary and exalted quartet to be found anywhere in Edwardian Europe', alongside the king himself, Queen Alexandra and the Portuguese Minister in London, Luis, Marquis de Soveral.[5]

Together the quartet shared a *confiance* never known before in royal circles and an influence that was far-reaching. The role of mistress to King Edward VII held by Alice for almost twelve years was to be virtually unique in the history of royal adultery. Because of it Alice Keppel was to be the most sought-out woman in political, diplomatic and Civil Service circles and she was consulted by men and women at all levels.

From her place in Society, Alice Keppel had a greater public profile than Agnes Keyser, and by temperament and character became the most ideal of all Edward VII's mistresses as friend, courtier and intimate. The king's style of ruling was to extend the way that he had dominated Society from his homes at Sandringham and Marlborough House. He did so through a fluctuating and all-knowing caucus of friends and acquaintances. His inner corps of friends formed his link with key members of Society and Alice Keppel gradually became chief of the 'Committee of Seven', comprising the Marquis de Soveral, Sir Ernest Cassel, Sir William Esher, Admiral Lord Fisher, Lord Hardinge and Sir Francis Knollys, who advised and informed the king. Agnes Keyser, too, was a conduit of gossip.

Alice Keppel had a different role from Edward VII's mistresses in other ways too. She offered the king a rare cocktail of sexual passion, amelioration of ire and relaxation under stress. She excited him physically – important in a man whose appetite for life's good things drove him towards impotency – she helped smooth over social irritations and she eased mental tensions. She cherished him as a wife would, she loved him for himself as well as his crown and she supported him with devotion and prudence.

Not everyone had thought highly of Alice Keppel. Over the years she was to attract caustic comments from those like Reginald Baliol Brett, 2nd Viscount Esher (1852–1930), royal archivist and intimate of every Prime Minister from Rosebery to Baldwin, who believed that she deliberately lied in Society about certain royal happenings to enhance her own reputation.[6] Virginia Woolf had some particularly acid things to say in her diary about Alice. Under the date Thursday 10 March 1932, she wrote:

> I had lunched with Raymond [Mortimer, critic] to meet Mrs Keppel; a swarthy thick set raddled direct – 'My dear', she calls one – old grasper: whose fists had been in the moneybags these 50 years: And she has a flat in the Ritz; old furniture; &c. I like her on the surface of the old courtezan: who has lost all bloom; & acquired a kind of cordiality, humour, directness instead. No sensibilities as far as I could see; no snobberies, immense superficial knowledge, & going to Berlin to hear Hitler speak. Shabby under dress: magnificent furs, great pearls: a Rolls Royce waiting.[7]

Alice Keppel shamelessly milked her royal relationship. As Charles Robert Wynn-Carrington, 3rd Baron Warrington and Marquess of Lincolnshire, was to say in conversation: she enjoyed being 'much toadied by everyone'. Alice Keppel's place as royal mistress was something that few cared to mention within royal hearing. The staid George V was always acutely embarrassed by the memory of his father's philandering, and Queen Mary, his wife May, was not the stuff of which mistresses are made. Queen Mary, to whom the physical, romantic side of marriage was uncomfortable, had empathy with her mother-in-law Queen Alexandra who had reluctantly publicly accepted Alice Keppel – in a long line of such mistresses – as a sharer of her husband's bed. It had saved her the bother of having him in hers.

King George V, as Duke of York, had always dreaded Alice Keppel's arrival on the scene when his mother Queen Alexandra was due. During the week of Cowes Regatta in 1902, Princess May, Duchess of York (who did not join the party aboard the royal yacht *Britannia* because she was a poor sailor), wrote to her husband asking how things were in the racing circle. Was there a dreadful atmosphere; was he having problems? The duke replied that peace had reigned, there had been no royal rumblings of discontent or rows, but he added: 'Alas, Mrs K. arrives tomorrow and stops here in a yacht, I am afraid that peace and quiet will not remain.' Princess May sympathised in her next: 'What a pity Mrs G. K. is again to the fore! How annoyed Mama will be!'[8]

HRH Princess Alice, Countess of Athlone (1883–1980), the last survivor of Queen Victoria's thirty-seven grandchildren, was one of the few members of the royal family ever to acknowledge Alice Keppel in print, although she seems, erroneously, to give too rosy a picture of Queen Alexandra's attitude to Alice. The princess recollected in old age:

> Uncle Bertie used to invite us [her widowed mother, Princess Helena of Waldeck-Pyrmont, Duchess of Albany, and her brother Charles Edward, Duke of Saxe-Coburg-Gotha] to some shooting parties he used to give at Sandringham. Alice Keppel, whom I found to be a most charming and tactful woman, was usually present . . . Our conversation inevitably turned to Uncle Bertie, and I told her that, much as I loved him, I found it difficult when sitting next to him at table not to be distracted by his habit of fiddling with his cutlery and almost impossible to keep up a consecutive conversation with him. 'Don't worry about that', she replied, 'we all experience that trouble. He likes to join in general conversation interjecting remarks at intervals,

but he prefers to listen to others than talk himself. Often he starts a discussion, but as soon as he can get others involved in it he is content to listen and make occasional comments.'

Princess Alice continued:

Uncle Bertie was deeply attached to Alice, who talked easily and was a vivacious personality. She never flaunted herself or took advantage of her position as the king's favourite. Aunt Alix [Queen Alexandra] was also very fond of her and encouraged her friendship with Uncle Bertie. Aunt Alix was renowned for her beauty, very lovely, with a gracious presence and a disposition which endeared her to the public who worshipped her. But being stone deaf and not mentally bright, she was not much of a companion for an intelligent man like Uncle Bertie . . . Of course, there was a lot of gossip and public disapproval of their relationship and unnecessary sympathy for Aunt Alix, who did not need it, as she welcomed the arrangement.[9]

It should be realised that Princess Alice's opinion was entirely her own. Courtiers like the 2nd Viscount Esher recorded that the queen could not stand Alice, but condoned the affair, despite several rows with her husband over the relationship, because Alice generally helped keep him genial.

Osbert Sitwell also attested that not all royalty shunned Keppel society. He remarked on the fact that Alice's younger daughter Sonia (Mrs Roland Cubitt) held lunch parties at her home which the Duke and Duchess of York (later King George VI and Queen Elizabeth) attended.[10] Again at the 'coming-out' dance for Sonia's daughter Rosalind Maud Cubitt, on 6 July 1939 at Holland House, London, property of family friend the 6th Earl of Ilchester, King George VI and Queen Elizabeth made an appearance. In conversation with the author Angela Lambert, a guest that day, Mrs John Miller (née Christian Grant) mentioned that people had gossiped about how forbearing the king was in attending a dance 'given by the daughter of his grandfather's mistress': 'It was rather special,' went on Mrs Miller, 'because there was that slight aura of naughtiness about it . . . We all thought it rather broad-minded and nice of them to accept the situation, but it did make it a bit conspiratorial and glamorous.'[11] There were others there that day who averred into their gin and tonics that King George was being *exceptionally* broad-minded. If rumours were correct that Sonia Keppel was the daughter of Edward VII, she was thus half-sister to George VI's father and her children Henry, Jeremy and Rosalind were his first cousins.

The memory of Alice Keppel has been long in Society and her name can still touch a raw nerve. In 1985 the Prince and Princess of Wales visited Florence and stayed at La Pietra, the home of Sir Harold Acton who had a love-hate relationship for years with Alice's elder daughter Violet.

Diana, Princess of Wales (1961–97) was particularly interested in hearing details of the great-grandparents of her rival in the Prince of Wales's affections, Camilla Parker-Bowles, wrote Nigel Dempster and Peter Evans in their *Behind Palace Doors* (1993). Sir Harold obliged, dwelling on a strong dislike of Camilla's great-aunt. He recounted in florid detail her lesbian affair with Vita Sackville-West and her eccentric 'ungentlemanly' behaviour in Florentine society. Violet, said Sir Harold with distaste, liked to be called 'Highness' in her erroneous belief that she was Edward VII's daughter. 'What a dreadful family they seem to have been,' Diana remarked.

In her best-selling novel *The Edwardians* (1930), Vita Sackville-West describes Alice Keppel's personality in the guise of her fictional character Mrs Romola Cheyne:

Mrs Cheyne was a woman of strong personality and vigorous courage . . . [she] had a real spaciousness in her nature; a woman who erred and aspired with a certain magnificence. She brought to everything the quality of the superlative. When she was worldly, it was on the grand scale. When she was mercenary, she challenged the richest fortunes. When she loved, it was in the highest quarters. When she admitted ambition, it was for the highest power. When she suffered, it would be on the plane of tragedy. Romola Cheyne, for all her hardness, all her materialism, was no mean soul.

She had, however, one weakness: she could not allow anyone to be better informed than herself. Whether it was politics, finance, or merely the affairs of her friends, the last word, the eventual bombshell of information, must proceed from her and no other. On the whole she preferred her information to be good; and although she was quite prepared to invent what she could not ascertain, she would first make an assault on the main and most reliable source of knowledge.[12]

Soon after the novel was published Marion Purves, whose family had known Alice from her youth, wrote:

On the fly-leaf of *The Edwardians* Vita Sackville-West had written, 'No character in this book is wholly fictitious', and I reflected how Vita had summed up for us all what we thought of Freddie [the diminutive by which Alice was known to her early childhood friends from her middle name of Frederica]; Mrs Cheyne was Freddie to a tee. When Margot Asquith [the second wife of Liberal Prime Minister Herbert Henry Asquith, 1st Earl of Oxford and Asquith] said that Freddie would be nicknamed as a 'character of history', it was not until later that I realised that she meant our history. I thought then what a wonderful book Freddie's life would have made, for then we would have had a glimpse behind palace doors where enquiries were hardly welcome. I knew though that it was not to be; Freddie was naturally a reticent person on certain subjects and was certainly not an intellectual with a book in her. All of us who remembered Marlborough House and Buckingham Palace in 'good old Teddy's day' knew that silence about what went on there was the price one paid for a repeat invitation. But maybe one day Freddie's place as the king's friend will be properly recorded.[13]

Everyone in Society knew Alice Keppel. She had that rare distinction of being known to high and low by a single name. You rarely had to explain which woman you meant when you referred to 'Alice'. Agnes Keyser was also known by a sobriquet. When she began her hospital charity work she had asked her royal admirer what she should call herself. 'Sister Agnes,' Edward had replied. And so she was known throughout Society, although she had had no formal medical training.

Yet no one outside Alice Keppel's family circle really knew much about her background. She kept her royal private life a closed book; people could wonder at her rapid rise to predominance as a royal mistress, but no one before or since could emulate her skill and talent as the perfect royal concubine who shaped adultery into a social accomplishment. In her lifetime Alice encountered few who would publicly speak a word against her; she had a kind of hypnotic charm and confidence that could defuse antagonism towards her.

When Agnes Keyser died on 11 May 1941, long-forgotten memories of her royal relationship with King Edward VII were brought to the recollection of old friends who read her obituary in *The Times*.[14] Agnes was buried in the Keyser vault in the churchyard of St John the Evangelist at Great Stanmore, Middlesex, with her parents and siblings. The service was conducted by the Rt Revd Eric Knightly Chetwode Hamilton, Bishop Suffragan of Shrewsbury, a Keyser friend who had married into the Cassel family of financiers; he was assisted by the chaplain of Agnes's foundation of the King Edward VII's Hospital for Officers, the Revd R.S. Swann-Mason. Queen Mary sent her equerry Maj. the Hon. John Spencer Coke.

Reflecting 'her extreme public dislike of publicity',[15] the 'Appreciation' of Agnes Keyser in *The Times* was very different from the fulsome praise of Alice Keppel in being succinct and unrevealing. Written by a pre-1914 junior subaltern, identified by the initials C.J.W., the appreciation mentions only, in a plethora of words, her kind good humour and absorption when dealing with patients and staff at the hospital she had founded with King Edward

VII's enthusiastic support. Alice had been publicly sociable, Agnes remained the self-effacing administrator.

Yet Agnes rivalled Alice for the Prince's affections, and there was a certain gritting of teeth on Alice's part when Agnes joined her and the Prince of Wales at the bridge table. When court life bored him Edward would go for a quiet drive to Agnes's home at 17 Grosvenor Crescent to dine on Irish stew and rice pudding, the fare of the nursery, which she prescribed to wean him off the rich food in which he so delighted. On Monday 2 May 1910, on his return to London from Sandringham, Edward, his chest badly inflamed and racked by a severe cough, eschewed his bed and went to Agnes's house to seek comfort, much to Alice's annoyance. It was to be his last dalliance for he died four days later.

Between Agnes and Edward a strong romantic relationship sprang up as quickly as his affections had been captured by Alice. Agnes Keyser was a sympathetic, forceful, selfless, wise, practical and severe person whose main role in Edward's later life was to keep the prematurely aged, bronchial and grossly overweight monarch alive as long as possible. Just as he loved Alice's attention, Edward thrived on Agnes's role as nanny, mother, confidante with the unstated sexual chemistry as an added frisson.

In contrast to Alice, Agnes Keyser, whom the Prince of Wales met in the same year as Alice Keppel, did not make herself rich at Edward's expense or through his influence; unlike her, she was not a social gad-about, and cared naught for Society. Agnes exploited Edward and his circle only to promote her and her sister's hospital foundation. And in immediate royal circles Agnes was not to encounter the court antagonism engendered by Alice. When Edward VII died the new king George V became patron of her hospital and both he and Queen Mary were to be her firm friends.

Her relationship with Edward as Prince of Wales and king never caused more than a flickering of eyebrows at Buckingham Palace. Yet writers like Anita Leslie, great-niece of Lady Randolph Churchill who sat with Alice Keppel at Edward VII's coronation (although then as Mrs George Cornwallis-West), averred that

Edward VII's 'affairs' with Alice and Agnes were of equal merit. She and others looked upon Alice as *la maîtresse du roi*, in the European sense of a mistress – a physical lover, who also dispensed favours to others from her position in Society – whereas the tiny, blonde Agnes Keyser was an *amitié amoureuse* – a loving friend with whom sex might occur as a flavouring. Both gave Edward a distinct 'home' to satisfy his needs.

Today for the researcher of Alice Keppel's and Agnes Keyser's lives, large deserts have to be crossed before an oasis of material is discovered. Details of both prove to be the most elusive of those for all Edward VII's loves. There are but the briefest mentions and chapters in royal biographies and, unlike other royal mistresses, such as Mrs Edward 'Lillie' Langtry, and Frances 'Daisy' Brooke, Countess of Warwick, neither Alice nor Agnes – for whom it would have been an anathema – wrote her memoirs.

Around the time of their marriage, George Keppel began a book of photographs for his sister-in-law Gertie Keppel; it is known as the 'Quidenham Park Book' and is in the archives of the Norfolk Record Office, Norwich. Yet its pages are strangely silent on royal visits to Quidenham and the presence of Alice. Violet Keppel, their daughter, also averred that her father was writing memoirs; if he did, they have never been published.

In the Edwardian royal circle Alice Keppel and Agnes Keyser lived parallel lives that were of enormous importance to Britain's royal social history. One woman offered the king a deeply felt romantic love, physical satisfaction and abiding loyalty. The other supplemented this role with an affection and the motherly fussing he had craved for all his days. They were the two perfect loves of Edward's later life, and theirs is a story waiting to be told.

CHAPTER 1

BORN A KEYSER AND BORN AN EDMONSTONE

On 27 July 1852 Margaret Keyser (1823–90), younger daughter of Edward Blore, architect, gave birth to her fifth child and fourth daughter at the Keyser family home of Warren House, Wood Lane, Great Stanmore, Middlesex. As she and her husband Charles Keyser (1813–92) had not decided on a name for the child, the infant was registered by the mother before Registrar Alfred Green just as a 'girl' on 27 August. On 9 September the baby was christened Elizabeth Agnes at St John the Evangelist Church, Great Stanmore.

The Keysers' eldest child was Marian Charlotte (1846–1931), who married Rowland Money Sperling (1841–73) in 1873. In due time their son Sir Rowland Arthur Charles Sperling (1874–1965) was to enter the Foreign Office wherein his Aunt Agnes attempted to pull strings with King George V to obtain him a better post. Next came Charles Edward born on 10 September 1847 at the Keyser London town-house of 1 Chester Place; he was educated at Eton from 1856 and Trinity College, Cambridge, during 1866–70. In 1871 he married Mary Emma Bagnall and lived at the family home of Warren House and Merry Hill House, Bushey, as well as his palatial mansion at Aldermaston where he died in 1929. They were to have four children, an heir Charles Norman, and daughters Dorothy, Muriel Agnes and Sybil Violet. Agnes Keyser's siblings were completed with twins Margaret Fanny (d. 1926) and Nelly (d. 1890), born around 1850 – Nelly was to marry Charles Newton; and, lastly, Anna Julia (1854–81).

Family traditions aver that the original Keyser representative had come to Britain to continue as banker to Prince William of Orange, and was one of the prince's Dutch entourage. In 1689 William and his wife Mary Stuart, eldest child of King James II and VII, were jointly to accept the throne of Great Britain and Ireland, when her father was deposed. Charles Keyser of Warren House carried on the financial traditions and made a fortune on the London Stock Exchange and through wise ventures that were backed by his friend and banker Sir John Lubbock, MP, 1st Baron Avebury, of Robert Lubbock & Co.[1] A partner in the firm of Ricardo & Keyser, Charles Keyser was the great-nephew of David Ricardo (1772–1823), one of the handful of Jews who had early on embraced Christianity through the Anglican Church to further a career in politics. Ricardo, the son of a Dutch Jew, also made a fortune on the London Stock Exchange and, inspired by the Scots economist and philosopher Adam Smith's *Wealth of Nations*, took up the study of the scientific management of economics. In time he became a leading authority on the subject and in 1817 published his own famous *Principles of Political Economy and Taxation*. Ricardo had retired from business to settle at Gatcombe House, Gloucestershire in 1814 and from 1819 to 1823 he was an independent-minded Radical Whig MP for the Irish rotten borough of Portarlington, Co. Laois, having turned Christian when he married his Quaker wife Pricilla Anne Wilkinson.

Agnes Keyser and her siblings were brought up in great prosperity and inherited the independence of mind that had engendered the family wealth. Her affluence, though, was to make Agnes a crashing snob.

During the sixteen years that separated the births of his last two romantic flings, Agnes Keyser and Alice Keppel, HRH Prince Albert Edward, Prince of Wales and Duke of Cornwall, born at Buckingham Palace on 9 November 1841, struggled into his teenage years against the restrictive and badly contrived plans his parents devised for his education and upbringing. By 1852 he developed as a disobedient, wilful and recalcitrant youth, undermined by the fact that he was an unwanted child. Queen

Victoria had resented greatly her second pregnancy coming so soon after the birth on 21 November 1840 of Victoria Adelaide, the Princess Royal. As a teenager the Prince of Wales showed more interest in clothes than books, pleasure than duty, and at the age of sixteen developed a taste for female company and intimacy that would be a lifetime's occupation.

In August 1855, Queen Victoria and Prince Albert, along with the Princess Royal and the Prince of Wales, made an official visit to Emperor Napoleon III and his Empress Eugénie at Paris. It was to be a sexually heady experience for the pubescent Prince of Wales as writer Philippe Jullian noted:

> In the Tuileries [residence of the French sovereigns in the centre of Paris, burned by revolutionaries during the Commune de Paris, 1871] he breathed for the first time the *odore di femina* whose trail he was to follow for the rest of his life. The scented alluring women not only kissed him (was he not still a child?) but also curtsied to him, and as they bent forward, their decolletage revealed delights that were veiled at Windsor.[2]

Two years later the Prince of Wales was fumbling with and kissing publicly for the first time a pretty young girl at Königswinter on the Rhine.[3] It was to be a memory never forgotten in the recall of his young companions who were to introduce him to a whole range of pretty young women. There was a certain frisson in pimping for the Prince of Wales and some of his lifelong friends took great pleasure in doing it. There was Harry Tyrwhitt-Wilson, his equerry, Charles Lindley Wood, later 2nd Viscount Halifax, in those earlier days, and George Henry Cadogan, later 5th Earl of Cadogan, Frederick Arthur Stanley, later 16th Earl of Derby and William Henry Gladstone, eldest son of Liberal Prime Minister William Ewart Gladstone.

The Prince of Wales's earliest sexual encounter on record occurred in 1861 when he was with the 2nd Battalion of the Grenadier Guards at The Curragh military camp some twenty miles from Dublin on a ten-week infantry training course. It seems that on the machinations of his brother officers, led by future Marlborough House Set regular Charles Robert Wynn-Carrington, a young, promiscuous – and, alas, loquaciously indiscreet – Burlington Arcade tart turned 'actress' called Nellie Clifden was introduced to the Prince of Wales's bed; thereafter the heir to the throne preferred to have a female bedmate rather than sleep alone.[4] This led to an unending series of court scandals, many never reported.

The Prince of Wales married, at St George's Chapel, Windsor, on 10 March 1863, his fourth cousin Princess Alexandra Caroline Marie Charlotte Louise Julie, daughter of Prince Christian of Schleswig-Holstein-Sonderburg-Glucksburg, heir to the Danish throne, and his wife Princess Louise of Hesse-Cassel. Handicapped by the hereditary deafness otosclerosis, the nineteen-year-old, deep-blue-eyed, brown-haired and peachlike-complexioned Alexandra was a beautiful, superficial and self-centred aristocrat who probably never relinquished the psychological umbilical cord which tied her to her childhood home of the Yellow Palace, Amaliengade, Copenhagen. Worse than that for lusty Edward, his bride was frigid, but deeply affectionate in a sickly way to her children and favourites. Soon after their marriage Edward became bored with his wife.

The Prince of Wales bored, or at a loose end, was a powerful sexual cocktail. Thus when she was pregnant for the third time, Alexandra was unable to accompany Edward to St Petersburg for the nuptials of her sister Dagmar to the Czarevich, later to be Czar Alexander III, at the Winter Palace, on 9 November 1866. Reports soon came to the British court that he was paying too much attention to the Russian beauties.[5] Adultery at home and abroad was to be the pattern for the rest of his life.

Alexandra's 'charm and manner', and 'natural tact and dignity', so remarked on by those who met her, did not make up for her woefully neglected education which rendered her virtually illiterate. Academic matters remained as naught to her and although

Edward was by no means an intellectual he enjoyed the company of adroit people, particularly clever women who could cure his boredom, especially with sexual satisfaction as a bonus. So in time both Agnes Keyser and Alice Keppel were to be his perfect women in an amalgam of these necessities.

Many in Victoria's court considered that Edward and Alexandra were never in love in a deeply passionate long-term way. One such, who believed that they were never in love at all, was the Keeper of the Privy Purse, Sir Charles Beaumont Phipps. He wrote to Queen Victoria from Brussels on the day of the couple's engagement, 9 September 1862 at Laeken Castle, that it was 'absurd to suppose that a real feeling of *love* could as yet exist for a person whom His Royal Highness has only seen for a few hours'.[6] In her heart the queen had to agree, but gave her permission for the marriage.

Although Edward and Alexandra had six children it is likely that all marital sexual relations ceased after the birth of the little-mentioned sixth Wales child in 1871, Alexander John Charles Albert, who lived only twenty-four hours. Consequently, Edward, who had inherited the strong sex drive of his Hanoverian forebears, sought satisfaction in the arms of society beauties, and a host of *demi-mondaines*.

The future lover of Alice Frederica Keppel, née Edmonstone, had been Prince of Wales for twenty-eight years, and married for six, when she was born on 29 April 1868. The Princess of Wales gave birth to her fourth child, the Princess Victoria – 'Toria' (d. 1935) – a few months after Alice's birth. Alice's parents, the 58-year-old Commander William Edmonstone, RN and his wife Mary Elizabeth, née Parsons, younger than himself by almost two decades, had not yet succeeded to the family baronetcy. So Alice was not born at the Scottish ancestral home, but at Henry VIII's royal dockyard Woolwich, then a pleasant Kent town on the River Thames, where her father had been Superintendent since 1866. The commander had been so taken up with naval business in the soon-to-be-closed Royal Navy establishment that he did not register his last child until 16 May.

When Alice Edmonstone was seven in 1875, a genealogical account of her family was published by her uncle Sir Archibald Edmonstone, 3rd baronet (1795–1871).[7] His wife, Aunt Emma, née Wilbrahame (1804–91), was to add to the account verbally for family entertainment; she remained a source of ancestral gossip for Alice until her death the year Alice married. From these sources Alice knew her family tree and the lifestyle of her Scottish ancestors whose actions were shaped by the 'happy Highland home', established in 1852 at Balmoral by Queen Victoria.

By the time of Alice's birth Queen Victoria had established her annual pattern of visits to Scotland. From April to June and from September to November – maybe with a trip to Europe in between – the queen was in residence at Balmoral. Around her she had two Scottish courts, one ceremonial and hereditary, the other practical. Her ceremonial court was led by the Hay family, the Earls of Errol, as hereditary Lord High Constables of Scotland, and the Campbells, Dukes of Argyll, as hereditary Masters of the Household. In due time the queen's son-in-law John Campbell, Marquis of Lorne (1845–1914), would assume the role when he became 9th Duke of Argyll; Campbell married Princess Louise (1848–1939) when Alice Edmonstone was three. The queen's personal household was run by the Lord Chamberlain as Commissioner at Balmoral and the estate factor.

During Alice's first year at the Superintendent's lodging at Woolwich, her prospective lover had been busy. The Prince of Wales visited Ireland, Egypt and Palestine, and laid the foundations of new buidings at the University of Glasgow. It had been a sweltering year with the extremes of heat claiming 20,000 deaths, and come August the Waleses were ready for their two-month break at Abergeldie Castle, a neighbouring property to Balmoral. The Edmonstones had been involved in royal visits to Scotland since Victoria's first trip in 1842. As landowners, deputy lieutenants and leaders of Society they were expected to 'make an attendance' at court when needed.

The Scotland Alice was to know in childhood, and the class into which she was born, had already begun to change. When Queen Victoria came to the throne in 1837 there were still two Scotlands: the Lowlands and the Highlands. By 1868 it was beginning to divide East–West, largely because of the Hibernisation of Glasgow. Scotland's industries were fast coming under the control of the English capitalism in which the Keysers were rooted; and those of the aristocracy entering the professions looked to London for advancement.

The Society into which Agnes Keyser and Alice Edmonstone were born was obsessed with class; it was a cult more zealous than any religion. Everyone belonged to the upper, middle, or working class; and even the latter was divided into the deserving 'hard-working, church-going' and the undeserving (feckless) poor. The upper and middle classes employed one in ten of Britain's populace as domestic servants, so both Agnes and Alice had their own servants from birth.

To those who were Agnes Keyser's and Alice Edmonstone's social companions, rank and riches were as divine rights. Poverty, with its indignity and squalor, was expected to be borne with resignation and Christian fortitude. Thus the nobility and upper classes of Victoria's Scotland lived, like their Anglo-Saxon compeers, in feudal splendour. Provided one had access to capital a fortune could be made without much anguish. The year Alice was born, income tax – which Liberal Prime Minister W.E. Gladstone promised to abolish – was 5d in the pound sterling on incomes above £150. As Agnes and Alice entered womanhood, those who had made money in mines and mills squeezed into the upper crust, albeit to be tolerated, patronised and snubbed.

The Edmonstones belonged to the part of Scottish society that functioned on a national rather than a local level, and conformed with the seasonal migrations of Anglo-Saxon rather than Scottish life. Like most of the upper-class Scots, the Edmonstones were educated at English schools and universities. Thus Alice's childhood followed the pattern of well-off English girls like Agnes Keyser.

Alice's uncle, the 3rd baronet, had identified the Edmonstones as having originated in the parish of Newton, some four miles east of Edinburgh, wherein Henricus de Edmoundiston had his principal residence in the reign of King Alexander III of Scots, 1249–86. He further averred that the family were of Saxon stock, arriving in Scotland when Edgar the Atheling, grandson of Edmund Ironside, fled to Dunfermline with his sister Margaret from the court of William the Conqueror. Margaret was to become spouse to King Malcolm Canmore, around 1069, and the Edmonstones believed that their royal service dated from the eleventh-century court of Canmore. The estate of Newton was to remain in the family until its sale in 1626.

The Duntreath Edmonstones sprang from a branch of the family which had property at Culloden, Inverness. The barony of Duntreath, in the parish of Strathblane, Stirlingshire, once the portion of the Earls of Lennox, was acquired by the Edmondstones around 1434 when James I gave it to his brother-in-law William Edmonstone of Culloden who had been espoused as her fourth husband by the Princess Mary Stewart, Countess of Angus, second daughter of Robert III; her bones still rest beneath the floorboards of the Edmonstones' tutelary church at Strathblane.[8] Thus did the Edmonstones boast royal Stewart blood in the salons of polite Victorian and Edwardian society, and the attractiveness and charm of their most famous family member, Alice, was to supply sexual and emotional balm that kept phlegmatic the Hanoverian-Saxe-Coburg-Gotha successor of the Stewarts, King Edward VII.

King James II of Scots had erected Duntreath into a barony in 1452 and, on 20 May 1774, the lawyer Archibald Edmonstone of Duntreath (1717–1807), MP for Dumbartonshire, thence Ayr, had been created a hereditary baronet by George III.[9] Their motto was to be gazetted as *Virtus auget Honorem* ('Virtue increases Honour'), which Alice neatly parodied in her lifetime. Alice's father, Sir William Edmonstone, succeeded his half-brother to the baronetcy in 1871 to become the 4th Baronet.

Born 29 January 1810 at Hampton, Middlesex, Alice's father was the son of Sir Charles Edmonstone (1764–1821), MP for

Dumbartonshire and Stirlingshire, and his second wife Louisa Beaumont Hotham (1778–1832), daughter of the 2nd Baron Hotham of South Dalton, whom he had married in 1804. Edmonstone entered the Royal Navy on 5 September 1822, was posted by October 1823 to Captain Samuel John Brooke Pechell's frigate *Sybille* and saw service in the Mediterranean. For a while young Edmonstone served aboard Captain Timothy Curtis's *Medina* but returned to the *Sybille* and was severely wounded in the arm and face – wherein he lost part of his lower jaw – while directing the boats in a fierce action with pirates off the island of Candia (Crete) in June 1826.

In 1827 Edmonstone joined the sloop *Columbine* bound for India, and in 1828 the elderly *Undaunted* under captains William Symonds and Augustus Clifford, and accompanied Governor-General Lord William Cavendish-Bentinck to India; the governor general's kinswoman Venetia, Mrs Arthur James, was to become, like Alice and Agnes, a favourite of Edward VII. In 1829 Edmonstone was promoted lieutenant and was transferred to Captain the Hon. William Waldegrave's vessel *Seringapatam*, for a trip to South America. Service followed during 1832–6 aboard the *Belvidere*, the *Alfred*, and the newly built *Vanguard* on the Mediterranean station and in 1838 he joined the *Impregnable*, flagship of Admiral Sir Graham Moore. The next year Edmonstone was given his own command of the brig-sloop *Weazel*. By 1841 he had become commander and, paying off *Weazel* in 1842, he was appointed Inspecting Commander of the Coast Guard, 1844–9, with an area from the West Country to Ireland.

In 1852 Edmonstone was nominated second captain of the *St George*, guardship in ordinary at Devonport, and was promoted full captain in 1853. By 1860 he was appointed to the *Dauntless*, thence the *Arrogant* to serve on the West Coast of Africa station. Edmonstone also saw service during 1861–2 against the kings of Porto Novo and Badibu. He was awarded a CB in 1863, the year he took command of the *Indus*, now serving as HQ of reserve ships, Devonport; he was promoted rear-admiral in 1869, and proceeded to be vice-admiral on the retired list in 1876 and admiral in 1880. He served as a naval ADC to Queen Victoria during 1865–9.[10]

Edmonstones had held seats in Parliament since the sixteenth century, and when Alice was six years old in 1874, Sir William was elected Conservative MP for Stirlingshire. Like the Keysers the Edmonstones were staunch Tories and it was a time when Conservatism had a firm footing in Scotland, following their enfranchising of all male householders who paid burgh rates, and of £5 and £14 tenants in 1868 during Disraeli's first Tory ministry. Edmonstone was to be an MP for the whole of Benjamin Disraeli's second Tory ministry, 1874–80, being defeated in the 1880 general election by the Liberal East India merchant Joseph Cheney Bolton.

As a Scottish laird, the proprietor of a country estate, Edmonstone enjoyed a position of privilege that was onerous. Unlike his opposite numbers, the English Keyser squires, he was not regarded with deference, but as a respected father-figure and custodian of the heritage of his estate.

Behind Edmonstone's attitude to politics lay his Presbyterian religion. In Parliament he was to champion the right of the Scottish Church to retain the privileges of choosing its own ministers. As Dr W.R. McNair was to write: 'Ministers formed a class all by themselves, and were a constant source of interest and discussion. Everybody sat "under" one or other of them, and it was a point of honour to uphold your choice as the finest preacher in the country.'[11] When at Duntreath Edmonstone consistently attended the Presbyterian church of Strathblane of which he was hereditary patron. The Edmonstones had shown great interest in the fabric of the church since the new one had been opened, on the site of a pre-Reformation edifice, in 1804. Alice and her siblings regularly sat in the 'Edmonstone gallery', fronting the pulpit wherein the minister of Alice's childhood was Daniel John Ferguson. The Edmonstones, of course, had a fine chapel of their own at Duntreath; although Presbyterian in rite, its tone would fit High Anglicanism as a setting and its religious imagery would make Calvinist rabble-rouser John Knox spin in his long-forgotten grave.

Admiral Edmonstone was a supporter of the right that tenant-farmers could enjoy the game on their lands without interference from superiors, and he jockeyed in the corridors of power for the abolition of the Hypothec Law wherein a tradesman could have the tools of his trade impounded as security against debt. Although absent often on parliamentary business, Edmonstone was not the hated 'absentee landlord' of history. He personally ran his estate from the farms to the quarries at Blairgar and served on such bodies as the Strathblane Mutual Improvement Association.

Alice was to be the mirror of her father's character and philosophy. Like the Scot of James Anthony Froude's writings Edmonstone was a devotee of 'Long-headed, thrifty industry, [had] a sound hatred of waste, imprudence, idleness, extravagance – the feet planted firmly upon the earth – a conscientious sense that the worldly virtues are nevertheless, very necessary virtues, that without these, honesty for one thing is not possible'. And then there was the humour that Alice was to inherit: 'genial humour, which half loves what it laughs at'.[12] Alice's daughter Violet was to note what all who met Alice were to see: that she exhibited many of the facets of a typical Scots character in that she was nimble-witted and astute, down to earth and sharp, but without small-mindedness and partiality.[13] From her early years Alice enjoyed a vigorous debate, particularly a political one.

While on the Mediterranean station William Edmonstone had met Mary Elizabeth, daughter of Lieutenant-Colonel John Whitchell Parsons, CMG, sometime British Resident of Zante (Zakinthos) in the Ionian Islands. Mary Elizabeth and William Edmonstone were married on 13 July 1841. Writing in her own memoir, Alice's younger daughter Sonia noted:

I cannot remember my maternal grandmother. My grandfather was born two years before Napoleon's retreat from Moscow and was much older than she was, and was nearly sixty when my mother was born. My grandmother had been brought up in Greece. Throughout her life apparently she preserved a fascinatingly nymph-like quality, rather oddly reproduced in some of her daughters.[14]

When Alice's father succeeded to the title, the focus of his family changed. He inherited the Edmonstone Stirlingshire residences of Colzium, near Kilsyth, and Duntreath, Strathblane. After he was elected MP in 1874, Edmonstone conducted his parliamentary business from such London locations as Smith's Hotel, Bury Street, his house at 2 Wilton Terrace, and the Tory Carlton Club. In 1875 he acquired a property as a town-house base at 11 Ainslie Place, Edinburgh and held the house until he died there on 18 February 1888. His widow died on 11 August 1902 at Cramond House, Edinburgh.

In Admiral Sir William's half-brother's time the fortunes of the Edmonstones were in decline, but these were enriched through selling land to build the railway, agricultural tenancies and the mineral rights of the estate of Colzium leased out to coal-mining companies from around 1870; Edmonstone owned some two-thirds of Kilsyth, but most of the family properties hereabouts were sold off in the 1920s. By 1883 Admiral Edmonstone had an income of £7,677 from his estates and £8,451 royalties from his mineral rights. Even so, his nine surviving children were a drain on his purse, so Alice although well-off and privileged was not of the very rich families like the Keysers or those who vacillated around the royal court. Alice's siblings were to exhibit in their careers the patronage they won from politics, their association with the aristocratic network which touched the rims of royal circles, and, in her brother Archie's case, her ardent relationship with the Prince of Wales.

Admiral Sir William and Lady Edmonstone had eleven children; two, Archibald William and Mary Emma Frances, died young. The eldest surviving daughter Louisa Anne or 'Louie' (d. 1921), married Henry Pipton (d. 1924) in 1872; he later rose to be a Major-General and served at the Tower of London. She was followed by Charlotte Henrietta, 'Dolly' (d. 1931), who married in

1866 the Revd John Francis Kisson (d. 1907), vicar of Antony, Cornwall. Next came Jessie (d. 1937), married in 1884 to Edward John Winnington-Ingram (d. 1892) of the Royal Warwickshire Regiment. Of Jessie, her niece Violet Keppel wrote that she had a countenance that summed up all of the Edmonstones' facial features for centuries. In particular Jessie favoured Violet and Sonia's grandfather the admiral, and she was always promoted as a nonpareil to the heterodox Alice.[15] To this Sonia Keppel was able to add:

> Aunt Jessie had scant sympathy for the nervous evasiveness of her diffident sister [Frances]. To her, indecisiveness and lack of courage were alike contemptible. To my dismay, one day she discovered my own shrinking terror of spiders. 'What, afraid of spiders?' severely she queried. 'And you a direct descendant of Robert Bruce!' No doubt her scorn was intended to have an astringent effect but, if so, I am afraid that it failed in its purpose.[16]

Then came Frances Euphemia (d. 1921), married in 1873 to Alexander R. Duncan (d. 1927), advocate of Parkhill, Forfar. Sonia Keppel said this about Aunt Frances:

> [She] was the most diffident . . . with a crab-like approach to reality. Once she asked Uncle Archie why her holly did not berry, like his. 'You must plant male and female bushes together', he told her. The next year he asked her whether the hollies had berried at last. Blushing, Aunt Frances answered: 'I don't know, Archie dear. I was too shy to look.'[17]

Frances was followed by Sophia, 'Sophy' (d. 1924), who was married in 1880 to James Edward Hope (1852–1917) of Belmont, Murrayfield, Midlothian. The eighth child was Susanna Emily, who married Johnathan Bucknill in 1885 and died soon after. Mary Clementina, 'May', came next and was married in 1874 to Andrew

Graham Murray (1849–1942) as his first wife. He served as Conservative MP for Buteshire 1891–1905 and as Lord Advocate 1896–1903 with a seat in the Cabinet, and was Secretary for Scotland 1903–5 and Lord of Appeal 1913. He became the 1st Baron (later Viscount) Dunedin. Andrew Murray was to stir up gossip with his devotion to Queen Marie of Romania (1875–1938), wife of King Ferdinand I of the House of Hohenzollern-Sigmaringen. Born Princess Marie Alexandra Victoria, 'Missy', the Romanian queen was the second child and eldest daughter of Queen Victoria's second son, Prince Alfred, Duke of Edinburgh (1844–1900), and Andrew Murray became her *cavaliere servente*. Dame Rebecca West, in a passage which neatly summed up the social life of the Edmonstones and Keysers and their peers, remembered Alice's brother-in-law:

> Graham Murray, a favourite guest . . . had an exceedingly good brain which he showed in his later years – he struck his own very critical profession as a great judge – and he was a remarkable linguist; his French and German and his classics were formidable. He was a good shot and a good golfer, and came handsomely through the programme of reels and strathspays at Highland balls, but he was also remembered as a rackets player, a cyclist, an elegant waltzer and a master of the new American ballroom dances such as the two-step, and as a skilled amateur photographer. Over and above this was the obligation to sit down after dinner, distended with food and wine, and play a really good game of bridge, and to do that very thing for hour after hour of the night. The nineteenth century had its own puritanism: it mortified the flesh, but it confused the issue by calling the chosen means of mortification by the name of pleasure.[18]

Sonia Keppel remembered that like Aunt Jessie, Aunt May was perpetually apprehensive and afraid of the 'unexpected'.[19] May and Graham Murray had four children, Eva, Gladys, Marjorie and Ronnie, of whom Sonia was to offer this:

Gladys [was] the most eccentric. To the end of her life, Gladys was convinced that she was the reincarnation of Bonnie Prince Charlie, which led her to wear the inevitable kilt and man's jacket, and to wish to visit the gentlemen's lavatory at every hotel she frequented . . . But, although decades older than [Sonia and her sister Violet], the term 'cousin' gave them a spurious juvenile status, ranging them with ourselves on a contemporary rung of relationship.[20]

As Sonia was to point out, although these Edmonstone relatives met regularly at Duntreath, to the young Keppels they were 'strangers'.[21] Most of them survived to realise that their sister and aunt, Alice, was to share the Prince of Wales's bed; in public they ignored it, or met public comments with stony silence, but in private voiced their disapproval and in some cases their hurt and humiliation.[22]

Next in age to Alice was the tenth Edmonstone child Archibald – her adored brother 'Archie' – his father's heir. He was born on 30 May 1867 at Woolwich Dockyard. Archie served in the Argyll and Sutherland Highlanders and was promoted, undoubtedly through his sister's lover's patronage, to be groom-in-waiting to the court, 1907–10. On 30 November 1895 he married Ida Agnes Eleanor Forbes (b. 1870) who became honorary woman of the bedchamber to Princess Helena, wife of Prince Christian of Schleswig-Holstein (1846–1923) and fifth child of Queen Victoria.

Archie and Ida Edmonstone had three children: William George, born 1896; Archibald Charles, born 1898; and Edward St John, born 1901, who was sponsored in person at his christening by Edward VII. Sonia Keppel remarked: 'No one quite knew how [Uncle Archie] and Aunt Ida had achieved this sturdy family, as Uncle Archie lived at the top of one tower and Aunt Ida, at the bottom of another.'[23] Ida died 21 December 1946, and Sonia wrote:

Of all my maternal aunts I preferred Aunt Ida. I admired her elegance and her neatness and the way she sewed. My other aunts knitted shapeless mufflers and serviceable stockings. Aunt Ida embroidered handkerchiefs and little samplers with bright threads from a gilt work-basket. She sewed more often than she spoke, but sometimes she asked my mother childlike questions. At the time of the South African War, she asked her: 'Alice dear, who *is* Majuba Hill?'[24]

In childhood Archie had been both worshipped and dominated by Alice, but because of the closeness of age they developed what Sonia Keppel called a 'love for each other [*which*] had the beauty of a theme in a Greek legend. Both had a great sense of family affection, but neither emotion transcended the white flame of their love for each other.'[25] Archie was to outlive his idolised sister by seven years, dying on 1 April 1954. On Alice's death [1947] he erected a plaque in the family burial plot at Strathblane to their great lifelong friendship. In memory of their youthful rambles on the Strathblane Hills he chose for the plaque the first verse of the 'Song of Degrees' (Psalm 121): 'I will lift up mine eyes unto the hills.'

Ironically although Archibald Edmonstone was succeeded by his son Archibald Charles, the 6th baronet was to die only two months after his father. The eldest son, William George had been killed at the battle of the Somme, on 15 September 1916, a loss deeply felt by Alice's family. Edward St John became a commander in the Royal Navy and died in 1983.

Alice was most close to her sisters May and Sophie as well as Archie, so in the days before the Second World War, she was a frequent visitor at their homes at Stenton, Belmont and Duntreath respectively. And in due time she took her daughters to visit. Violet remembered well her visits to aunts May and Sophie. To her childlike senses Stenton was a house of some eccentricity of décor, wherein furnishings had been placed almost in a frenzy of housekeeping activity, but with little real taste in their choice. The outside of the house was unprepossessing, and inside were to be found the usual piles of hideous Victorian *bric-à-brac*. Even as a child Violet thought that Stenton desecrated the fashion values of the era and was given relief only by a wide range of sporting equipment from croquet mallets to gaffs (hooks for landing large fish). She noted, too, that although there was nothing in the drawing-room to make a child tarry with interest, it was the only room at Stenton that displayed any normality of furnishing. She remembered the screens, lamp-shades of frilly material, and the wall-hung landscape pictures which appeared to have been bought as one would purchase wallpaper. Indeed not one piece in the drawing-room had a value of ten sovereigns.[26] When Alice took her daughters to visit her sisters' households her girls noticed the contrasts in the characters of the homes. Violet again noted the fun atmosphere at Aunt Sophie's house at Belmont, in the environs of Edinburgh. This home was stuffed with flowers and Italian canvasses.[27]

As with other well-to-do females the Keyser and Edmonstone women were separated into their own sphere of life with hearth and home as their sole theatre of influence. Alice and Agnes were to rebel against all this in their own ways. They were not going to let the prevailing narrowness of a woman's life or the limitations of a patriarchal society impede their progress or position. Despite being conditioned from babyhood to accept their lots philosophically Alice Edmonstone and Agnes Keyser were determined to be different.

CHAPTER 2

Two Childhoods

Warren House, Wood Lane, Great Stanmore, Middlesex, stands on an estate that once belonged to the Lord of the Manor of Stanmore and was the home of the medieval warrener, who supplied rabbits for the lord's use. In time the manor house which developed on the site was sold off by the trustees of the Brydges family, who became Dukes of Chandos, to pay off the debts of a contemporary duke's son. Once owned by James Forbes of the Honourable East India Company and then the Smirkes, it passed to the Keyser family by 1860. In 1890 the house and estate were sold by Agnes's brother Charles Edward to the financier Henry Louis Bischoffsheim (1829–1908) of the firm of Bischoffsheim & Goldschmidt. It was then occupied by Major Sir John Peter Gerald Maurice Fitzgerald (1884–1957), grandson of Henry Bischoffsheim, who moved in around 1925 after the death of his grandmother. Following the death of his mother, the former Amelia Bischoffsheim, in 1947, Fitzgerald disposed of the house to the National Corporation for the Care of Old People in 1951 and it was in use in 1972 as a hospital called Springbok House. In the 1990s the property became the Hussein Shia Islamic Centre. In the Bischoffsheims' time Warren House was to be visited by the Prince of Wales and Alice Keppel, to make the friendship link with the Keysers that was to become a famous piece of royal history.

Warren House was to be the milieu of Agnes Keyser's childhood, and as an adult she was a regular visitor to her brother's several homes. Charles Edward was to secure a high public profile and be of lasting financial support to his sisters.

In 1893 Charles Edward purchased the deer park and estate of Aldermaston Court from the Burr family and this became his main home. The house, with its imposing tower, had been built during 1848–51 for Higford Burr, MP; Keyser altered and enlarged the house in 1893 and it still exists as the Manor House and Conference Centre. Although he read for the Bar as a member of the Inner Temple, and in the chambers of Sir Richard Harrington, Charles Edward Keyser never practised law, as his wealth allowed him to pursue unpaid charity work, philanthropy and independent academic study. In 1872 he became one of the founders of the Colne Valley Water Co. (now within Three Valleys Water plc at Hatfield, Hertfordshire) and was its chairman from 1904.

Keyser became a keen antiquary, a nationally known Freemason and a prominent leader in the public life of Hertfordshire and Berkshire. His scholarly catalogues of ecclesiastical art, architecture and artefacts are still used by antiquaries. He spent much of his time and personal fortune on enhancing the village facilities of Aldermaston and its church, of which he was a prominent parishioner and lay reader. The church remains virtually a monument to the Edwardian Keysers. He unsuccessfully fought the parliamentary seat of Reading as a Conservative candidate on three occasions. Keyser died on 23 May 1929.[1]

Alice Keppel's family properties were to be as historically significant as the Keysers'. Originally a part of the large earldom of Lennox, a family with strong claims to the Scottish throne, the estate of Colzium, near modern Kilsyth, south Stirlingshire, was well established when it was formed as a part of the dowry in 1214 of Lady Eva Lennox on her marriage to Malcolm de Callander. In 1783 the estate was sold to Sir Archibald Edmonstone for some £40,000, which he had raised by selling the Edmonstone Irish estates. At the time there was no suitable dwelling on the estate, both Kilsyth and Colzium castles – which had existed since medieval times – having been destroyed and the Livingstone mansion was almost derelict.

Sir Archibald therefore undertook the building of a new house during the year of his purchase of the estate. The Edmonstones now made this their chief residence and the buildings of Colzium

House were added to in 1861. After Alice's father succeeded to the baronetcy in 1871, he moved the family to Duntreath Castle as their main residence around 1877. Thus for several of her nursery years Colzium House was Alice's family home.

The Edmonstones held Colzium as a part of their estate until the First World War, after which they began to dispose of it. In 1930 they sold Colzium House and its policies to W. Mackay Lennox, a lawyer and town clerk of Kilsyth; and on his death in 1937 it was gifted in his will to the burgh of Kilsyth. Its gardens now form a public park.

Duntreath Castle lies in Strathblane on the level land at the bottom of the Blane Valley, by the Blane Water, 1½ miles north-west of Blanefield, Stirlingshire. In Alice's day the Blane Valley branch of the North British Railway ran behind the castle. Flanking the castle are the hills of Dumgoyne and Dumfoyne of the Strathblane range that gives the area its particular character. In 1452 James II erected the estate into a free barony and the castle of this year was probably a tower house which had been added to a late fourteenth-century building.

Duntreath developed into a complex that was probably meant to be a full quadrangular plan with keep to the north, a gatehouse to the west, domestic range to the east and an uncompleted south range. The last of the major construction phases of antiquity was undertaken by Sir James Edmonstone (d. 1618), who was to make an extremely foolish move. By association he became involved with the coterie of Alexander, Master of Ruthven (c. 1581–1600), who – according to the testimony of James VI – planned to kidnap the king. The supposed plot – for what really happened is likely to remain a mystery – was known as the Gowrie Conspiracy, and Sir James was arrested for complicity and indicted for high treason. By throwing himself on the king's mercy he managed to obtain a pardon and retired to his estate. By 1609 Sir James had finally decided to transplant his family to Ireland and acquired the estate of Broadisland, Antrim, and the new mansion of Redhall there became the main residence.

As a consequence of this move, Duntreath fell into some neglect and there is talk that it was deroofed by the estate factor as a source of slates for a nearby farm. Be that as it may, when Sir Archibald Edmonstone succeeded to the title in 1851 he undertook an extensive renovation of the property and many of the ruined medieval buildings were destroyed by 1857. A new south-west range was added to begin a huge reconstruction plan by the Glasgow architect Charles Wilson. Work continued in one form or another until Alice's father assumed the title. During 1888–9 Alice's brother Archie added more to the castle which was greatly reconstructed in 1958. The Victorian south-west range remains as Alice knew it, but the keep is now free-standing and an ornamental lake replaces a fir wood of Alice's childhood.

The late-Victorian castle was sumptuously decorated and hung with heavy curtains of the period, the whole setting off the corniced ceilings and panelled rooms and the collection of family furniture of differing eras. In time the castle was to have its own electric light powered from a private generator.

Sonia Keppel remembered the castle of her mother's day:

> Duntreath was a square castle built round a courtyard, strengthened at each corner by four pepperpot towers. Twin arches governed the approach to the courtyard, punctured by twin doors of admittance. Each side of the house had a separate entity, but the arches welded the two sides together like clasps of a box . . .
>
> One of the doors was the front door which led into a long, low, panelled hall, filled with beautiful plants . . . The pervading smell of tuberoses was delicious.[2]

To this account can be added that of Marion Purves:

> [14 June 1904] Papa [Colonel Richard Purves] announced that Ida [Lady Edmonstone] had suggested that I join the party from Edinburgh travelling to the shoot. Freddie [Alice's diminutive]

was to be there from London, with Violet and the baby [Sonia] and while the men went off shooting we were to potter and lunch. It had been ages since I saw Freddie and I was delighted at the thought of seeing her and lovely Duntreath again. It was to be an early train from Princes Street Station with Papa's Purdeys [shooting guns] in their leather case, and his shooting basket taking up a rack to themselves. A gig collected us at Blanefield station and took us to the castle. I had been to Duntreath before for the Edmonstones had been friends of the Purveses when both families lived in Edinburgh; Alice had come to tea at our house in Pentland Terrace and had joined our jaunts to walk in the Pentland Hills and our trips to the seaside at Portobello.

Duntreath was always at its best in the hot sunshine. The long driveway from the East Lodge led up to what I always thought of as a huge, but kindly, fortress, with its lovely sunken garden. Inside there was an air of pure luxury from old Lady Edmonstone's [Alice's mother's] day; she had loved flowers and the panelled rooms and corridors were always full of vases of the most exquisitely smelling flowers from the huge garden arrangements.

My favourite rooms at Duntreath were the music room, with its ornate mirrors and beautiful ceiling, the ballroom, where the Edmonstones also held receptions, the library with its beamed ceiling and old Lady Edmonstone's boudoir. Everywhere was richly furnished in the most elegant style.

Freddie, Ida and the menfolk greeted us as the gig descended the last part of the drive and down through the twin-towered gateway. What a change I saw in Violet, now grown into a pretty young ten-year-old, but oh! so precocious! At length the men drove off in the waggonette to shoot. I, Freddie, Ida and Violet, who entertained us en route with mimicry of some people she had met in the village, went off for a walk. Freddie allowed Violet to mimic some aunts too, in a very rude way. Over the railway we went and up the hill to overlook the castle. The views were stunning and Archie [Alice's brother] has immortalised

them in his studio; really his canvasses are quite good. We hadn't
gone far when the courtyard bell rang for lunch; so we all
trooped back again to the beautiful dining-room with its huge
canopied fireplace. On the way down Violet had fallen and
muddied her dress; she blamed one of her cousins for pushing
her; the child continually looks for excuses to explain her (often
very bad) behaviour.

After lunch Freddie and Violet took me on a tour of the
armoury and the dungeon, where Violet demonstrated, with
great relish, the uses of the thumb-screws. She had just
discovered tales of the Dumb Laird [William Edmonston of
Duntreath, *fl.* 1647–90] who is said to haunt the oak room, and
recounted all she knew with great verve; what an imagination
the child has.

At last the children went off about their own business and we
womenfolk chatted about the gossip of the day. Now 'marooned'
in London, Freddie was missing Duntreath, but really she is a
town-person. She looked so gay and happier than I had ever seen
her, and, of course, we never mentioned a certain royal person.

Freddie had us laughing at some of the social pretentions of the
'wee lairds' and the kirk elders of the nearby parish. She said that
on the last Sabbath they had had the hymn with the words:

> The rich man in his castle,
> The poor man at his gate,
> God made them high and lowly,
> And ordered their estate.

Freddie said that it always made her giggle to see some of the
local 'rich men' with their ever expanding stomachs who had
just stuffed themselves at breakfast with kidneys and lamb chops
singing lustily and looking down on their humbler porage-for-
breakfast neighbours. Freddie is the least snobbish person I know
although she has a lot to be snobbish about.

At length the men returned from the shoot with full baskets

and it was back in the gig to Blanefield. This time Freddie and Ida came with us as far as the station; she was returning to London later in the week and would not be at Duntreath again until after Christmas.[3]

For the most part Alice's childhood was spent at Duntreath and at 11 Ainslie Place, her father's Edinburgh town-house. Set in the capital's New Town, above the cliff of the Leith Water, Regency Ainslie Place is made up of two facing crescents, and has been the home to a wide range of famous Scots from William Blackwood the Tory publisher to Lord Corehouse the Session Judge. In Alice's childhood days the neighbours made up a coterie of lawyers, physicians and landed gentlefolk whose children shared Edmonstone society.

The plot of Alice Edmonstone's and Agnes Keyser's childhoods was that of any Victorian upper-class family, and related almost entirely to raising them for emerging into prosperous society, and, as they were girls, with a once-over-lightly attitude to education. As with all upper-class families, Alice and Agnes saw their parents, singly or together, usually no more than once a day and more often than not only after tea. They saw more of their mothers than of their fathers, and in Alice's case much of her father's time was spent in Parliament during her childhood.

George Cornwallis-West, godson of Alice's future royal lover and stepfather of Winston Churchill, summed up the sentiment of the age:

> Children in my early days were looked upon partly as a nuisance and partly as a kind of animated toy, to be shown, if they were sufficiently attractive, to callers. We were always brought down [from the nursery] and shown after lunch, but were never expected to utter, and were consequently all abominably shy.[4]

Shyness and silence were not to be Alice's characteristics, nor did she show any inclination to be a bluestocking. Through the

Education (Scotland) Act of 1872, the state, for the first time, accepted direct responsibility for educating children. But the 3*d* weekly schools of Stirlingshire and Edinburgh were not for Alice. In fact there was very little in the way of education. A contemporary of Alice, and a close friend of her future brother-in-law Sir Derek Keppel, Mabell, Countess of Airlie (1866–1956), was to feel deprived by her inadequate instruction:

> I have always regarded my inferior education as a handicap, but it was almost universal among girls of the upper classes in my day. I remember one of my friends of later years – Lady Kinnaird – telling me that when she married at seventeen her husband had been so ashamed by her ignorance that immediately after the honeymoon he had opened up the family schoolroom and engaged a governess for her.[5]

Alice learned to read and write from her devoted nanny Betsy Wells and had some formal education from transistory governesses. To this was added a few dancing classes and educational trips to Edinburgh Castle, Holyrood Palace and the beaches of East Lothian.

For a while Alice shared a nursery, which doubled as a daytime schoolroom, with her brother Archie. Alice's education was intended to give her a patina of culture, and prepared her for society and the organised idleness that marked the upper-class female. Alice was devastated when Archie left home for further education when he was around thirteen or so. For a while he was tutored at the rectory of the Revd William Henry Draper of Middleton Stoney, Bicester, Oxfordshire. There he was crammed for Oxford; Archie was in residence at Christ Church during 1886–9, but like so many well-to-do undergraduates, took no degree.[6]

Although they were inseparable as children, Archie and Alice were very different in character. Archie was an artistic and sensitive child, and, although vulnerable and anxious, proved to have a keen sense of humour. In due time he was to convert a room in one of the Duntreath turrets as a studio, and spent many an hour painting shepherdesses and pastoral scenes. Violet averred that Archie hated sports of all kinds and 'winced through the glorious 12th'. He was more interested in gardening.[7] Even Alice's adult visits to Duntreath were filled with gardening alongside her brother. She designed the rock garden and waterfalls adjacent to the old stable (now main) entrance to Duntreath. She also planted the shrubberies and ordered shrub-bordered paths laid out on Dumgoyne and Dumfoyne.[8]

Alice was a doer: she was stifled by the schoolroom and longed to be out with her friends James Blair the groom and John Arthur the coachman, the stable boys, the gardeners James Graham and Alex Patterson and the gamekeepers Nicol Weir and William Kerr. As the youngest of the family, with much older brothers and sisters, Alice was given more flexibility of activity than her siblings ever had; their upbringing had been to conform to what Harriet Grey of Fallodon, Northumberland, had expressed as making 'life go smoothly [for the male members of her family]' and shrinking 'from argument'; she 'was always prepared to efface herself'.[9] Not so Alice; she resented boys being given privileges because of gender and formulated her own nonconformity.

As with two other mistresses of the Prince of Wales, Lillie Langtry and Daisy Warwick, Alice was a tomboy. This rumbustiousness led to the air of high spirits that HRH liked and found so attractive in women. Archie did not like violent exertion or kicking over the traces, but Alice loved the indecorous ploy and took pleasure in a good game of cricket, an Anglo-Saxon game enjoyed by the Scottish aristocratic families, but which never really took off at Strathblane village. Alice played with the estate staff at Duntreath. 'Rin, Allus, Rin' (Run, Alice, Run) they would shout encouragingly in the Lowland accent, while her older sisters looked away in some embarrassment.[10]

Alice was an outspoken and assertive little girl; a trait that was to be reflected in both her daughters. Her great-niece Lady McGrigor remembers the family story of how, when Alice and Archie were at the family home of 11 Ainslie Place, Edinburgh, they had looked out of the window to see a hearse and its cortège convey a neighbour to the grave. Archie was much alarmed with the Stygian procession of sombre carriages, horses and mutes. Alice comforted him assuring her brother that the coachman was certainly alive![11]

Violet also recollected another family tale of Alice's childhood wilfulness. While she was still in the nursery, Alice's parents had decided that it was time to teach the rumbustious and naughty child that her ways were not acceptable. Always one step ahead of anyone, Alice confronted her elders. With ostentatiously contrite mien she confessed that she had a 'wicked heart'. Her parents were mollified: but only for a few seconds. For Alice added that the wickedness was also possessed by the family paragon Jessie. Quite satisfied by the scene she had made, the unrepentant Alice was off to practise on her Shetland pony the stunts she had seen at the circus.[12]

Never in her life would Alice allow herself to be browbeaten; if she thought she was thwarted she would even cuff an impudent stable lad. Sonia Keppel remembered breaking her collar-bone during some nursery ploy; the doctor setting it was rough with her and her mother 'boxed his ears'.[13] Agnes Keyser was also to be held in awe, and no little fear, by her staff.

In later life Alice would discuss her childhood with her friends at dinner parties and social gatherings. And at the house of her friends the Asquiths she concurred with the opinion of Violet Bonham-Carter, later Baroness Asquith of Yarnbury, the Liberal politician:

> as a child, asking my governess how I was going to spend my life . . . Her answer came without a moment's hesitation. 'Until you are eighteen you will do lessons.' 'And afterwards?' 'And afterwards you will do *nothing*.' . . . The deep river, the Rubicon which flowed between, was called 'Coming Out' . . . One day one had a pigtail down one's back — short skirts barely cleared the knees. The next day, hair pulled high on top of one's head . . .

It used to be a sin to be vain – but now it became a sin to be plain . . . 'lessons' were of course thrown to the winds . . . In fact I remember being warned by a well-wisher to *conceal* any knowledge I *had* managed to acquire . . . 'Men are afraid of clever girls.'[14]

Little is known of Agnes Keyser's childhood beyond its privileged background, its focus on 'doing good' in the Great Stanmore milieu – and the social round of St John the Evangelist's parish – and journeys to and from Keyser properties in London and Warren House. The late biographer Anita Leslie recalled her grandmother talking of the young Agnes and her strange dislike of women, which old Mrs Leslie put down to a harsh nanny, and the constant company of women when 'she ached for the attention of young men'.

Unlike her sisters, continued Mrs Leslie, Agnes was always 'restless', the restrictions of her sex and class were always an 'irritation' to her, and the 'conventional social round' bored and frustrated her. She enjoyed giving orders, and was bold when addressing men, in a society that ruled that she should be demure. Anita Leslie averred that one of the things that attracted the Prince of Wales to her was that she was not afraid of him and 'Edward obeyed her orders like a small boy'. Her character, explicit from an early age, was that of a 'bachelor girl', said Anita Leslie; and it was that which was to give her a 'unique' position in the Prince of Wales's affections. From her childhood Agnes honed her will of iron.[15]

Agnes Keyser was small, blonde and pretty from her teens, yet as her teenage developed Alice Edmonstone retained the Latin looks of her grandmother and added to them a lively personality and a seductive air. Her generosity of spirit became a strong part of her emerging character. Although to those she liked Agnes Keyser gave complete devotion, she was bossy and snobbish. Alice had neither of these traits.

Violet Keppel was to write that her mother rarely lost her composure, and was not often moved to anger. If she was aroused, she would offer the miscreant who had caused her ire a few frosty statements. Alice had the character trait of never harbouring spite, and if she thought she was in the wrong would apologise immediately. Her great gift was to make people at their ease on meeting her, and happy in her company. Agnes Keyser tended to intimidate those with whom she did not have an immediate rapport. Violet likened her mother to a Christmas tree hung with goodies for all, and said that there was never any boundary to her generosity. Added to this, Alice could make all comers, high and low, feel welcome in her circle.[16] Agnes Keyser had little interest in those lower than her station.

'Manipulation' was to be a key in both Alice's and Agnes's characters; they could mould people to their will with charm and vivacity. And from their teens Alice and Agnes were determined not to become seemly women of submissive mien. Alice was not intent on giving up her life entirely for others without personal return. Yet Agnes craved to move in a man's world.

Alice became a very desirable young woman. Her father's political and naval connections called upon her to support her mother as hostess. Admiral Edmonstone rented various London houses for the 'Season' and the Edmonstones' table was always a place for lively conversation. John Buchan's wife Susan, later Lady Tweedsmuir, described such a table:

> there might be one or two Cabinet Ministers who welcomed the opportunity of quiet conversation, or there might be a Viceroy or high official from a far-off corner of the Empire, anxious to make someone in the government of the day realise a little more the difficulties of a particular experiment that Britain had delegated to him to carry out. These parties often included . . . a painter, and almost certainly a musician who played to some of the company in the evenings. Besides these eminent people there was usually a sprinkling of women famous for their beauty or wit, or both, who either gave the conversation a sparkling turn, or were wise enough not to interrupt good talk.[17]

41

And in such company Alice 'sat looking statuesque or flower-like' as the mood took her.

It was the British essayist Sir Richard Steele who first coined the word 'Season' in the *Tatler* (1709): 'the Company was gone and the Season over', he wrote. The Season always took place in London. So a house in London – whether rented or owned – was a must although for many rural-based well-to-do folk it was a detested upheaval. Not to be in the throes of the Season was unthinkable for those who sought advancement in Society; to be 'invited' and be 'seen' was vital for a girl's smooth entry into Society.

Like the Season, a girl's 'coming out' was an eighteenth-century invention. It is mentioned as an entity by the novelist Fanny Burney, Madame d'Arblay, in *Cecilia* (1782); she noted: '. . . she has never been presented yet, so is not come out.' Neither Alice nor Agnes 'came out' in the sense of a debutante being presented at court; but Alice emerged into Society as had Mabell, Countess of Airlie with the clear target of a rapid proposal of marriage:

> Unless a girl was quite exceptional . . . her fate was decided by her first impact on society. Anyone who failed to secure a proposal within six months of coming out could only wait for her second season with diminished chances. After a third there remained nothing but India as a last resort before the spectre of the Old Maid became a reality.[18]

Agnes was unmoved by such opinions. An activity which older women in Society took up with zeal was the art of matchmaking, and this was an important part of the Season. Alice and Agnes were introduced to the round of adult parties, country-house weekends and the gatherings held to view eligible bachelors. Alice viewed; Agnes looked away.

Alice and Agnes came out into a Society dominated by political and army service hostesses who were the representatives of a powerful social force. In the 1880s all social life and hospitality among the upper classes was private, though lavish. A lady of birth did not dine in such public places as restaurants. Thus Society for the unattached female remained a small chaperoned group that had not changed for centuries. Men did not seduce their friends' sisters, but copulated with women of a lower class. The bloodlines had to be kept pure.

The late 1880s were not all bright for Alice. The year 1888, for instance, was to be a traumatic one; the year was not far advanced when it became more than evident that her beloved father was dying. The twenty-year-old Alice and her mother never left his bedside for long and on Saturday, 18 February he died at 11 Ainslie Place, Edinburgh.

The admiral's body was brought from Edinburgh to Strathblane by train, and the long cortège of mourning carriages made their way up the slope to the kirk on the hill where the admiral had been a keen worshipper. The route was lined with the families of those who worked on the estate, and a group of his workers were waiting at the kirk door to bear his body into the service and thence to the family vault abutting the church.

There were many in the congregation that day who were to receive bequests from the admiral's will, but as they filed out after the service they thought more of his kindly smile and his jollity whenever something amused him. They remembered him as a man who spoke only when he felt he had something to say. *The Times*, in a short obituary of 22 February, reflected the admiral's quiet nature: 'He spoke very seldom [*in the House of Commons*], indeed, it is said, but once – but he was noticeable for the assiduous fidelity with which he cheered the utterances from the Ministerial bench.' Things were now to change at Duntreath: Alice's brother Archie was the new baronet and in London her future royal lover had given orders that Marlborough House was to be lit with electricity in time for his silver wedding celebrations.

The London Society that Alice and Agnes became a part of was extremely assured of itself. It was controlled by around ten thousand people from fifteen hundred families and they all 'knew' each other. By the late 1880s money could obtain most entrepreneurs a place in a once aristocratically closed Society. The fact that the Keysers were of Jewish origin now mattered not a jot; their financial skills assured their status. In future years Alice was to become rich from advice given by the new Society folk of her lover's court, such as Baron Nathaniel Rothschild. Another of Alice's acquaintances, Lady Frances Balfour, sister-in-law of the Prime Minister Arthur Balfour (1848–1930), summed up the confidence of Society: 'Social life was centred in the home and its interests. Outward distractions were few, and "entertainment" meant by the gifts and talents of the hosts and guests. It was a circle intimately interwoven . . . They were all known to one another; to be left out, or forgotten, was an unthinkable misfortune. The old were established facts, and over all was the grace and beauty of the best manners and the ease which accompanies people who are sure of themselves, and need no advertisement.'[19]

Alice Edmonstone and Agnes Keyser were to be among the most self-assured girls of their generation. Whereas Society bored Agnes, Alice was in her element. Despite flirting with young men from both north and south of the Border, Alice was to make her greatest impression among the young naval and military officers who frequented her father's house. And it was through this network that she met the Keppels.

CHAPTER 3

ALICE'S MARRIAGE AND THE ALBEMARLES

A year before Agnes Keyser was born, the official census of 1851 reported that out of a population of 27,396,629, there were over 600,000 more females in the UK than males. Almost 20 per cent of women never married, and by the time Agnes was twenty-four the average age of first marriage for women of her class had risen to twenty-six. Yet Agnes was in no need and no hurry to pursue a man who was available and willing to support her.

Exactly when Agnes decided to have a 'genuine normal life' of her own without marriage, as Geraldine Jewsbury had written to Jane Welsh Carlyle in 1849, is not known; but while liking men enormously, she found the social ideal of a woman subjecting herself to a man in matrimony abhorrent. The *Englishwoman's Review* summed up her attitude perfectly when in its columns it averred that 'the higher a woman's nature is, the more likely it is that she will prefer rather to forgo marriage altogether, than surrender herself to a union that would sink her below her own ideal.' Because Agnes Keyser was wealthy she was never considered a social failure.

Furthermore, as a spinster, Agnes Keyser was far more independent than a married woman, being able to act as a trustee, an executrix, or an administratrix should she wish to, and to enjoy a franchise in parish matters. Agnes Keyser became a member of the Victorian group of women who slowly developed new lifestyles which in time would influence all women. And as a terrible snob, Agnes intended to be *somebody*.

Incidentally, in Agnes's day snobbery was looking up the social scale rather than looking down on others.

Alice Edmonstone had a similar sentiment, but she was bent on using the marriage state for her ends. The spirit of her age that women could not choose whom they married, even for love if necessary, was not what Alice had in mind at all. She wished to get married, but in her own social, nonconformist way; it was to be on her terms and she was going to play the field like men. Like Agnes, Alice adored men; she was highly sexed and she came to realise that marriage (any marriage) was a respectable entry into Edwardian Society. Many girls had a kind of instant success in using London Society as a marriage market, others succeeded only after much delay. The longer the delay the greater the likelihood of being on the shelf. London Society was full of such girls; Alice was determined not to be one of them, but she was going to take her time and enjoy coquettish encounters with the young men who came to the London house her father rented for the Season. No wonder her nickname among her most intimate friends was 'flirtatious Freddie' . . . remembering the diminutive of her middle name.[1]

The Society that Alice found in London, and the *louche* essence of the era among the aristocracy, were to suit her perfectly. The flavour of extravagance and lavish living, the style of the Prince of Wales and the Marlborough House Set, the chic set, the decadent set and the *avant-garde* – the whole ambience of the 1890s – were to be all to Alice's liking. She was to see the regeneration in the 'Naughty Nineties' of the raffishness that had been subdued in Victorian England since Regency days.

It was a period of 'manliness' – of cock-fighting, pugilist shows, card-playing and abstinence from church attendance among the London Society gentry. The 1890s aristocracy's idea was that God approved more of bicycling and boating, cricketing and croqueting than the churchgoing of the Victorian Sunday. As a female Alice was as yet proscribed much of this, but she delighted in meeting young men who indulged. And her future lover the Prince of

Wales and his friend the Earl of Rosebery encouraged the young men of their circle to be libertine men-of-the-world as a contrast to the High Victorian Christian accomplished manliness of the 1870s and 1880s. One of the reasons cited for the flamboyance of the 1890s was the invasion into Society of a wide range of raffish people from Americans to actors, and from artists, writers and bohemians to Jews – all of whom became denizens of Alice's future lover's court.

When she entered royal circles, Alice was to take up in earnest the new vogue of ostentation. Although the mid-Victorians had lived by the standards of money – under an Evangelical God – opulence was reserved for such events as the queen's Golden Jubilee of 29 June 1887. By the time the queen had her Diamond Jubilee in 1897 ostentation was a day-to-day affair among Society.

Ease of communications in the 1890s gave the pleasure-seekers new opportunities to diversify. And London's Society was more expansive. Constance Gladys, Countess de Grey, later Marchioness of Ripon, who dined regularly at such places as Romano's, made it easier for girls like Alice Edmonstone to be seen in certain select restaurants, and weekend parties became usual. At one such Alice was to meet the Hon. George Keppel, son of the 7th Earl of Albemarle, whose family had many naval connections which touched those of Alice's father.

The earldom of Albemarle had been created in 1697 for Arnold Joost van Keppel (1670–1718), *Heer van der Voorst* in Guelderland, attendant of the Prince of Orange in 1688 as page of honour. Soon after the prince's accession to the English throne as William III in 1689, van Keppel became an important courtier with a grant of 108,634 acres of forfeited Irish lands. Lord Macaulay's *History of England* (1848–61), describes van Keppel as having 'a sweet and obliging temper, winning manners and a quick though not a profound understanding'. Van Keppel's position was assured as the monarch fancied him for his bed.

Van Keppel retired to Holland after the death of King William in 1701 and sat thereafter with the nobles of the States General, commanding their forces as general at such battles as Ramillies (1706) during the Spanish Succession War. Van Keppel died at the Hague.

William Anne, 2nd Earl of Albemarle (1702–54), godson of Queen Anne, was educated in Holland and became a general in the service of the United Provinces. At the age of twenty he entered the court as a lord of the bedchamber to the Prince of Wales and in 1724 was elevated to ADC to King George I. Albemarle became Governor of Virginia in 1737 – a post he held until his death – and was present at the battle of Culloden in 1746 after which he was made commander-in-chief of the forces in Scotland; he was also ambassador to France during 1749–54.

George Keppel, 3rd Earl of Albemarle (1724–72), followed a military career in which he was lord of the bedchamber to HRH William Augustus, Duke of Cumberland, second son of George II. By 1761 as Lieutenant-General, Keppel was Keeper and Governor of Jersey. His son William Charles, 4th Earl of Albemarle (1772–1849), was Master of the Horse to William IV and to Queen Victoria. His wife, Charlotte Susannah, nicknamed 'the Rowdy Dow' (Rowdy Dowager), managed to disperse Keppel heirlooms with extravagant eccentricity; they were restored by Gertrude, wife of the 8th Earl.[2]

Augustus Frederick Keppel, 5th Earl of Albemarle (1794–1851), was an officer of the 1st Regiment of Foot Guards at Waterloo and served as MP for Arundel 1820–6; he died insane. His brother George Thomas succeeded as 6th Earl of Albemarle (1799–1891). He also served at Waterloo and as MP for East Norfolk 1834–5 and Lymington 1847–50, was secretary to Prime Minister Lord John Russell, and equerry to HRH Prince Augustus Frederick, Duke of Sussex; he was groom-in-waiting to Queen Victoria 1838–41.[3] Of him the *Gentleman's Magazine* for February 1857 said: 'His voice is loud, his manner confident and somewhat overbearing.' These attributes were to be passed on to his grandson George Keppel.

Alice's future father-in-law, William Coutts Keppel, 7th Earl of Albemarle, was born on 15 April 1832 at London. He was educated at Eton and entered the army as ensign and lieutenant in the 43rd Foot in 1843; he served in the Scots Guards during 1848–53. Keppel was ADC to the future King William IV's fifth illegitimate child by actress Mrs Dorothy Jordan, Lord Frederick Fitzclarence, in India. He was MP at various times during 1851–74 for Norwich, Wick Burghs and Berwick-upon-Tweed. His royal service included being Treasurer for the Queen's Household during 1859–66 and Volunteer ADC to Queen Victoria, 1881. In 1876 he sat in the Lords as Baron Ashford and became a Roman Catholic in 1879. He had married on 15 November 1855 at Dundrum, Canada – while he was Superintendent of Indian Affairs – Sophia Mary McNab, daughter of Sir Allen McNab (sometime Prime Minister of Canada). He succeeded to the earldom and estates in Norfolk and Co. Leitrim in 1891; he died on 28 August 1894 and was buried at Quidenham, Attleborough.

George Keppel was the third son and fifth child of the 7th Earl of Albemarle. He had been born on 14 October 1865. Sonia Keppel left this memory of his boyhood:

> As a boy, he had outgrown his strength (he was known as 'The Wolf' for his cadaverous appearance at school), and, at the age of 19, had been out to South Africa for a year, in the care of Cecil Rhodes. Later, he had worked as a lumberjack, in Canada; and in a mining-camp in Colorado.[4]

In February 1884, George Keppel was admitted to the Royal Military Academy at Sandhurst. After an undistinguished career at Sandhurst, where his performance rose from 'Fair' to 'Good', Keppel was commissioned in the Gordon Highlanders in 1886.[5] He was described as a lieutenant in the 92nd Gordon Highlanders on his marriage.[6] He resigned his commission in 1892, the year after he married Alice Edmonstone. As the son of a peer he took the title of 'the Honourable', a style for written communications and not verbal introductions; in due course Alice took her husband's rank.

Violet Keppel was to leave the most detailed description of her mother's husband – her father to Society. Although not as devoted to him as she was to her mother, Violet described him as sympathetic, mild, friendly, obliging, benign, solicitous, lenient and caring, easily gratified and simply pacified when annoyed. A French linguist of some skill, Violet saw her father as a supreme example of *bon public*, full of helpfulness. Devoted to his country, true to his friends and faithful to his family, Violet said, George Keppel seemed to have a quality in common with the author of *Peter Pan*; he, like Sir James Matthew Barrie, 'never really grew up'.[7]

Alice was greatly attracted to George from the first meeting. The records at Sandhurst showed that he was just under 6 feet 3 inches, and he was handsome and dashing. Rebecca West noted that 'George . . . was the only real beauty of the two'.[8] And Consuelo Vanderbilt Balsan, Duchess of Marlborough, added: 'The Honourable George Keppel was one of those tall and handsome Englishmen who, immaculately dressed, proclaim the perfect gentleman.'[9] An anonymous hand writing of George Keppel in his obituary in *The Times* underlined too his 'exquisite manners', his 'benign gentility' and his 'sense of fun'.[10] More than anything else though, George was a good step up into the next stratum of Society that Alice wished to cultivate; she, of course, brought some colour into the Albemarle circle, as the Duchess of Marlborough noted: 'and in bringing his wife into the somewhat cloistered family circle of the Earl of Albemarle [he] had introduced a note of gaiety and Gallic bonhomie that previously had been lacking'.[11]

Yet, Alice was to make one error that she would never repeat again in her life. She was of a very avaricious nature when it came to finance and she believed that the Albemarles had a large amount of money and that George would have a plentiful share of it. In truth the Albemarles had 7,500 acres in Norfolk and 2,500 in Co. Leitrim, Ireland, which produced an income of some £8,300, but that was not to be reckoned by the standards of the day as being in the forefront of wealth. Ironically the much less prestigious Edmonstone Scottish estates produced more wherewithal.[12]

Despite this miscalculation there were other social attractions which made George Keppel good husband potential. He was not the first to propose to Alice, family gossip has it, but his ardour and devotion were the strongest. The match was acceptable to both families in rank and dynasty. Some time in late 1890 Alice accepted George's proposal, and a short engagement was arranged. The formal engagement was announced at The Hyde, Luton, the home of the senior Keppels. An elegant party took place during 19–21 January 1891, with Alice being chaperoned by her brother Archie. As to nuptial settlements, they were to live off a capital sum of £20,000. Alice received some £15,000 in shares and cash from Archie, and George had a bequest of £5,000 from an aunt.[13]

George and Alice were married at the fashionable St Paul's Church, Knightsbridge, London, by the Revd Henry Montague Villiers on 1 June 1891; she was twenty-three and he was twenty-five. Alice left for her wedding from 33 Belgrave Square, which the Edmonstones had rented for the Season from their family friend Vice-Admiral George Edward John Mowbray Rous, Earl of Stradbroke; and George left from the nearby Alexandra Hotel, with his best man, his brother Viscount Bury. Alice was given away by Archie, her father being dead. The register was signed by Alice's mother and brother, her new father-, mother- and brother-in-law.[14] Sonia Keppel wrote this of the nuptials:

> At their wedding the combined beauty of my father and mother had been sensational. In an age of giants he stood six feet four inches high, and in his Gordon Highlander bonnet, at nearly eight feet . . . And his magnificent breadth was a foil to her slender figure.[15]

George Keppel's siblings were a characterful mixture. Of the marriage between his father and mother ('Grannie B' to Alice's children) there were nine children, two short of Alice's own siblings. Arnold Allan Cecil (1858–1942), who married Gertrude

Lucia Wilbraham (Alice's children's 'Aunt Gertie') in 1881, was the eldest son – and the 8th Earl of Albemarle from 1894; he himself had five children who flitted in and out of Alice's life: Walter Egerton George Lucian (1882–1970); Arnold Joost William (1884–1964), 'Cousin Arno'; Rupert Oswald Derek (1886–1964); Albert Edward George (1898–1917; he was killed in action on 1 August), for whom the Prince of Wales stood sponsor; and Elizabeth Mary Gertrude (1890–1963), 'Cousin Betty'. After Arnold, who held the courtesy title of Viscount Bury, came Theodora (1862–1945), who married Major William Leslie Davidson; this was 'Aunt Theo' who served as matron in a French military hospital in the First World War. Then came Derek William George (1863–1944), who married, in 1898, the Hon. Bridget Harbord. His career in royal circles, initially as equerry to George, Duke of York when Prince of Wales, was to bring him close to George and Alice and no little embarrassment when Alice became royal mistress.[16] Mary Hilda (1864–1964) – 'Aunt Hilda', was next in line and she served in the VAD during the First World War. Leopoldina Olivia (1866–1945), 'Aunt Lena', named for her godfather Leopold II, King of the Belgians, followed; she became a Carmelite nun as Mother Keppel of a Brighton convent. The family was completed by Susan Mary (1868–1953), who married Walter Townley; Mary Stuart (1869–1906); and Florence Cecilia (1871–1963), who married William Henry Dudley Boyle.

There had been a Keppel in the Prince of Wales's entourage from the first days of his setting up his household at his marriage to Alexandra on 10 March 1863. This was his equerry Lieutenant-Colonel Frederick Charles Keppel. Again the family were not themselves without skeletons and one scandalous story was kept alive in the memories of many, concerning Alice's great-uncle-in-law.

Rear-Admiral Sir Henry Keppel (1809–1904) was erstwhile groom-in-waiting to Queen Victoria and an intimate of the Prince of Wales; he followed his royal friend in his adulterous behaviour. The incident that became infamous as the 'Keppel Affair' occurred when the steam frigate HMS *Forte* had sailed from Plymouth on

30 April 1860 with Sir Henry aboard; he was to assume naval command at the Cape of Good Hope and the *Forte* was to be his flagship. During the voyage a reported adulterous relationship sprang up between him and Eliza Lucy, Lady Grey, the wife of the Governor of New Zealand, the womanising Sir George Grey. There was great scandal but Keppel survived the public opprobrium; he was promoted Admiral of the Fleet in 1877 and was one of the first to be given the Order of Merit. Sir George Grey died the year that Alice had become the Prince of Wales's lover. Incidentally Keppel's career was to jettison the idea that 'the breath of sexual scandal damned a public man in mid–Victorian England'.[17]

The main Keppel family home was the red-brick Quidenham Hall, near Norwich. The hall was set on the site of a now vanished Elizabethan mansion, and in the Keppels' time it had been developed as a Georgian pile. Sir Thomas Holland had acquired the estate in 1572. By 1673 it was the seat of John Holland of a strongly parliamentarian family. The house and estate were sold by the last of the Holland line to John Bristow, a merchant of Portuguese goods in Bristol, who in turn sold it to General George Keppel, the 3rd Earl of Albemarle, in 1762.

Quidenham was to be a regular part of the lives of George, Alice and their daughters. Easter was always spent at spartan Quidenham, with Violet and Sonia taking part in a variety of outdoor activities never encountered at Duntreath, from boisterous birds'–egg collecting expeditions with Keppel cousins to salty water sports on the Norfolk coast with 'Uncle Arnold', the 8th Earl of Albemarle.[18]

Indeed the centre of Quidenham life for the Keppel girls was their uncle and his wife 'Aunt Gertie'. Both girls remarked on Arnold Keppel's artistic skills as a sculptor and painter, to say nothing of his expertise as a boat-builder and sailor. Quidenham was full of his statuary, with a huge female nude in the front hall which gave rise to Sonia's remark that Aunt Gertie had thought it wise to chaperone her husband when he had live models at his London studio.[19]

Quidenham was crammed with relics of the Keppel 'fighting tradition' with the bedrooms named after battles in which they had fought, from the Duke of Marlborough's third great victory at Oudenarde in 1708 to the Duke of Cumberland's rout of Bonnie Prince Charlie's Jacobites at Culloden in 1746.[20] The mansion was also a treasure-house of paintings, including many family portraits by Sir Joshua Reynolds who as a boy had been a protégé of a Keppel during a career at sea.[21]

George Keppel was to make several visits to Quidenham without Alice, to take part in family shoots. It was an ideal bolt-hole for him when his presence was not required on 'Mrs George jaunts' with the Prince of Wales. George also regularly pursued an interest in local militia matters. He was an officer in the Prince of Wales's Own Norfolk Militia Artillery. When it was founded in 1875 the Albemarles had taken a prominent part in its ranks. It was renamed the 1st Norfolk Artillery Volunteers in 1880, then the 2nd Bde Eastern District Royal Artillery (Prince of Wales' Own Norfolk Militia Artillery in 1882). In 1902 it was renamed again and became the 1st Norfolk Royal Garrison Artillery (Volunteers) retaining the patronage of the new monarch.

Quidenham, of course, was not George's only 'bolt-hole'. The Albemarle records show that he made regular solo visits to Keppel friends at such places as Palace House, Beaulieu, Southampton, and favourite spots in Scotland like the homes of the Earl of March and Wemyss at Gosford, Longniddry, East Lothian, and Wemyss Castle, Fife. It was to be an increasing solo pattern for the whole of his married life.[22]

CHAPTER 4

FIRST LOVER, FIRST CHILD

As the closing years of Queen Victoria's reign began to slip away the Keysers were a part of the financial coterie of socialites who had taken over London Society. In Agnes Keyser's youth the influence of titles and breeding was all that was needed to be in the front rank of London Society; by the 1890s stocks, shares and money-making skills pushed into the social limelight a whole range of families backed by purchased land and money which had not been inherited. As the *Saturday Review* was to say later in 1905, the peerage was adulterated by 'mere wealth'.

Alice and George Keppel now became one of the fifteen hundred families who dominated London Society, but with a position secured according to the old rules of Society by George's pedigree rather than wealth. Their first London home was 7 West Halkin Street, off Belgrave Square, which they were to hold until 1896, when they moved to nearby 2 Wilton Crescent. Both properties were in the heart of Belgravia. George Keppel leased the West Halkin Street premises from the now defunct Lowndes Estate in 1892–6 and he and Alice then leased 2 Wilton Crescent from the Grosvenor Estate, where they stayed until 1899. West Halkin Street was not built as a grand street and as it developed west it became less prestigious. Wilton Crescent was elegant and impressive, having been constructed in 1827 by Seth-Smith and Cubitt. In the 1820s Lord Grosvenor had come to an agreement with Thomas Cubitt to develop the open spaces with a centrepiece at Belgrave Square. Her half-uncle Sir Archibald Edmonstone had leased property at 34 Wilton Place. Alice's daughter Sonia was to marry into the Cubitt family.[1]

Money was to remain tight but they managed to preserve a place in Society and gave modest dinner parties. Their connections brought them into the circles which touched those of the Prince and Princess of Wales's Marlborough House Set and the *louche* society therein, with the relaxed attitude to discreet adultery. May, June and July were the months of the Season's greatest activities, with a regular programme of grand receptions at such places as Lansdowne House. Here the queen's Secretary of State for Foreign Affairs, Henry Charles Keith Petty-Fitzmaurice, Lord Lansdowne, entertained, and at Montague House Louisa Jane, Duchess of Buccleuch, the queen's Mistress of the Robes, dispensed hospitality with regal splendour.

Alice's personality and still fresh beauty made her a jewel of these smart circles concentric to the inner at Marlborough House. Alice and George were the personification of the Victorian belief that love could flourish quite apart from sex. George loved Alice dearly, and would do so for the rest of his life; but social gossip averred that he was sexually cold while Alice had a raging need for sexual congress.[2] If Alice had ever really loved George in anything but a romantic sense, her ardour was beginning to wane. The Keppels were somewhat stuffy and for all his kindly nature and sense of fun, George was Alice's intellectual inferior and did not stimulate her to the level of cerebral and physical excitement she needed to survive. As an incorrigible flirt, Alice shone among the pare-nymphomaniacs who permeated London Society. She had many gentlemen callers in the style of the period and they would just 'pop in' for a cup of tea when she was expected to be 'at home'.

Whenever she could she would be seen in a carriage when the fashionable ladies took drives in Hyde Park. As society hostess Sibyl Colefax (1874–1950) remembered:

There were drives in the park 'when it was the fashion for barouches and victorias to progress in close formation, two lines westward and two eastward between Stanhope Gate . . . and the Hyde Park Hotel, all at a foot's pace and all looking at each other, parasol up and two men on the box and all that . . . I can feel the heat, the cramped position, the imbecility of the proceeding, but above all the intolerable boredom of it'.[3]

The key, as Consuelo, Duchess of Marlborough noted, was to have your carriage positioned near Grosvenor Gate 'to see the Princess of Wales pass, lovely and gracious as she bowed right and left'.[4] As she made her respectful obeisance Alice had no idea that within a short time she would rival the beautiful princess for her husband's heart.

Alice took to accepting carriage rides from a rich new acquaintance, Ernest William Beckett, the future 2nd Baron Grimthorpe (1856–1917). He had become MP for Whitby in 1885 and was a partner in the banking firm of Beckett & Co. of Leeds. In 1883 he had married Lucy Tracy Lee of New York, who had died in 1891 leaving him with three children. Alice ran a dreadful risk of social admonition in dallying with a widower, particularly visiting him regularly at his town-house at 138 Piccadilly. Yet the hazards were worth it; Beckett, who was rich and influential, showered her with presents of money and gowns, all of which were a godsend to the Keppels' strained budget. Some time around 1893 they became physical lovers.

By the end of the year Alice was pregnant, allegedly with Beckett's child; and Violet was born at 2 Wilton Crescent on 6 June 1894. For her first child's name Alice eschewed Edmonstone and Keppel favourites and audaciously christened her child after Beckett's sister Violet.[5] No one doubted the child's parentage.

Violet was to become a precocious, cheeky child, greatly spoiled by her parents as she herself averred.[6] From an early age she was attention-seeking, even indulging in shoplifting from such as Bumpus's bookshop to heighten notice.[7] Violet disingenuously called herself retarded, which she never was, and prone to floods of tears.[8] Undoubtedly she was obsessively jealous and possessive, but no one who saw her disputed that she exhibited her natural father's broad brow and the 'Beckett nose'.

Life for Violet, and later her sister Sonia, included regular visits to their maternal grandmother at 2 Wilton Terrace, home of Alice's widowed sister Mrs Jessie Winnington-Ingram. They visited their grandmother again during August–November at Duntreath and made journeys to Quidenham at Easter.

At Duntreath young Violet mixed with ease with both the estate workers and family visitors and in her autobiography identifies her favourites as the Strachans who were keepers of the West Lodge and Miss Laurie of the Moss House, with whom she stayed when Edward VII (as Prince of Wales) made his first visit to his lover's family home.[9] Violet was despatched there not for propriety's sake but because they had run out of beds at Duntreath.

It was at Duntreath incidentally, a little later in 1905, that Violet began a lifelong acquaintance with the writer (Sir) Hugh Walpole. Walpole had been engaged to tutor Violet's cousin Willie Edmonstone in the school holidays. When Walpole's parents, Dr and Mrs Somerset Walpole, realised that Alice would be present at Duntreath during their son's visit they 'strongly disapproved' of his going. Walpole argued his corner in a letter from Cambridge in which he noted that at university he had 'come into contact with men just as bad as Mrs Keppel'.[10] At Duntreath Walpole found Alice 'very beautiful and charming. She is very nice to me but I should never rave about her.'[11] Alas, he overheard Alice tell a friend after an afternoon walk alone with Walpole that 'Even the nicest people can be bores sometimes'.[12]

Violet got to know her Keppel cousins at the Easter Quidenham visits, which were decidedly more rumbustious than those at Duntreath. Certainly the Keppel cousins were more active in aesthetic pursuits than the Edmonstones, but still found time to seek birds' nests, hunt for the headless coachman who haunted the grounds and vie to be the best *enfant terrible*.[13]

Like all Society families the Keppels had a memorable summer in 1897. It was the occasion of the queen's Diamond Jubilee. London was full of royal personages and the hotels and town-houses bulged with European nobility. Events proper began with such occasions as a commemoration concert on Sunday, 20 June at the Queen's Hall; the Queen's Jubilee Dinner at Buckingham Palace was held the next day. Every Society hostess gave a Jubilee dinner, receptions and balls, with Alice attending that given by the Duke and Duchess of Devonshire (see pages 62–3).

When the Devonshires' ball was over in the early hours of the morning, the guests meandered home through Green Park. As Alice and George walked down the paths they could not but notice the dregs of humanity, some drunk, some just demoralised through want of work or food, sprawled on the grass. In her stunning period dress Alice looked a vision of prosperity, health and beauty. Her thoughts echoed those of Consuelo Marlborough: 'How they must have hated me.'[14]

For a long time Alice was developing what would now be called a social conscience. Her daughter Sonia was to recount two incidents to substantiate her mother's generosity. On one occasion she was looking in Morrell's toy-shop window in Stratford Place, London, when the young Sonia's eye rested on a beautiful doll she instantly coveted. Next to them an urchin similarly expressed her delight. Alice entered the shop and bought the doll; and, to Sonia's chagrin, Alice gave the doll to the ragged mite. 'Call her Alice,' she said. To a crestfallen Sonia she said: 'I thought she needed it more than you did.'[15]

The other occasion Sonia mentions concerns Humphrey Napier Sturt, 2nd Baron Alington (1859–1919); he and his wife Lady Feodorovna Yorke, daughter of the Earl and Countess of Hardwicke, were the Keppels' neighbours when they moved to Portman Square. Alington was much taken with Alice – and would be intimately involved with gossip over Alice in the future – and enjoyed taking her for carriage rides. One day Alice indicated that she would like to be driven to Hoxton. A survey of London life and labour in the 1890s described Hoxton as 'one of the worst parts of London, where poverty and overcrowding are characteristic of practically the whole district'. Alington was an extensive property owner in Hoxton and was somewhat embarrassed at the poverty which Alice shamed him into witnessing. (It appears that

Alington had never visited his slum properties.) On arriving back home Alice thanked him for the drive and expressed her hope that what she had seen would be improved in the future.[16]

Despite her family's High Tory principles, in party politics Alice veered more to the left and admired Lord Rosebery's Liberal cabinet, formed in March 1894, more than Lord Salisbury's Tory third cabinet, formed in June 1895. Salisbury's Tories were to rule until A.J. Balfour succeeded as Prime Minister in 1902, and, of course, it was among the Salisbury circle that Alice was to receive the most opprobrious comment as royal mistress. But as Queen Victoria's reign came to an end Alice's main preoccupation was not party politics but the increasingly necessary economic and social advancement of herself. Yet it was to be the party politicians she most skilfully manipulated, as the Duchess of Marlborough was to comment: 'Alice . . . knew how to choose her friends with shrewd appraisal.'[17]

CHAPTER 5

AGNES AND ALICE MEET THE PRINCE OF WALES

As with many aspects of Agnes Keyser's and Alice Keppel's parallel lives in royal circles, how and when they first met Albert Edward, Prince of Wales is something of a conundrum. The year 1898 for the initial presentation is generally accepted as accurate. Yet there are a few extant versions of the first meeting between the 30-year-old Alice Keppel and the 57-year-old Prince of Wales.

First there is the recollection of the not wholly reliable Baroness Agnes de Stoeckel, the 24-year-old wife of a London-based diplomat. She averred that she had presented Alice to the prince at a private lunch party. She recalled the event thus:

> Staying at Villa Kazbeck [with Grand Duke Mikhail Mikhailovich, 1861–1929, cousin of Czar Nicholas II] was Mrs George Keppel. She was entertaining, handsome and very refreshing. It was decided she might amuse the Prince [during his annual spring holiday on the French Riviera] so my husband [Sasha – Baron Alexander de Stoeckel] was told to arrange a small luncheon party – just the Grand Duke Mikhail and Countess Torby [the morganatic wife of the Grand Duke], Mrs Keppel, Sasha and myself and the prince. He saw her then for the first time and from that day started their friendship.'[1]

For the next version the writer Anita Leslie noted how her grandfather, Colonel [later Sir] John Leslie, had figured in the purported first meeting.

HRH first set eyes on the delectable Alice when he was inspecting the Norfolk Yeomanry [in reality the Prince of Wales's Own Norfolk Militia Artillery] in which her husband was an officer. He asked old Lord Leicester [Thomas William Coke, 2nd Earl of Leicester, of Holkham] who she was and requested she be presented to him. A few days later, at Sandown Races [20 April], the Prince noticed my grandfather strolling happily along with the lovely Mrs Keppel on his arm. Waving his stick in salutation, the prince summoned him for a chat, but his eye continued to rest on the lady at his side.

After acceding to Leslie's request to introduce Alice, the prince stated that he was C-in-C of George Keppel's regiment and that he had already met Alice. It was clear, too, that he wished Leslie to make himself scarce, whereupon the prince strolled off with Alice.[2]

The Prince of Wales's biographer Sir Philip Magnus [Allcroft] was to state that the Keppels had 'entertained the Prince to dinner for the first time on 27 February 1898'. Hence the prince's comment of 20 April. It is logical that Alice would have been presented to him by then, for protocol dictated that he could not accept an invitation to the home of people he did not know. The dinner would have taken place at 2 Wilton Crescent, as the Prince of Wales rarely dined in public except with very old friends. It should be remembered too that the prince had visited Quidenham in 1897, where he might have met Alice.

Even so there is proof positive that Alice had been in the presence of the Prince of Wales on at least one occasion the year before the dinner party, although it cannot be proved either way that she was or was not presented to him.

On 2 July 1897, Spencer Compton Cavendish, the 8th Duke of Devonshire, held a costume ball at Devonshire House, Piccadilly, which had been built for the 3rd duke during 1734–7. The event was to celebrate Queen Victoria's Diamond Jubilee. Arranged by his wife Eleanor, it was attended by the Prince and Princess of Wales and the Duke and Duchess of York, and by all of the brilliant and ostentatious drawn from the fifteen hundred privileged families of London Society.

Alice Keppel – dressed as one of Marie Antoinette's courtiers, the Duchesse de Polignac – is listed among the guests. George Keppel is not mentioned, but Alice's fastidiousness with her dress is alluded to. For her paniered costume she obtained genuine eighteenth-century material.[3]

Incidentally the homosexual Prince Edmond de Polignac, a descendant of the *duchesse*, was to be a visitor to Alice's Florentine home of The Ombrellino in the 1920s and 1930s and his estranged wife Winnaretta was an intimate of the Keppel set in Florence.

If Alice Keppel deliberately set herself out to be fatally attractive to the Prince of Wales she could have considered herself to be wholly successful. A contemporary description of how she appeared to Society highlighted her special features:

Alice Keppel had a short, generously proportioned figure, with small hands and feet, of which she was very proud. When she got older she ran to stoutness, and was a perfect match for her portly royal lover. Once when Queen Alexandra saw them together squeezed into a carriage she shook with laughter calling a lady in waiting to share the joke. [Her] head was large and set upon broad shoulders. Her luxuriant chestnut hair was worn in high arrangements. Lustrous, blue-green eyes were set off attractively by her alabaster skin. Her lips were full, and her deep, throaty voice suggested sensuousness. She had a particular vocal mannerism. Usually she spoke in powerful tones, but when she had a special piece of gossip to emphasise she would allow her voice to drop to a whisper, incline her head and then increase the volume to a sonorous bellow as the key point she was making was reached. She was funny, bright and her flirtatiousness showed a deeply felt liking for men. In time she was to exhibit the most important qualification of a mistress – she was a good listener. When one spoke to her, she gave, or seemed to give, the whole of her attention, looking the speaker full in the face. She had no rival for the Prince of Wales's affections except the beautiful but brainless Queen Alexandra. Alice Keppel took her time to enter a room so that she achieved the right effect on those present. Her every movement seemed to be studied, her every gesture looked almost rehearsed as if aimed at projecting her personality and her use of her long cigarette holder was positively balletic.[4]

Alice Keppel had a sensuous effect on men; her daughter Sonia noted how Alice always took time to raise her veil in male company; as she did so, a watching gentleman 'seemed to catch his breath a little as he beheld her beautiful face'.[5]

From his first enamoration of Alice, the Prince of Wales subjected her to his own particular style of courtship. There was his chuckling Germanic guttural laugh, his way of rolling his 'r's in a Teutonic manner, his complimentary asides, the caressing, the undressing glance, and the absorbed expression. His full beard, now grey and nicotine-stained, added raffishness to cover his weak Hanoverian chin. Alice would know full well that his attention to her at the race meeting and dinner would lead to an afternoon call. In due course Alice received a note from the Prince of Wales's private secretary Sir Francis Knollys (1837–1924, later 1st Viscount Knollys), to suggest the first afternoon appointment, when George would not be expected to be at home.

In fact, it is said that the Prince of Wales had a hand in giving George an excuse to be out. George Keppel had been up for membership of the St James's Club, 106 Piccadilly, since 1896. Founded in 1859 for members of the Diplomatic Service, by the 1890s it was electing members from a wide spectrum of society. George's membership was sponsored by Cuthbert Lacking and the wealthy Irish peer James Frederick Daly, Lord Dunsandle and Clanconal, erstwhile assistant private secretary to Benjamin Disraeli. On 2 March 1898 – a few days after Magnus says the Prince of Wales dined with the Keppels – George's membership was confirmed following enquiries concerning its progress by Francis Knollys.[6]

The developing intimacy with the prince led Alice, chaperoned by George, to be a member of the 'Marlborough House Set'. Soon after their marriage, during April 1863, the Prince and Princess of Wales moved into Marlborough House. The house, set at the north side of London's Pall Mall, was originally built by Sir Christopher Wren for Sarah, Duchess of Marlborough, and was finished in 1711. With additions and renovations, the house remained in the Marlborough family until 1817. It was acquired by the Crown and was lived in by Queen Victoria's uncle Prince Leopold of Saxe-Coburg-Saalfeld until he became first king of the Belgians in 1831. From 1837 the dowager queen Adelaide of Saxe-Meiningen, relict of King William IV, lived there until her death in 1849. From then until the renovations by Sir James Pennethorne in 1861–3 it was an art gallery.

Marlborough House, birthplace of the future George V, was to become the focus of a rival court to Queen Victoria's. Society was now divided into two camps, that of the retired and dismal circle around the widowed queen, and the rumbustious group around the Waleses. The couple entertained their guests both formally and informally and accepted invitations to visit their friends' houses. And for many, the Marlborough House Set, as they were dubbed, were the epitome of decadence. As Charles Wynn-Carrington, who had first procured Nellie Clifden for the Prince of Wales's bed, said, 'When the Marlborough House Set fall out, husbands need no longer sleep alone.'[7]

The socialites of London pencilled into their diaries the 'Marlborough House Season' with the hope that invitations would come their way. For every hostess knew by heart the pattern of annual activity of Edward both as Prince of Wales and as king. During January–February he was at Sandringham; mid-March he would be in residence at Marlborough House and at the end of July he was at Cowes. Alice Keppel was to be introduced to Marlborough House, but she came to know Sandringham and Buckingham Palace best as these were the places Edward frequented most after he became king. In August to October Edward was in Germany or Austria, thence at Abergeldie and

Balmoral, finishing off the year at Sandringham. Autumn was the season for 'Society house weekends' after the debutantes had been presented at court and when Henley Regatta and Ascot race meetings were over. These weekends occurred from Saturday to Monday and at them adultery was honed to a fine art.

Society slavishly supplied and aped the racy tastes of the amiably tyrannical Prince of Wales. They loved and feared him, and indulged him in his sexual appetites. Docile acceptance of the role of cuckolded husband – of which Alice Keppel's husband George was to become the best example in the history of kingly adultery – showed how Edward could command subservience from those who were prepared to sacrifice all for his favour and patronage. The Prince of Wales was fatally easily bored, so the whole credo of the Marlborough House Set was to stave off his ennui. This meant supplying him with a train of vivacious women.

The Marlborough House hothouse of intrigue was a male-orientated society, although the Prince of Wales, as Margot Tennant (later Margot Asquith) noted, was not interested for long in men's company alone. She further commented that he loved women's gossip about their amours, sought their advice on his social programme and gave them a lifelong loyalty if deserved; in all his dealings with females he 'was a professional love-maker'.[8]

High society promiscuity was carried on in a set pattern and was indulged in almost entirely between married people or a married woman and a single man. The permanence of marriage in a society where women's main function was to look beautiful, entertain brilliantly and bear children was therefore the secure background against which adultery took place. Marriage was for life in high society, divorce was out of the question. There was a certain disregard for *meum* and *tuum* when it came to personal possessions too. A number of high society members purloined moveable effects when they visited each others' houses. Virginia Woolf quotes Alice Keppel as saying how outrageously Society women used to filch from country houses. 'One woman purloined any jewelled bag left lying,' Alice had confided.[9]

The Marlborough House Set evolved a pattern for high society adultery. First would begin the *flirtation*, then the *definite courtship* would be continued with *ardent letters* and snatched moments at house weekends. Then, if both parties agreed, an *affair* would be *established*. This would lead to *discreet appearances* on the part of the male at the home of the lady involved at a time when her husband would not be expected to be at home. At house parties the hostess would ensure that the pair would be given bedrooms in proximity. In her novel *The Edwardians* (1930), Vita Sackville-West gave a flavour of the arrangements:

The name of each guest would be neatly written on a card slipped into a tiny brass frame on the bedroom door. This question of the disposition of bedrooms always gave [the hostess] cause for anxious thought. It was so necessary to be tactful, and at the same time discreet. The professional Lothario would be furious if he found himself in a room surrounded by ladies who were all accompanied by their husbands.'[10]

This was the exact practice of her mother Victoria, Lady Sackville, at the family home of Knole: *chacun à sa chacune* Alice Keppel is said to have commented.

The Marlborough House Set were soon able to define the kind of woman the prince wanted. She must be beautiful, witty, attentive, non-opiniative, but clever, or, if not, appear so. Alice Keppel immediately realised that Edward did not like women to assume intellectualism or strongmindedness; but if the conversation flagged they must jump in with a subject upon which he could comment.

The prince's rule for physical sexual expression was: 'Trifle not with unmarried women'. Thus his attraction to Agnes Keyser was not deemed to be physically sexual – although her unstated sexuality drew him – and probably did not go beyond hand-holding and maybe a caress or two. Edward was a sex opportunist and indulged whenever he could, although some hostesses whispered he was all fingers and emotions and not much action.

Alice Keppel was to find that her royal lover's court was filled with a motley crowd of rakes, gamblers, high-born trollopes and hell-raisers. It was to be the forcing ground of the Society she was to know well and manipulate. Among the prince's special friends certain names occurred regularly on invitation lists. One was Sir Frederick Johnstone of Westerhall, Dumfries, a womaniser later to be associated with the Mordaunt divorce case, wherein the prince appeared in court to testify whether or not he had slept, in a long line of others, with Sir Charles Mordaunt's wife Harriet. Then there was Spencer Cavendish, 'Harty-Tarty', 8th Duke of Devonshire, later Chief Secretary for Ireland in Gladstone's Liberal cabinet, whose affair with Louise, Duchess of Manchester was an ongoing scandal; Devonshire had also set up the notorious Liverpudlian whore, Catherine 'Skittles' Walters with a house in Mayfair. The racy Mary Georgina Caroline, Lady Filmer, wife of Sir Edward Filmer; Charles Wynn-Carrington, Marquis of Lincolnshire who shared the prince's tastes for gambling and pornographic books, which they exchanged; and the royal toady who ruined himself trying to keep up with the expense of entertaining the Prince and Princess of Wales, Christopher Sykes of Brantingham Thorpe, Yorkshire: these also appeared on the list but Sykes died the year of Alice's entry into court circles.

One way or another they all procured for Edward's bed, but Society knew the open secret that the chief go-between and pimp was the prince's secretary Sir Francis Knollys. Knollys arranged for Edward's raffish parties to be peopled with 'actress friends' and when required to do so he set up cockfighting for the benefit of those who preferred gambling to girls.[11]

Few had the courage, or lack of self-seeking patronage, to deny the prince's carnal requests. One such was Archibald Philip Primrose, 5th Earl of Rosebery. On the prince's instructions Knollys had approached Rosebery to use his house at 2 Berkeley Square, London, for himself and his brother Prince Alfred Ernest (1844–1900), Duke of Edinburgh and Saxe-Coburg-Gotha, to dally with trollopes from the chorus of London's theatreland. Rosebery refused but accompanied the prince's party on the same night to Frank Lawley's (of the *Daily Telegraph*) at 2 Brook Street, for drinking, lechery and cockfighting. Years later Alice and her daughter Violet were to visit the Roseberys at Dalmeny Park, West Lothian, Scotland.

Edward liked nothing better than gossip about amatory pursuits, and his mother's court regularly supplied tales of adultery. There was Baroness Arundel who dallied with the artist Basil Hodges; the Countess of Jersey and the Earl of Abingdon; the Marchioness of Ailesbury and the Earl of Wilton; the Countess of Lincoln and Lord Walpole; and the desirable Hermione, Duchess of Leinster with Hugo Charteris, Lord Elcho, who became the Earl of Wemyss and March. Alice Keppel soon fell in with the scions of all these noble houses, extracting all the gossip she could to delight her royal lover. Agnes Keyser was to serve a similar purpose for both Edward and George V, particularly providing the latter with titbits about his wayward son who as the Duke of Windsor married Wallis Simpson.

The Prince of Wales's visits to Alice were soon established into a set pattern when he was in London. He would arrive from Marlborough House in a discreet brougham, which would park further up the street. The maid would bring tea and the prince's favourite cakes and bobbing a curtsey would leave, knowing that she should not return until summoned. There outside the drawing-room, on the upstairs landing, Alice's butler kept a discreet watch that no one should enter while the prince was present. What happened in the drawing-room was common knowledge, for many a former inamorata had indiscreetly spilled the beans at functions. There would be a little flirtatious conversation, a caress or two, leading to a bout of passionate kissing, and if the right circumstances prevailed full sexual intercourse.[12] 'Right circumstances', of course, included if HRH could manage full intercourse there and then because of his bulk. Being younger Alice would be more supple in a sexual role, but when in the prince's own quarters they could use the 'hanging harness, complete with footholds' that he had had made.[13]

Life was to change rapidly for Alice Keppel as soon as it became common knowledge that she was the Prince of Wales's new mistress. No more boring days with or without George: her social diary was to be crammed. Her predecessor in the royal bed, Lillie Langtry, summed up what life for Alice now became:

> to pass in a few weeks from being an absolute 'nobody' to what the Scotch so aptly describe as a 'person'; to find myself not only invited to, but watched at all the great balls and parties; to hear the murmur as I entered the room; to be compelled to close the yard gates in order to avoid the curious, waiting crowds outside, before I could mount my horse for my daily canter in the Row . . . surely, I thought London had gone mad.[14]

Society began to know Alice well as the acknowledged royal mistress; George being present or not did not raise eyebrows. Consuelo, Duchess of Marlborough noted how Society was accepting Alice:

> Alice Keppel was handsome and of genial and easy approach . . . Even her enemies, and they were few, she treated kindly, which, considering the influence she wielded with the Prince, indicated a generous nature. She invariably knew the choicest scandal, the price of stocks, the latest political move; no one could better amuse the Prince during the tediousness of the long dinners etiquette decreed.[15]

All her life thereafter people maintained an exaggerated respect for Alice which she came to expect and connive at. She fast became a connoisseur of good food at the new houses to which she was invited. Her own cook, Mrs Wright, was a fine caterer but at the houses of the rich the food was exceptional, particularly if the prince was present. At first Alice ate largely in silence, but eagerly absorbed the structure of royal conversation. It was to be a trait she used to good effect. As the prince aged and his girth made sexual intercourse more jockey-style, Alice's fundamental role was to be one of amuser and mollifier, and in preventing him from being bored. She was to keep conversation going, but knew when silence was called for.[16]

Like so many of the women who had been in the Prince of Wales's bed, Alice found herself in love with his title and wanted to be associated with it. She now filled her diary with what the prince was doing, so that when he was in London she was available; more than that she held herself ready, with or without George, to accept invitations to where the Prince of Wales was going. She knew that the prince adored her, as she worshipped and admired him. She was to feel pangs of jealousy when he seemed to be paying too much attention to other women, and he was uneasy if her 'flirtatious Freddie' personality was wrapped round another man.[17]

As Consuelo, Duchess of Marlborough had pointed out, Alice was very well informed (for the prince's entertainment and information) about what was going on in Society. And one of her first tasks on becoming royal mistress was to make herself familiar with the workings of the prince's court and with those who served him.

Like the queen, the Prince of Wales had his own 'court'. At the top of the heap were the lords of the bedchamber, Baron Suffield (whose daughter married Alice's brother-in-law, Derek Keppel) and the Earl of Gosford. Sir Dighton Macnaughten Probyn VC was Comptroller and Treasurer, and Sir Francis Knollys (also the prince's private secretary) and Henry Stonor were grooms of the bedchamber. The Groom of the Stole was the Duke of Abercorn, and next came nine equerries, mostly service officers and one peer in Baron Wantage.

Eight medical men were also members of the prince's court, headed by such famous names as Sir William Jenner and Sir James Paget, as Physician and Surgeon in Ordinary, respectively. Other age-old court positions were the prince's Lord Warden of the Stannaries (the tin-mining districts of Cornwall and Devon, which had their own court until 1897), in the Earl of Ducie; the Keeper of the Privy Seal was the Earl of Leicester (who featured in Anita Leslie's story), while the court was completed with C.A. Cripps as Attorney-General and Colonel Sir Robert Kingscote as Receiver-General.

Alice was to get to know all of these people; some of them treated her well, some icily, others with disdain, depending upon their opinion of royal mistresses. She was also to come across another wide range of court officials because the Princess of Wales had her own, and after hers came the minor courts of the Duke and Duchess of York (the prince's son George and his wife May), the Duchess of Connaught (his sister-in-law Princess Louise of Prussia), the Duchess of Albany (his sister-in-law Princess Helena of Waldeck-Pyrmont), Prince and Princess Christian of Schleswig-Holstein (his brother-in-law and sister Princess Helena), and the entourages of his sisters Princesses Louise (Marchioness of Lorne) and Princess Beatrice, widow of Prince Henry of Battenberg.

So, for the next twelve years Alice Keppel's life was dictated by the comings and goings of the prince's court. During May 1898 he left for Mentone with the Duchess of York and by 28 May he was in Copenhagen with the Princess of Wales. On 11 June he made an official visit to Reading.

June 1898 was to be a busy family month too for Alice. On 20 June George's brother Derek married the Hon. Bridget Harbord, younger daughter of the 5th Baron Suffield, a lord of the bedchamber of her new lover's court. Educated at Charterhouse, Derek Keppel was a lieutenant-colonel in the Prince of Wales's Own Civil Service Rifles and during 1893–1910 was equerry-in-ordinary to George, Duke of York and held the same position when George in turn became Prince of Wales; Derek Keppel was to continue court service to George V and Edward VIII, retiring in 1936.

Combined with her love for the Prince of Wales, Alice had a deep maternal feeling towards him and as her love grew so did her worries about his health. She knew that the 16-stone prince lived an unhealthy life of heavy smoking, eating and drinking and he was prone to tripping over. For instance, after a visit to Edinburgh, on 18 July 1898 the Prince of Wales visited Waddesdon Manor, Aylesbury, Buckinghamshire, the lavish home of Baron Ferdinand de Rothschild, when he slipped and fell. A memory of the incident was recorded by the 12th Earl of Warwick, the husband of Prince of Wales's former mistress Daisy Warwick, in his *Memoirs of Sixty Years* (1917):

I was out early and sitting on a chair in front of the house talking to one of the guests – I can't remember to whom. Suddenly the butler came out and asked anxiously if I knew where the Baron was. I replied I had not yet seen him, and asked if anything was amiss, as the poor man was greatly agitated. 'I fear', he replied, 'that the Prince of Wales has met with a bad accident. He slipped heavily on the spiral staircase [West Stairs], and is now sitting down there unable to move.' I hurried into the house, and found the Prince where the butler had left him, sitting on a step of the main circular staircase. He smiled reassuringly at me, although I could see at a glance that he must be in great pain, and said: 'I fear I have broken something in my leg; my foot slipped, and as I fell I heard a bone crack.' Two servants came up at that moment bearing a long invalid chair, and fearing from what the Prince had said that he had split or broken his knee-cap, I tied his leg straight out onto one of the parallel carrying poles. Then the local doctor arrived, and the Prince was allowed to sit on a sofa with his leg down, to have his breakfast before leaving. I have always thought that but for the severe strain involved by his straightened leg the subsequent illness would not have been so long or so difficult – but I will not blame the doctor. The Prince was ever the kindliest of men, and his great anxiety was to reassure Baron Ferdinand, who was too grieved to think he should have met with a serious accident under his roof.

In trying to find out at their request, years later, if the prince had been treated at the Royal Bucks Hospital, Mrs James de Rothschild discovered that when the prince was being transported to the line for Windsor at Aylesbury station, the chair in which he was being carried broke. The prince was undignifiedly dropped on the passenger bridge.[18]

Alice Keppel was continually anxious about the prince's health and from time to time tried to persuade him to accept more care. When a direct approach failed she tried through the help of another mutual friend. Proof of this was found by Gordon Brook-Shepherd when he was researching the papers of the Marquis de Soveral. He discovered an undated letter from Alice which included the comment:

> I want you to try and get the [by then] King to see a proper doctor about his knee. Perhaps the Queen could make him do so. He writes that it is very painful and stiff and that massage does it no good or rather harm as there is a slight 'effusion' on it. This I know ought to be seen at once, for if he gets water on the knee this might mean a stiff knee for life . . . do try what you can with your famous tact and, of course, don't tell anyone *I* wrote to you . . . Cher Soveral, From your affectionate old friend, Alice Keppel.[19]

The Prince of Wales was incapacitated for eight weeks following the Waddesdon Manor accident, but he was at Balmoral by 14 September. On 18 September he presented new colours to George Keppel's old regiment the Gordon Highlanders at Balmoral. Then there were visits to Cowes and Weymouth and a trip to Mount Edgcumbe, Plymouth, the home of William Henry, 4th Earl of Mount Edgcumbe, who had been one of the 'three very distinguished young men' – as Prince Albert described them – who had been the Prince of Wales's youthful companions (really junior gentlemen equerries) at White Lodge, Richmond Park, way back in the 1860s.

Autumn was overshadowed in court circles by the death of Queen Louise of Denmark, the Princess of Wales's mother, on

9 September. Princess Alexandra went into something of a depression and the prince was concerned about her health. It did not stop him enjoying himself with Alice. Even the crowds which gathered when people found out that the Prince of Wales was to be present at a function were beginning to look for Alice to arrive too. Alice quickly came to terms with the public interest, playing it down with her own innate discretion. Gossip about her was to be heard at every Society function. Princess Daisy of Pless said: 'As for dear Alice Keppel, she was inimitable! What spirit, wit and resilience the woman has!'[20] And many too remarked about George Keppel's fortitude in accepting with equanimity the role of most famous cuckold in Society.

The Prince of Wales's association with Agnes Keyser developed at a much slower pace than his with Alice Keppel, and was not to increase in intensity until after he became king and his health entered its steady decline. Alice would never lose her place as *maîtresse du roi*, but the monarch's need for Agnes evolved as a loving friendship. It is likely too, that Edward was a regular visitor to the London house of the Keyser sisters at 17 Grosvenor Crescent, which the family leased from the Duke of Westminster.

Exactly when and where the Prince of Wales met Agnes Keyser for the first time in 1898 is difficult to tell. The prince – with Alice Keppel – was to visit the former Keyser home of Warren House on a number of occasions and knew the Keysers well, but it is likely that they first met in London through mutual friends, within the network of Anglo-Jewry which vacillated at the edge of Edward's court. In particular the Bischoffsheims and their relatives the Goldschmidts, the Sassoons, the Cassels and the Wernhers, were all members of the prince's court circle. Many of their friends were to be further linked with Agnes and her new royal admirer through the advent of the South African War.

CHAPTER 6

WAR, ASSASSINATIONS AND ALARMS

For the second time in two decades Britain found herself at war with the Afrikaners, by-named the Boers in British newspapers and the music hall. Fundamentally the causes of the Boer War, or the South African War as it was known to Edwardians, lay in the grievances of the mostly British 'Uitlanders' (foreigners) who had flocked to the Transvaal when gold was discovered in the Rand in 1886. Paying heavy taxes and commodity prices to the Transvaal government, the Uitlanders were virtually excluded from the franchise and their dissatisfaction with the Boer government was inflamed by such as the ambitious Cecil Rhodes, the British diamond millionaire, who was also Prime Minister of Cape Colony. Rhodes wished to absorb into the British Empire Boer territory including the South African Republic, whose president was the xenophobic Paul Kruger. This political powder-keg exploded and the South African War was to last for almost three years from the Boers' ultimatum to the British government on 9 October 1899 to the Peace of Vereeniging of 31 May 1902.

War became the main talking-point in Society which continued with its social life, but as the casualties began to mount and young men disappeared from Society functions, the minds of the well-to-do became focused on charitable activities to raise money for soldiers' comforts. Many Society women went to South Africa with their soldier husbands; alas a goodly number were sensation-seekers and were of little service to the cause parading around Johannesburg dressed as for Ascot rather than for doing useful war work. Unmarried women had the best record, many joining together to work in the nursing service or relief organisations. Among them were Agnes and Fanny Keyser.[1]

From the early days of his public duties, the Prince of Wales had shown great interest in promoting and supporting hospitals. In the year of his marriage (1863) he became patron of eight hospitals alone, including the London Fever Hospital. In the Keyser sisters he saw worthy (and wealthy) promoters of his favourite charity theme and suggested that they set up a hospital for sick and wounded in the current war. So in 1899 a hospital was founded at the sisters' home of 17 Grosvenor Crescent. But at Agnes's insistence it was to be for officers, as her snobbism could not countenance other ranks. From the War Office Field-Marshal Sir Henry Evelyn Wood sent written recognition of the hospital's existence on behalf of the Marquis of Lansdowne, Secretary of State for War, and Viscount Wolseley, C-in-C of the British Army.

Funded by the two sisters the hospital was to nurse 275 officers during the period of the war and Agnes showed herself to be an able administrator, although she had no medical training.[2] The hospital was not to take the whole of Fanny Keyser's efforts. She decided to go to South Africa. Before 1899 there were few female nurses in the British Medical Corps, and at first there was an official reluctance to send women as nurses to South Africa. Fanny Keyser joined a civilian hospital at Johannesburg, from 5 November 1900 to 28 February 1901, whereupon she rejoined her sister.[3] Meanwhile brother Charles Edward founded a Home for Convalescent Soldiers at Aldermaston.

While the Keyser sisters busied themselves with war work, Alice Keppel was establishing herself in royal circles and began to appear regularly at the Prince of Wales's main haunts. And people increasingly gossiped about her. Mary Victoria, Lady Curzon was among them, noting that the Prince of Wales was being 'made fun of, and there is a new story of him and "Favorita" [Alice] every day. The whole scandal is public property.'

Queen Victoria and Prince Albert had decided that, on his 21st birthday in 1861, the Prince of Wales should quit the family home and occupy a house of his own. Marlborough House, assigned by Act of Parliament as his London base, made him 'too available' to Society, and his parents wished him to have a private residence, preferably in the country, where he could take up 'healthy' pursuits.

The search for such a house was brought to a halt on 14 December 1861 with the death of Prince Albert. Queen Victoria, however, then insisted that all should proceed as her consort would have wished, and that an option on a house that had come up when Albert was still alive should be investigated immediately.

The Hon. Charles Spencer Cowper (stepson of Queen Victoria's Prime Minister Henry John Temple, 3rd Viscount Palmerston) had made it known that he wanted to sell his Norfolk estate at Sandringham. Cowper had recently married his mistress Lady Harriet d'Orsay, and they found the lady's reputation did not fit in well with staid Norfolk society. On 4 February 1862 the Prince of Wales went to see Sandringham with Sir Charles Beaumont Phipps, Keeper of the Privy Purse. Phipps had reported favourably to Queen Victoria and with the prince's further enthusiasm, the queen agreed to purchase the estate for £220,000.

Sandringham had been built in the late eighteenth century by Cornish Henley, who had replaced a former house with a stuccoed Georgian pile. Charles Spencer Cowper had inherited it from a friend in 1843, and although he had made some alterations the house was now somewhat shabby. The Prince of Wales was to pull down the old house, preserving the conservatory as a billiard room, and to the design of A.J. Humbert a new red-brick Victorian-Jacobean house was ready in 1870.

For the whole of their married life thereafter the Prince and Princess of Wales made it a rule that they would be at Sandringham for the prince's birthday (9 November) and the princess's birthday (1 December) and for Christmas. And these occasions were usually accompanied by a large house party. Alice and George Keppel's first invitation to a specifically royal gathering was at Sandringham around early 1899, the year they moved into 30 Portman Square.

Invitations to dine and sleep at Sandringham came via the Prince of

Wales's secretary, on a large printed card, bearing on the reverse the words, usual on royal invitations: 'Should the Ladies and Gentlemen to whom the Invitations are sent be out of Town, and not expected to return in time to obey Their Royal Highnesses' commands on the days the Invitations are for, the cards are to be brought back.' Alice and George received separate cards as a matter of course, so that a compliant George could be 'otherwise engaged' if necessary.

Guests usually arrived at Sandringham House by train at the small station of Wolferton, some two miles away, to be met by smartly turned-out carriages with coachmen in the Prince of Wales's livery; luggage and servants arrived separately in less ostentatious vehicles.[4] Usually George took a manservant and Alice her personal maid; and if Violet and Sonia were present, their nanny.

Alice soon became used to arriving at Sandringham through the magnificent Norwich Gates as the Prince of Wales's carriage bowled up the drive to the large *porte-cochère*. There they were greeted by their royal host and hostess, and taken into the hall for a curious ritual. Guests were placed in a leather-seated weighing chair to have their weight recorded. (They were also weighed at the end of the visit.) After tea George and Alice, and the other guests, were conducted to their rooms by the Prince of Wales so that he could see personally that nothing was lacking for their comfort.

The first time they went to Sandringham, Alice and George were given the customary pep-talk by one of the prince's equerries as to the 'house rules'. Edward was a punctilious and generous host and planned his weekends in great detail. Alice soon became used to her lover's routine. Walking, riding and driving round the estate were obligatory, and there was ice-skating in winter, with the whole household playing ice-hockey; non-skaters were pushed around in basket chairs on sleds and sledges; lanterns were set round the ponds when darkness fell. Most guests had two main reasons to be disgruntled with Sandringham: the chilly Norfolk climate and the very late hours kept by the royal couple. Sometimes the parlour games went on until three o'clock in the morning.

After dinner came a multitude of entertainments in the Main

Drawing-Room described by Queen Victoria in 1871 as 'very long and handsome . . . with painted ceiling and panels with two fireplaces'.[5] The gentlemen usually played billiards and bowls, while the ladies played cards. The Prince of Wales was a very keen bridge player and Alice, herself a skilled player, was often at his table. She soon became skilled too in soothing his sulks when he lost. Plays, charades and games were also planned for various parts of the weekend. The atmosphere at Sandringham was genial and casual. One guest, Victor Montagu (brother of Queen Alexandra's devoted courtier Oliver Montagu), commented: 'It is very jolly here indeed, very unstiff and only a certain amount of etiquette, very quiet and gentlemanlike altogether.'[6]

Sunday was set aside with its own routines. The whole household attended religious devotions in the morning, walking across the park to Sandringham's Church of St Mary Magdalene which the Prince of Wales had had altered in 1890. After lunch there were tours of the home farm, kennels and stables. Often the ladies walked to York Cottage, that small house, once called Bachelor's Cottage, in the parkland, the home of the Duke and Duchess of York. The Princess of Wales presided for tea in the model dairy and then the company would walk back to the house through the gardens.

On the days when there was shooting, the ladies joined the men for lunch alfresco from the Prince of Wales's 'hot box', and watched the rest of the shoot despite the cold winds off the North Sea. The walk back to Sandringham was made more delightful with the thought of copious afternoon teas and roaring fires.

Life at Sandringham was informal with a noticeable lack of the Germanic protocol which Queen Victoria insisted upon at Windsor Castle and Buckingham Palace. If guests remembered not to be familiar, and did not forget etiquette, the Prince of Wales would always be an accessible and friendly host able to put aside strict royal ceremony but remain dignified. Breakfast was served between nine and ten at small tables; the fare was of gargantuan proportions. The Prince of Wales breakfasted alone in his rooms as did the Princess of Wales who never appeared in company before eleven.

Luncheon was served at one-thirty sharp – not that this meant anything to the unpunctual Princess of Wales – and tea at five o'clock in the Saloon, into which the front door led. Here in the principal reception room of the house was set out what Alice would see as a Scottish meal; with sandwiches and pastries of all kinds and heaped plates of the prince's favourite Scottish shortbread. Dinner at eight-thirty was elegant and elaborate with the ladies on their fourth change of clothes of the day. Thus a large part of the Keppel household budget went on Alice's clothes.

Alice had rapidly learned too that her lover required in his women impeccability of dress, a trait which came naturally to her. The tiara, the decorations, the petticoat and underclothes, the stockings and shoes; every flounce had to be just right. The Princess of Wales often drove Edward to distraction by her laxity in the protocol of couture. If he remarked that an Order clashed with a jewel she had chosen, she would move the Order from its proper place, say on the left breast, and wear it on the wrong side. Edward had long given up reprimanding her, but other women were given short shrift. The Duchess of Manchester once omitted to wear a prescribed tiara and was rebuked for it by the Prince of Wales.

In May 1899 Alice went to Cannes with the Prince of Wales for the first time and on 2 July he made a royal visit to Edinburgh. During his Scottish tour, the Prince of Wales was able to call at Duntreath for the first time to see his new lover's childhood home. It was a low-key visit, but as the *Glasgow Herald* was to say, Alice and her brother Archie were able to show their royal visitor some of the glories of a romantic and highly picturesque country.

During late 1899, Alice found herself pregnant again. When Society gained the information, the gossips began to speculate again and came to the conclusion that this time the child's father was no less a person than the Prince of Wales. Alice never let her pregnancies cramp her style; she still drove a tandem of mettlesome ponies in a dog-cart.[7]

Yet she was to receive a 'scare' on 4 April 1900. At the time the Prince and Princess of Wales were en route for Copenhagen, and during the first stage of their journey arrived in Brussels. The Prince of Wales's diary commented: 'Walk about the [Nord] station. Just as the train is leaving, 5.30, a man fires a pistol at [the Prince of Wales] through open window of carriage (no harm done).' The would-be assassin was a Belgian youth, Jean Baptiste Sipido, who had fired maintaining that the prince deserved to die because of the thousands of Boers who had died during the South African War.[8] The Prince of Wales had remained unperturbed, saying only, 'Poor fool.' But he was anxious that Alice might hear of the attempt and be worried. At the time Alice was enjoying a few days at Devonshire House, Devonshire Buildings, Weymouth, as a guest of Montague John Guest, the brother of the 1st Baron Wimborne, whose wife Lady Cornelia was a daughter of the 6th Duke of Marlborough. Alice had met Guest in the Spencer Churchill circle.[9] The prince's telegram to Alice read: 'Tirelmont: As we were leaving Brussels a man jumped on the step of our carriage and fired a pistol at us through the open window. I don't think there was a bullet in it. He was at once seized. A[lbert] E[dward].'[10]

In Edward VII's time there was no Royal Protection Squad of armed police to protect his every public movement; when the king ventured out to have one of his favourite strolls incognito, he invariably had only one equerry and a detective with him; often when in Paris (under his travelling guise of 'Baron Renfrew') he was accompanied by a solitary *aide*. Alice was to be continually concerned about her royal lover's safety; when strolling arm-in-arm with her from his suite at the Hotel Bristol down the boulevards of Paris the king would often stop and chat with people and a nervous Alice would encourage the king to keep walking and was not happy until she steered him safely back to the hotel.

On one occasion the king was lunching at a restaurant at Saint-Cloud, wherein various parties of people were at tables in arbours around the garden. A secretary from the British Embassy, Alice, the king and a smattering of French nobility were eating together in a prominent position. Alice became agitated at the sight of a man at a nearby table who she averred had a criminal-looking face. Glancing around she noted that the restaurant's garden had openings through which an apache bent on an opportunistic robbery or an assassin might appear at any moment. The king's private secretary Sir Frederick Ponsonby assured her that the monarch had ample police protection nearby. Alice became more distressed and Ponsonby, to reassure her, sought out the head of the French police, M. Lepine, to check on the police presence. He returned to the table with a broad smile. He whispered to Alice that each of the tables around the king was occupied by police and their wives including the policeman with the 'criminal face'.[11]

Alice and George attended the parties held after 18 May 1900 to celebrate the relief of Mafeking, the town in Bophutha Tswana, South Africa, which had been besieged by the Boers for 217 days, and held by Colonel Robert Baden-Powell. After one such occasion, as she and George went home, in her exuberance she sat 'astride a lion in Trafalgar Square'. On 24 May Alice gave birth to Sonia Rosemary at 30 Portman Square.[12] It was the day of Queen Victoria's eighty-first birthday, and six days later the Prince of Wales's horse 'Diamond Jubilee' won the Derby.

On the announcement of the birth, Alice's house was swamped with flowers, the Prince of Wales's garlands of yellow Maréchal Niel roses being delivered by a liveried coachman.[13] And those who saw the child had no doubt that her face — though blemished with eczema — mirrored the baby features of the Prince of Wales captured in 1843 by court painter Sir William Ross. The likeness to the prince was also noted when close friends of the Keppels saw the miniature portrait of Sonia by Gertrude Massey of around 1904. Sonia's sister Violet always resented the inference that her sibling was a 'royal brat' and fantasised that she herself was the true Fitzedward.[14]

Long before she met the Prince of Wales, Society had made Alice aware of his so-called 'Fitzedwards', so rife was the common knowledge about the royal bratlings. There was George Cornwallis-West, grandson of the Marquis of Headford, whose mother Mary 'Patsy' Cornwallis-West was a court favourite. He married in 1900 the beautiful widowed Lady Randolph Churchill.

Then was mentioned the child of Lady Susan Pelham-Clinton, daughter of the 5th Duke of Newcastle who had been one of the Princess Royal's bridesmaids in 1858. She had married the alcoholic Lord Adolphus Vane-Tempest in 1860. Lady Susan's supposed child with the Prince of Wales was born in 1871 and the prince was asked to contribute financially to the child's upbringing. Edward James the surrealist poet, art collector and eccentric, averred that his mother Evelyn 'Evie' Forbes was the daughter of the Prince of Wales; Jones had the prince as his godfather.

Gossips further inferred that Chief Constable of Edinburgh, Roderick Ross, was also a child of the Prince, as was Sir Stewart Graham Menzies, 'C' of the British Secret Intelligence Service MI6. The Prince of Wales was further rumoured to have fathered a child by the Princesse Jeanne de Sagan; in 1873 he had visited the Château de Mello, a few hundred kilometres south of Paris, and dallied there with her. It was said that his favourite illegitimate child was Baroness Olga Alberta de Meyer, daughter of the Duchess di Caracciolo. The child had been brought up discreetly at Dieppe, and was to be one of Winnaretta, Princesse de Polignac's lovers, years before Violet Keppel shared her bed.[15]

Alice Keppel was in the habit of taking her daughters with her when she visited neighbours in Portman Square. And at No. 15 there was a royal connection in Alexander William George Duff, 1st Duke of Fife (1849–1912), and his wife Princess Louise of Wales (1867–1931), her royal lover's third child and eldest daughter. But the Keppels' great friends were Humphrey Sturt, Conservative MP for Dorset East, and his wife, Lady Feodorovna; they lived at 38 Portman Square. In 1904 Sturt became the 2nd Baron Alington, and gossips made him Alice's lover and named *him* Sonia's father!

In her book, Sonia Keppel describes visits to No. 38 and how she was tormented by Sturt's youngest daughter Lois, whom she called 'the monkey'.[16] Sonia noted: 'The Alington household was the hub of the big wheel of Edwardian fashion, setting in motion the gilded structure with its elegant concourse of people.'[17] Into this circle came people who were to figure prominently in Alice

Keppel's future life, men and women who were to become linch-pins in her progress in royal society. Here at the Alingtons' Prince Francis of Teck (1870–1910), the 'black sheep' younger brother of the future Queen Mary, Sir Ernest Cassel, Sir Thomas Lipton and Lady Sarah Churchill all sat down to dine. From the august gatherings Alice Keppel cultivated those whom she needed to oil her rise to prosperity, and from their number she chose three prominent godparents for Sonia.

First was Sonia's godfather the Grand Duke Mikhail Mikhailovitch, grandson of Czar Nicholas I of All the Russias, and his wife who was first godmother. Mikhail had morganatically married Sophie Nicholaievna (1868–1927), Countess of Merenberg, a daughter of Prince Nicholas of Nassau and his wife Nathalia Pushkin (daughter of the poet) in 1891; Sophie was created Countess Torby on her marriage. The second of Sonia's godmothers was the Hon. Margaret Helen Greville (1867–1942); the illegitimate daughter of the Liberal MP William McEwan by his cook in 1891 she had married the Hon. Ronald Greville, a friend of George Keppel, and became a millionairess in her own right on the death of her natural father. She was to become something of an Alice Keppel protégée in royal circles. Although she was to be a friend of Alice all her life, Margaret Greville pulled no punches when she felt that Alice was being pompous. On the outbreak of the Second World War in 1939, Mrs Greville was to note: 'To hear Alice talk about her escape from France, one would think she had swum the Channel with her maid between her teeth.' Mrs Greville, too, was to fall foul of Harold Nicolson's acid comments as he described her as 'a fat slug filled with venom'.[18]

The scenario for much of Alice's affair with the Prince of Wales took place largely at the six-storey 30 Portman Square. Alice and George maintained their own bedrooms and it is probable that by 1898 sexual relations had ceased between them.[19] The fact of separate bedrooms, of course, in itself was not significant to sexual relations, as in many aristocratic families husband and wife slept apart and lived 'separate sexual lives'.

Alice and George had the luxuries of electricity and a bathroom each – in an age when few people had bathrooms at all. The house was run by a staff of six, overseen by Rolfe the butler and Mrs Wright the cook. Alice was attended by her ladies' maid Draper, and maids Katie and Peggy did the hard slog assisted when necessary by George the bootboy.[20] With her eye for décor, Alice furnished the house on their limited budget, but managed to give her home an 'atmosphere of luxury' so that her boudoir was always immaculate when the Prince of Wales called.

The staff soon got used to the regular visits of His Royal Highness. Violet Keppel's friend and future lover, Vita Sackville-West, remembered as a child seeing the Prince of Wales's (then the king's) 'discreet little one-horse brougham' waiting outside the house. One day when she arrived to see Violet, Vita was gently pushed into a discreet corner of the hallway by Rolfe the butler with a 'One minute, miss, a gentleman is coming downstairs'.[21] Thus did the monarch pass her in the hall on a cloud of *eau de Portugal*.

The Princess of Wales knew soon after Alice became his lover that her husband was philandering again. Alice always gave the impression that she was a close friend of Princess Alexandra (soon to be Queen), who 'didn't mind' about her adulterous relationship with the Prince of Wales, but while retaining equanimity and good humour in public, Alexandra had a deep dislike of and resentment towards Alice.[22] Alice Keppel played a large part in the scaling-down of Alexandra's public appearances, and was certainly responsible for her increased reliance on her children and grandchildren; with them she could forget the growing frequency of Alice Keppel's presence in royal circles, particularly at the card table.

By the end of the nineteenth century, in Society whist had yielded to bridge-playing and among the most avid players were Alice and the Prince of Wales. Bridge became *de rigueur* at Edward's dinner parties. Depending on the number who wished to play, there were usually two bridge tables laid out after dinner. At Edward's table stakes could be substantial, but at Alexandra's they were modest to non-existent depending upon the queen's mood.

The bridge table was to supply a whole round of 'Mrs Keppel quotes'. On one occasion when, as king, Edward had admonished Alice for fluffing her cards she excused herself by saying she could not 'tell a King from a Knave'. Another time she was given a hand that was very difficult to play and said: 'God save the king, and preserve Mrs Keppel from his rage.'

Alice's increased presence made Alexandra a 'prisoner' at Sandringham. 'When she gets *stuck* at Sandringham it is difficult to move her . . . It does not look well either for her constantly to leave *him* alone as she does,' said Princess May of Teck, her daughter-in-law.[23]

As 1900 proceeded Alice became more and more knowledgeable about international affairs and was drawn into them in a way that no other of Edward's mistresses had ever been. With the events of the Second South African, or Boer, War, developing from 11 October 1899, she began to realise the rift between her lover and his nephew the Kaiser Wilhelm II.

The eldest child of the Prince of Wales's beloved elder sister Victoria and Frederick III (1831–88), King of Prussia and Emperor of Germany, Wilhelm II (1859–1941) was a flamboyant, anti-Semitic, repressed homosexual, whose moods were unpredictable. Mentally unstable, he had had a joyless childhood under a Calvinist tutor, and his breech birth had caused neurological damage; a withered arm led to his paranoid view of life. When he succeeded to the Imperial Throne of Germany in 1888, Wilhelm began to stiffen in his attitude towards his uncle; he admired the British, but hated them as possible stumbling-blocks in the international progress of the German Empire. So the relationship between uncle and nephew was a series of snubs and brushes, with irritation on the part of Edward at Wilhelm's intrigues against Britain with the Czar, his unwanted 'advice' on international affairs and his unwise public statements on such diverse subjects as the Boer War and the Boxer Rebellion in China. Alice encouraged her lover to be conciliatory towards his nephew at Cowes Regatta when Wilhelm appeared aboard the German imperial yacht *Hohenzollern*, but the state of Europe and the Empire was casting long shadows across Buckingham Palace where another cataclysmic event was to take place.

Worry over the Boer War had clearly affected Queen Victoria and her health was deteriorating. During December 1900 she paid a visit to the Irish Industries Exhibition at Windsor Town Hall. This was to be the last of her public appearances. She was greatly shocked, too, by the death of Jane, Lady Churchill who had become a lady of the bedchamber in 1854; Lady Churchill had remained in constant attendance on the queen for forty-six years.

At Osborne on 1 January 1901, the 82-year-old queen wrote in her journal: 'Another year begun, and I am feeling so weak and unwell that I enter upon it sadly. The same sort of night as I have been having lately, but I did get rather more sleep and was up earlier.'

During 2 January she conferred the Garter on Frederick Sleigh Roberts, Earl of Kandahar, Pretoria and Waterford, Commander-in-Chief of the Army; and her frailty and infirmity were noted by all. It was the gossip too at a house party at Chatsworth on 7 January. Spencer Cavendish, 8th Duke of Devonshire – the Prince of Wales's old friend 'Harty Tarty' – was the host. Devonshire was Lord President of the Council in Lord Salisbury's third Tory Cabinet and there was much discussion in sporting field and at dinner table on what was likely to happen when, not if, the old queen died in the next few months. Alice Keppel was now becoming used to these in-depth political and constitutional discussions and enjoyed them to the full. And there was the added excitement that her lover was to be sovereign of the largest empire the world had ever known.

The last time the queen was to leave Osborne alive was on Tuesday, 15 January when she went for a drive with the widowed Duchess of Coburg. On 17 January she suffered a mild stroke and her physician Sir James Reid knew that she was near the end. A public bulletin was issued on 19 January regarding her failing health. At last on 22 January the final bulletin read: 'Her Majesty breathed her last at 6.30 pm surrounded by her Children and Grandchildren.'

Back in London a few weeks earlier the Prince of Wales had been carrying out his private and public duties, with Alice joining him whenever possible. On Friday, 4 January, Alice accompanied the

Prince of Wales and his sister Princess Louise at the wedding of Amelia Mary Maud Cassel, the daughter of Sir Ernest Cassel, to Wilfred William Ashley (later 1st Baron Mount Temple) at fashionable St George's Church, Hanover Square. They were to be the parents of Edwina, named after her godfather as King Edward, and the future wife of Lord Louis Mountbatten (1900–79). Alice was to be a regular attender at the Cassel table after Edward had become king.

Alice and George Keppel received the news of the queen's death at 30 Portman Square, the Prince of Wales's secretary having telephoned them discreetly. For Alice it was news received with a mixture of real sorrow but intense intoxication. She was only a little hurt that Edward had spent his last evening before he went to Osborne with Sister Agnes Keyser and not with her. But Alice's future was undoubtedly rosy so the hurt passed quickly.

The Keppels took no invited part in the royal funeral. On 23 January Edward arrived in London and held his first council as monarch at St James's Palace. Next day he was proclaimed king. On 1 February Queen Victoria's body was brought from Osborne to Portsmouth and following a solemn funeral procession through London, on 4 February her body was laid to rest next to that of the Prince Consort in the mausoleum she had built at Frogmore.

On 14 February 1901, Edward carried out his first official ceremonial as monarch, presiding over the State Opening of Parliament. If anyone believed that the king was going to ditch his female friends on becoming monarch they were disabused by his guest list for his first Speech from the Throne. In his diary the English poet and traveller Wilfrid Scawen Blunt noted: 'When he succeeded to the throne he wrote to divers of [his] ladies to say that though called to other serious duties he hoped still to see them from time to time.'[24]

This was the first time that Alice saw her royal lover in all the panoply of British pageantry. He made a dramatic entrance into the chamber of the Lords dressed in his scarlet uniform with his red velvet state robes, an ermine cape across his shoulders, and carrying his white plumed helmet. Queen Alexandra walked at his side in a black dress under her own robes, the chamber sparkling with her diamonds. The royal speech was carried out with dignity and solemnity, but as he looked up to the Ladies' Gallery in the House of Lords, there was not a lady present, including Alice, who did not think he looked at her.

During 1901 a curious story circulated that Alice was pregnant again. The main perpetrator of the gossip was Lady Curzon who identified the putative father as Lord Stavordale or Humphrey Sturt, Baron Alington. Alice produced no third child, and no miscarriage was ever reported.[25]

Alice admitted to the Marquis de Soveral that she was very anxious about the king going abroad. She feared for his life. There was the Brussels incident still fresh in her mind, and only a short while previously, on 29 July 1900, King Umberto I of Italy had been assassinated at Monza, northern Italy, by the anarchist Gaetano Bresci. Yet, although Europe was awash with nihilism and potential regicides, the king was making plans to visit his sister Vicky, the Dowager Empress Frederick. Vicky was slowly dying from cancer and was at Friedrichshof, the castle near Cronberg in the Taunus mountains.

Before the German trip the king discussed details of his new royal household with Alice. He told her about the sweeping changes he had been making at Buckingham Palace and Windsor Castle. He had brushed away eighty years of Victoria's *bric-à-brac*. He had already rearranged and redecorated whole swathes of rooms, installed bathrooms and lavatories and made room for his new motor cars to which he had been introduced in 1898 at Warwick Castle with a trip in a 6hp Daimler. And he asked Alice's opinion about the candidates who were to make up his household; this was a thing that he did not do with Queen Alexandra.[26]

By now, Alice knew all the more prominent members of her lover's court, many of them being her new friends or, at the very least, acquaintances who tolerated her because they had to. At the top of the heap was the Master of the Royal Household, the financial wizard, Horace, Baron Farquhar (later Earl Farquhar); there were to be 'Mrs George' trips to Farquhar's residence of

Castle Rising, Norfolk. Then there was the Keeper of the Privy
Purse, the sharp-tongued and choleric General the Hon. Sir
Dighton Probyn, who had been in the new king's service since
1872. Edward retained his secretary Sir Francis Knollys, and an
assistant to both Farquhar and Knollys was Captain F.E.G.
Ponsonby (later Sir Frederick, and 1st Baron Syonsby, 1867–1935).
Edward's Treasurer was to be Unionist-Liberal MP of West
Derbyshire, Victor C.W. Cavendish and his Comptroller, Arthur,
12th Viscount Valentia. A plethora of other positions were quickly
filled, and among the equerries Alice could note was the great
marksman (Sir) Henry 'Harry' Stonor, whom she had met already
at several house parties.

Because of the imminent death of his sister, King Edward
planned that his diary would be free from mid- to late August 1901
so that he could go to Germany if necessary to be with her at the
end. In the meantime he would carry out his full programme. After
his accession Edward let it be known that he would no longer wish
to meet his friends at restaurants or clubs. But he would be
delighted to meet them in their homes. There followed a flurry of
renovation, building and refurbishment to bring properties up to
the king's standards.

Hostesses gossiped with each other as to the protocol of such a
visit. One hostess was to take the protocol very seriously. Shelagh,
first wife of Hugh Richard Arthur Grosvenor, 'Bendor', 2nd Duke
of Westminster, was unsure, for instance, if Alice should be invited
to Eaton Hall; the king was to enjoy his visits there in May for
Chester Races. She asked the Marquis de Soveral what to do:
'I want the king to be happy, but I don't want to annoy the queen.'
The marquis advised that if the queen was not present then he felt
that Alice could be asked.[27]

There were certain houses to which Alice was never invited, so
much did their owners disapprove of Alice and the king's so public
affair. The country's premier Roman Catholic, the Duke of
Norfolk, banned her from Arundel, his castle in West Sussex. Nor
was she invited to the Duke of Portland's house at Welbeck Abbey,

near Sherwood Forest, or to the seat of the Cecil family, headed by the Marquis of Salisbury, at Hatfield. Count Albert Mensdorff-Pouilly-Dietrichstein, representative of Emperor Franz Joseph of Austria-Hungary at the Court of St James's, and cousin of Queen Victoria, noted that Alice always dealt with such social snubs with aplomb. When the king was at a house where she was not invited, she would contrive to be at a neighbouring one. For instance, when the king was at Hatfield she would turn up at Lord Lytton's house at nearby Knebworth.[28]

Whichever were the king's favourite places, they were to live in Alice's memory too. Hall Barn, Beaconsfield, built by Edmund Waller the poet, was to be such a place, with its original gardens inspired by Versailles. Alice soon came to realise the influence that her royal lover exerted over Society and how they would go out of their way publicly and privately to accommodate his sexual needs. One such was Colonel the Hon. William Le-Poer Trench, third son of the 3rd Earl of Clancarty, and Commander-in-Chief of what was to become the Ordnance Survey. The colonel and his wife Harriet were well known in royal circles, as she was the daughter of Sir William Martins, Gentleman Usher of the Sword of State to Queen Victoria.

Trench owned the fine Bath-stone mansion of St Huberts, Gerrards Cross, Buckinghamshire, a country house which saw social history in the making. Despite its size and importance the eighteenth-century house, rebuilt for the Reid family in the early 1840s by the Victorian architect Edward Buckton Lamb, 'vanished' from local maps on Colonel Trench's orders to ensure the Prince of Wales's (and later the king's) privacy with whichever woman he deigned to entertain.

Again, around the same time and for the same reason, a road that ran close to the frontage of St Huberts was diverted by private Act of Parliament and over thirty members of the mansion's staff were rehoused away from the main buildings in cottages on the perimeter of the estate. Lillie Langtry, Daisy Warwick, Agnes Keyser and Alice were all romanced at St Huberts, local tradition has it.

Wherever she went, though, Alice shone; she had great resilience to withstand the snubs at court and was never more ebullient than when attending such occasions at Millicent, Duchess of Sutherland's receptions at Stafford House. They began with a dinner party for around two dozen people; then would come a coffee reception for invited guests around half past nine; and to round off the evening 'all comers' would be welcomed to what was known as the 'crush'. Millicent, like other hostesses, relied on Alice to put the more pushy attenders in their place. On one occasion the wife of the Jewish financier Sir Sigmund Neumann was being extra-presumptive in her monopolisation of guests. Alice gave her short shrift with the comment: 'My dear Maud, may I call you Lady Neumann?'[29]

Edward VII actually invented the Edwardian house party. The routine was laid down by him and carried out to the letter. Some twenty to forty guests would be invited. His protocol directed that none of the guests should be introduced to each other; after all, Edward supposed they all knew each other anyway. Apart from the part of the house visited that was designated for the king (and Alice if she were present alone), the host's abode would be open to any of the guests. Two important things had to be dealt with too. A telegraph room had to be set up so that the king could be in touch with his government. Again some hosts had to hire extra porters to deal with the huge amounts of luggage that came with the guests, their servants and the king's entourage of equerries and secretaries.[30]

One visitor to house parties who was not a favourite with every host was the King's dog Caesar. As far as the king was concerned the white fox-terrier 'could do no wrong'.[31] His collar proclaimed to the world on a silver plate, 'I am Caesar, the King's dog'. Caesar was a dog of extreme mischievousness and every admonition of the king – for pursuing his host's peacocks, or digging holes in the shrubbery – was met with vigorous tail-wagging. An armchair had to be supplied by the king's bed for Caesar to sleep in. The dog was given free run of Alice's homes at Portman Square and Gloucester Street to the delight of her daughters and the dismay of the servants. Caesar was too much for the Keppels' French governess who once gave him a Gallic booting for his misdeeds. A disconsolate Caesar, in the charge of a valet, trotted behind his master's coffin at the royal funeral.

The first private visit the king made after his accession was to Keele Hall, Newcastle under Lyme, Staffordshire. During 12–15 July 1901 the king visited the L-shaped, red sandstone house (now a part of the University of Keele), which since 1899 had been rented from its owner, Ralph Sneyd, by the Grand Duke Mikhail of Russia and his wife Countess Torby. The guests arrived by private train and were met by the Grand Duke at the station. Some guests enjoyed golf on the house's small eighteen-hole course and the king played croquet with Alice, the Grand Duke and Baroness de Stoeckel.[32] The king was his affable self and chatted animatedly in German with the Grand Duke's servants from Mecklenburg. Security was not what is necessary today; the king had his one detective, but drove out without a bodyguard with the Grand Duke to Whitmore.

The closing months of 1901 were sombre at court, and Alice had to be on hand to bring some lightness to the king's state of mind. The king had been making arrangements to travel to Germany when he heard of the death of his sister Vicky on 5 August. He and Queen Alexandra attended the funeral service at Homburg, and the burial at Potsdam where the German Empress was interred next to her husband in the imperial mausoleum of the Friedenskirche on 13 August.

The next day the king left for a 'cure' at the spas at Homburg, while the queen went on to Copenhagen. As well as the sorrows accompanying his sister's death, the king was irritated by her son the Kaiser turning her funeral cortège into a display of German military might. It was a bitter end to the year. The visits to the Duke of Fife's Mar Lodge in October, to Castle Rising in November and to Elveden Hall in December were not the bright occasions they had always been; and Christmas was held at Marlborough House instead of Sandringham because the king had severe chest problems. But there was always Alice to brighten his life and she was becoming indispensable.

CHAPTER 7

RAISING THE WIND

Edward VII's predecessor, HRH Prince William Henry, Duke of Clarence (1765–1837), who ruled Great Britain as William IV, was a very poor monetary provider for his long-suffering mistress the Irish actress Mrs Dorothy Jordan, who bore him ten illegitimate children, so she was constrained to return frequently to the stage to earn money. Not so King Edward VII. According to the traveller and diplomat Wilfrid Scawen Blunt, Edward's accumulated debts were taken care of by his friends on his assuming the throne, with extra capital being amassed in exchange for knighthoods.[1] The balance of £26,085 of this accrued capital the king handed over to the German Jew and erstwhile Roman Catholic Sir Ernest Cassel, financier of the Aswan Dam, the largest civil engineering project the world had ever seen.[2]

On her royal lover's becoming king, Alice's stock of privileges soared. The opportunities for her to be in the king's party at dinner and the theatre increased as Queen Alexandra's worsening deafness cut her out of Society and made her reluctant to accept invitations. Yet all this brought Alice difficulties. To be the king's companion and mistress cost money; her dress bill alone could keep many a poor family for years. The Keppels did not have much to spare, George was feckless about monetary matters, and from this time all the family financial arrangements were dealt with by Alice.

Being the sovereign's mistress brought Alice into the orbit of the world's finest financiers and the king encouraged them to help her. The most important of Alice's financial advisers was to be Sir Ernest Cassel. He had made his fortune in Sweden and in North American banking circles, and on the Mexican railroad. He was recognised in Britain as the leading financier in the Central London underground project and became the most influential and prosperous financier of Edward's reign.[3] Cassel had been a member of the Marlborough House Set since 1887 through his horse-racing activities.

Cassel was to remain a generous friend to Alice until his death in 1921. He gave the Keppel womenfolk bejewelled Fabergé Easter eggs, and Alice and her daughters passed many an Easter at his Villa Eugénie at Biarritz and his flat at the rue de Cirque, Paris, which Alice and her daughters used on their journeys to and from Biarritz.[4] When Sonia Keppel married Roland Cubitt in 1920, Cassel gave her a substantial cheque. Alice considered such presents vulgar and forced a reluctant Sonia to change it into Canadian sables.[5]

It was Cassel who advised Alice to invest in Canadian stocks which were to make her wealthy. She received important financial advice, too, from Herbert Stern (1851–1919), first Baron Michelham, Sir Alfred Charles William Harmsworth (1865–1922 – the newspaper mogul who became Lord Northcliffe) and later the Liberal minister Reginald McKenna (1863–1943), Financial Secretary to the Treasury and Home Secretary. Alice's niece Cecilia Keppel was to marry Reginald and Pamela McKenna's son David. Their daughter Miranda was a future guest at Florence.[6]

Another of the country's financiers to help Alice was the bachelor millionaire Thomas Johnstone Lipton (1850–1931), the Glasgow-tenement-born general provisions merchant. Lipton had worked for five years in America, going there when he was only fourteen and with no more than a pound or two in his pocket. He worked as a labourer in tobacco plantations and rice fields and as a tram driver. Finally he became an assistant in a grocery shop, and returned home to Glasgow in 1869.

Lipton opened his first store in Glasgow in 1871 and by the time he was thirty he was a millionaire. The year Alice and the Prince of Wales became lovers, 1898, Lipton launched his stores and Ceylon tea plantations on the Stock Exchange as a limited company for

£2.5 million, with himself as its head. His first attempts to attract royal attention failed, when at the Golden Jubilee of 1887 he offered Queen Victoria a monster cheese; the queen declined the gift, but in 1895 he was granted a royal warrant for his tea.

From his large mansion of Osidge Park, Southgate, Middlesex, Lipton honed his pretensions to enter royal society. He saw a good way into aristocratic circles in yachting, a sport given much royal support. Lipton endeavoured to win the America's Cup with successively numbered yachts called *Shamrock* (in 1889, 1901, 1904, 1920 and 1930) but to no avail; his ultimate prize, though, was to enter royal circles. His technique won him the admiration of Alice Keppel, who, soon after they had met, had him under her spell.

Lipton laid his plans well. In 1897 the Prince of Wales set up a trust fund to offer a Diamond Jubilee meal to 400,000 poor folk all over the UK. The prosperous public did not dip their hands very deep into their pockets, but Lipton contributed £25,000 anonymously. At length the public discovered the donor's identity and his entry into royal circles was assured, sealed with a further donation of £160,000 towards a Poor Persons' and Children's Restaurant in City Road, London, under the Alexandra Trust. With yachting as a social key, Lipton became a regular visitor to Balmoral, was knighted in Alice's magic year of 1898 and was made a baronet in 1902. The king was to use Lipton's steam yacht *Erin* as if it were his own, but the members of the Royal Yacht Squadron excluded the 'King's pretentious little grocer' from membership until 1931. The Kaiser lumped Lipton in with the unsuitable Keppel set, sneering that 'only in England would the king dine with his grocer'.

Alice quickly saw the potential that Lipton offered her own financial situation. Engaging her charm in its highest gear she wooed the Scottish grocer into giving George employment. It was to many in Society the ultimate humiliation; not only was George Keppel a complaisant husband, but now this scion of the noble house of Albemarle was reduced to being employed in trade. Whatever credibility George Keppel had was now in tatters as he joined Lipton's 'Buyers Association' at 70–4 Wigmore Street, London.

In researching the papers of the Marquis de Soveral, Gordon Brook-Shepherd came across a letter written by George Keppel, on the obvious promptings of Alice. The letter notes that Soveral was considering buying a car; George now offered a 'great bargain' of a 12hp Sidley from Lipton's stock at £300 instead of £440 new.[7] Soveral's reply is not recorded.

In 1919 Violet wrote to Vita Sackville-West that her mother was worth at least £20,000 a year.[8] On her death in 1947 Alice Keppel left the sum of £177,637 as a gross value estate in the UK. This did not include assets in North America and her estate in Italy.[9] When George Keppel died a few months after his wife, a large quantity of jewellery and *objets de vitrine* were sealed in a black strong-box and deposited with Drummond's Bank. There they remained for forty years. On the death of Alice's daughter Sonia in 1986 the items were sold by Sotheby's at the Hôtel Beau-Rivage, Geneva. The items formed a fabulous collection of *objets d'art* acquired and collected by Alice. They ranged from a William IV silver-gilt snuffbox by Joseph Lilly of Birmingham, dated 1833 (it sold for £1,320) to the Maundy Money set of 1916 (at £1,540) which Lloyd George had secured for her. It was difficult to identify the gifts that Alice had received from her royal lover, or from her other beau Ernest Beckett, or her many gentlemen friends. A certain prurient sniggering was to emanate concerning a diamond and enamel nautical motif brooch Alice had received from the prince. Its four enamelled nautical flags read: 'Position quarterly and open. I am about to fire a Whitehead torpedo ahead.'[10] The Fabergé items in the sale spoke of Alice's connection with the royal Fabergé collection.

Peter Carl Fabergé (1846–1920), court jeweller to the Czars, was the most remarkable of the goldsmiths of his age. The Fabergé firm had been established in St Petersburg by Fabergé's father Gustav in 1842, and in 1884 the first Imperial Easter egg was given to Empress Marie Feodorovna. The eggs were gem-encrusted miracles of the goldsmith's art. Each egg's shell would open to reveal a 'surprise'; maybe a basket of wildflowers made with white chalcedony petals and gold leaves; or a cockerel which crowed on the hour and flapped its wings. In all Fabergé created fifty-six Imperial Easter eggs for the Czars Alexander III and Nicholas II.

The London branch of the Fabergé company was begun in 1903, working out of Berners Hotel; and it was from the London premises that the British royal family made their purchases. The London branch was managed by Fabergé's son Nicholas and Henry Charles Bainbridge.

Records show that Alice Keppel was largely the inspiration for the creation of the Sandringham Fabergé animals: portraits of living animals at Sandringham during Edward VII's time. Bainbridge recounted the story of how around 1907 Sir Ray Lankester, the eminent zoologist, was a regular purchaser at the London shop at 48 Dover Street, and one day in conversation with himself had suggested that 'the owners of English pedigree animals should have models made of them' out of coloured stones to match the original colours of the animals. Bainbridge filed the idea in his memory.

Not long after, Alice Keppel called at the shop and Bainbridge and Alice had a chat about the royal Fabergé collection. Bainbridge mentioned Lankester's idea to reproduce the favourite animals of wealthy landowners. 'Why not some of the favourite Sandringham animals for the queen's collection, if the king will give his permission?' suggested Alice. That day Alice mentioned the idea to the king and the next day a telegram came from Sandringham to Bainbridge. 'The king agrees' it read and Bainbridge took the next train to Wolferton Station. Thus the royal collection was begun.[11]

At her death Alice Keppel's Fabergé collection in Florence included twelve items: a gold and enamel pedestal pill-box; five gold and enamel cigarette cases; an enamel vanity case; a gold, enamel and hardstone vesta case for matches; a gold, diamond and enamel egg pendant; a jewelled gold and enamel miniature Easter egg; a gold enamel and hardstone patch box; and a jewelled hardstone compact.

It was only to be expected that Alice, as one of the most fashionable women in Europe, would have one of the first powder compacts. Queen Alexandra was perhaps the first Edwardian royal lady to encourage the use of cosmetics. Philippe Jullian wrote: 'Long before it had ceased to be frowned on, she was wearing make-up, applying a mask of cold cream, face powder and rouge to her cheeks'.[12] However it was just like Alice to cut across fashion and smoke in public, when Society women did not.

The Fabergé piece most associated with Alice is the snake cigarette case. The case was given to Edward VII by Alice some time around 1908. It is of dark blue enamel over a *guilloché moiré* ground with red gold. Swathed over the case is a snake of pale green gold, its scales formed of rose diamonds. The case bears the Moscow factory mark and is punched for a gold mark of 56 *zolotniks*. After the death of the king, Queen Alexandra returned the case 'as a souvenir'. (The queen in fact did this with several items the king had received from friends.) In 1936 Alice gave the case to Queen Mary 'to place with the Russian collection of Fabergé things at Sandringham'. A note in Queen Mary's own hand tells of the case's provenance.

It is uncertain today how much cash was given to Alice Keppel by Edward as Prince of Wales and as king. The supposition that he did make substantial financial arrangements was considered without a doubt in Society, particularly among those who had connections with the king's secretariat.

A few months before his death Edward was writing to Sir Ernest Cassel from Biarritz with the cryptic thanks for counsel on 'the matter you generally report to me at this time of the year [which] is as satisfactory as the preceding ones'.[13] Some historians have hinted that this 'report' was on the special account the king had raised with Cassel as banker on behalf of Alice and her children.

Around this time too, Sir Francis Knollys returned to Sir Ernest an envelope containing £10,000 in bank-notes which the queen had found in the dying king's bedroom. Cassel himself returned the money to the palace with the comment that it was an 'interest

I gave the king in financial matters I am undertaking'. Again historians believe that the money was meant to go to Alice, and that the king had planned to hand it over to her on her next visit to him.[14]

It was through the king's financial circles that Alice made her first appearance at Balmoral. While Queen Victoria was alive Alice was, understandably, not invited to Balmoral. The new king now revived the Ghillies' Ball, which had not been given for a number of years because of the queen's increasing frailness. The 'ghillies', of course, were Victoria's esteemed Highland manservants and they had a reputation for quaffing large quantities of whisky; for reasons of her own, the queen, an abstemious drinker herself, turned a blind eye to their drunkenness, and was a generous hostess at their annual ball. Alice Keppel was to attend the first of the October shoots and the first Ghillies' Ball after the king's accession. Her presence was subtly done by having her as a member of the party that Sir Sigmund Neumann, the banker, brought over from his hunting lodge; and Alice and George merged decorously with Neumann's other guests Mrs Cornwallis-West, Major Wilfred Ashley and Major-General Sir Cecil Lowther.[15]

CHAPTER 8

'THE KING'S LOOSE-BOX'

As the new king's coronation approached Society buzzed with gossip and scandal. Writing to his mother Jennie Churchill, a young Winston wondered if Edward's accession would 'entirely revolutionise' his lifestyle and that of Society. Would he dissolve his Anglo-Jewish court; would such as 'Reuben Sassoon be enshrined among the crown jewels and other regalia?' Would the king continue his friendship with the Churchills, and would 'the Keppel be appointed 1st Lady of the Bedchamber'? Would the royal racehorses be scattered, Winston further asked?[1] Little was to change, and on the subject of the king's horses, Princess Alice, Countess of Athlone, recalled: 'When Uncle Bertie named one of his horses "Ecila", everyone realised that this transparent disguise was Alice's name in reverse and this caused a considerable scandal.'[2]

When the Royal Titles Bill was passed the new king was formally described as 'King of Great Britain and Northern Ireland and of the British Dominions beyond the Sea' – to Alice's children he became 'Kingy'. Alice's daughter Sonia recounted how her nanny always reminded her to curtsey to the king. Confused and shy, Sonia often took the bearded Sir Ernest Cassel as the king, and he was given a curtsey too. Kingy also played a game with Sonia in which he would position his seated legs so that Sonia could place two slices of buttered bread on them. Then penny wagers were betted as to which slice would slide down the trousers first.[3]

Alice maintained a state of controlled excitement when the king told her during one of their afternoons at Portman Square that he would like her to be present at his coronation. Alas, of course, with space being at a premium the invitation could not be extended to George.

The coronation was fixed for 26 June 1902, but in the meantime much work went on apace in the royal palaces as the king purged many of the artefacts of his mother's reign. Buckingham Palace, very rarely occupied, had remained as a mausoleum to the memory of the Prince Albert, with almost everything left as it had been when he died in December 1861. The new king dispelled the gloom and completely renovated the palace with electric light, telephones and modern plumbing; he was assisted by the Comptroller of the Lord Chamberlain's Department, Sir Arthur Ellis, and others. Alice Keppel's advice was sought by the king on this and that, but rarely did the monarch consult his wife. Edward took a definite hand in the refurbishment. 'I do not know much about ar-r-t,' he told Sir Lionel Cust, Surveyor and Keeper of the King's Pictures, in his guttural tones, 'but I think I know something about ar-r-rangement.'

Redecoration of Windsor Castle was completed by early 1902 under the eye of Sir Lionel Cust, and Edward and Alexandra were in residence by 14 January. The king saw Windsor as a venue for official visits by foreign heads of state and he innovatively intended opening the State Apartments to the public at set times.

Gossiping tongues clacked again around 25 January 1902 when Giles Stephen Holland Fox-Strangeways, Lord Stavordale (who later became the 6th Earl of Ilchester) married Helen Mary Teresa Vane-Tempest-Stewart, daughter of the 6th Marquess of Londonderry. For some time Society's tittle-tattlers had linked Alice's name with 'Stavey' as her lover when she was not engaged with the Prince of Wales. Certainly the Keppels were to remain firm friends of the Ilchesters spending New Year and other seasonal sojourns at the Ilchester mansion at Melbury, Dorchester, Dorset.[4] At the head of the gossiping pack on this occasion was the wife of the Marquis Curzon of Kedleston, Viceroy of India. She publicly remarked on 'Stavey's' impending marriage, and wrote to her husband that 'Mrs Keppel made a promise to Lady Ilchester to *allow* ['Stavey'] to marry at the end of this summer'.[5]

Alice's forward diary was getting filled for the early months of

1902. The king was going to lay a new foundation stone for the new Naval College at Dartmouth on 7 March. But on 25 March, Queen Alexandra was bound for Copenhagen. As she was to stay until 21 April that meant a potential of several private hours with the king. But uppermost in every Society hostess's mind was the impending coronation. It was all so exciting. No one could remember Queen Victoria's coronation of 29 June 1838 and all of Society was on tenterhooks to discover who would receive the coveted invitations. And there were the medal presentations. Both Alice Keppel and Agnes Keyser were honoured with the silver Coronation Medal, although Agnes was not given the dubious honour of sitting during the coronation with the monarch's bevy of women friends.

Alice was one of the first to be shown round Windsor Castle personally by the king who also extended this distinct privilege to scientific congresses, learned societies and various official delegations.

The first court held by Edward and Alexandra took place in the ballroom of Buckingham Palace on Friday, 14 March 1902. It was a glittering occasion of court dress, ostrich feathers, veils and long flowing trains. It was the new world of Alice Keppel, whose diary was filling with more royal occasions and visits to country houses.

The king was to be a frequent visitor to both Penn and Gopsall, near Atherstone, Warwickshire, where Sonia Keppel remembered spending Christmas. One Christmas she and her sister Violet attended a fancy dress ball at Gopsall, whereat Violet appeared as a Bacchante (a priestess of Bacchus, god of wine) and Sonia as the Albemarle ancestor Admiral Sir William Keppel. Alice appeared with Lord Herbert Vane-Tempest 'as a pair of immense twins, pushed into the room in an enormous double perambulator by Papa, as a very hirsute nurse'.[6] Royal visits to Penn and Gopsall were usually connected with shooting parties, and of the January 1902 visit, Lord Howe wrote in his game book, 'Memories such as these are not written in sand.'[7]

The king arrived at Penn on Thursday, 16 January by his special train from Baker Street, accompanied by his equerry Major-General Sir Stanley Clarke, who often accompanied the king on future 'Mrs Keppel trips' to Biarritz. Alice and George were among the large house party there to meet the king with Earl and Countess de Grey, Viscount Curzon and the ubiquitous Marquis de Soveral.

The *Middlesex and Buckingham Advertiser* recorded how 'King's weather' had favoured the party at their shoot, with Alice in attendance at the luncheon for the 'guns'. The Keppels joined the king at the church service on the following Sunday and in the afternoon the monarch accompanied Charles Wynn-Carrington, Earl of Carrington and his Countess Cecilia Margaret for tea at their home at Daw's Hill Lodge, High Wycombe. Alice remained at Penn. The king then returned to Windsor in his Daimler.

The king was greatly looking forward to his coronation with growing enthusiasm. It had been a long time coming and as Europe's premier expert on royal precedence and protocol, Edward would be not only central player but prime advisor. All the arrangements for the coronation were in the hands of Henry Fitzalan-Howard, Duke of Norfolk as Earl Marshal. And at 30 Portman Square, Edward never tired of telling his mistress the details which the police had worked out for the routes of the procession; nor did Alice tire of reflecting that it was to be her 'coronation' too as *maîtresse en titre*.

Despite the excitement Alice was worried about her lover's health. Their intimacy gave her a far from trivial knowledge of the abdominal pain he had been suffering of late. Edward, though, was in the very best of spirits. On 31 May the Boer War had come to an end; he and Queen Alexandra attended the service of thanksgiving for peace at St Paul's on Sunday, 8 June, and he enthusiastically joined the spring race meetings, taking great interest in the Coronation Derby at Epsom. The weather for that year was exceptionally foul and the king caught a chill; he was unable to attend Royal Ascot and rested at Windsor.

Alice had an instinctive feeling that there was something more seriously wrong with the king than a chill; nevertheless at court no one was gravely perturbed. The king refused to scale down his activities and on 23 June he left Windsor for London with due pomp. This was the day on which a massive luncheon party was given for visiting representatives of foreign powers in London for the coronation. It was followed by a rehearsal in Westminster Abbey, which Alice attended.

Edward was now in growing abdominal pain and his doctors became increasingly anxious. His Sergeant Surgeon Sir Frederick Treves gave his opinion to royal physicians Sir Francis Laking and Sir Thomas Barlow that unless the king was operated on immediately he would be in grave danger.

What if he refused an operation? the king enquired. Then he would die, came the blunt response. At first the king refused to have an operation as it would lead to his coronation being cancelled: 'I will go to the Abbey even if it kills me', he growled; so he would defer any operation. He could not let his people down, he insisted. Sir Francis Laking, in his most conciliatory manner to his irascible royal employer, went over the reasons why an operation must be carried out immediately. Eventually the monarch reluctantly agreed. The great coronation banquet for 250 guests which was to be held on 26 June had to be cancelled and the huge amount of food was distributed to charities; for once the poor folk of London were able to dine on jellied strawberries and snipe stuffed with foie gras.

With the help of Dr (later Sir) Frederick Hewitt as anaesthetist and of Nurse Haines, Sir Frederick Treves performed the necessary operation on 24 June and the following bulletin was posted on the railings of Buckingham Palace:

The King is undergoing a surgical operation. The King is suffering from perityphlitis [appendicitis]. His condition on Saturday was so satisfactory that it was hoped that with care His Majesty would be able to go through the Coronation ceremony. On Monday evening a recrudescence [a flaring up] became manifest, rendering a surgical operation necessary today. Signed: Lister, Thos. Smith, Francis Laking, Thos. Barlow.

Alice kept in touch concerning her royal lover's recuperation through his secretary Knollys and learned that the king was making steady progress. The monarch was able to walk about his room by 29 June and on 15 July he was well enough to embark on a three-week convalescence cruise aboard the royal yacht *Victoria and Albert*. The thought of not seeing her lover for so long since the scare about his health was hard to bear.

Early in the days after his operation, according to the journal of Viscount Esher, the king 'in a moment of weak emotion' wrote to Alice saying 'that if he was dying, he felt sure [the queen] would allow [Alice] to come to him'.[8] It was to be a letter that Alice was to keep and use during her embarrassing outburst following the king's death.

Once his convalescence was complete the king turned his attention to the rescheduling of his coronation. The revised date was 9 August and it was to be a less spectacular event than previously planned. In any case the huge number of European guests who had assembled for the first set date had gone home and were unable to return. But for the nation it was to be a double celebration; his crowning and a thanksgiving for his life.

Alice rose early on Coronation Day, her hairdresser arriving before breakfast. Violet and Sonia were dressed in new frocks and were to be taken by their nanny to see as much as their patience could stand once their mother had left for the abbey. The servants were to have their own party later in the day and the Keppel children were to join the Alingtons.[9]

Alice's memories of the coronation were built up on what she herself saw and the intimate gossip the king and she exchanged; he wanted to know what Society was saying when not overawed by his personal presence — a role, incidentally, Alice was ever to play — and she was eager to hear every morsel of tittle-tattle from Buckingham Palace. The king was still furious that Kaiser Wilhelm II was boycotting the ceremony, refusing even to allow Crown Prince Wilhelm to attend. On a previous visit the Crown Prince had availed himself of too many favours of Edward's court ladies, and the Kaiser thought that Alice was a bad influence. In fact, of course, the foreign princes had returned home following the cancellation of the first coronation, and only the Abyssinian Special Mission of Ras Makumen remained.

On the mantelpiece of her boudoir at 30 Portman Square, Alice displayed her invitation. It was headed:

CORONATION OF THEIR MAJESTIES KING EDWARD VII AND QUEEN ALEXANDRA, BY COMMAND OF THE KING THE EARL MARSHAL IS DIRECTED TO INVITE THE HON. MRS GEORGE KEPPEL TO BE PRESENT AT THE ABBEY CHURCH OF WESTMINSTER ON THE 9TH DAY OF AUGUST 1902. Signed NORFOLK EARL MARSHAL.

As Alice was getting ready, at Buckingham Palace her royal lover was joking with his grandchildren, whom he had summoned to see him in his robes. 'Good morning, children,' he had beamed, 'am I not a funny-looking old man?' Tradition has it that Queen Alexandra was late as she always was and the king scattered her ladies as he strode into her room, shouting: 'My dear Alix, if you don't come immediately you won't be crowned queen.'

From early morning huge crowds began to gather along the route of the royal procession. There had not been a coronation for sixty-five years. Alice and Feo Sturt (the future Lady Alington) shared a carriage to the abbey and soon became enmeshed in the log-jam of traffic at the abbey approaches. All around the crowds heaved to get a better look, often breaking out into song:

> We'll be merry,
> Drinking whisky, wine and sherry,
> Let's all be merry
> On co-ro-na-tion Day.

Now the regular cries of 'Where's Alice?' which rang out whenever the king had appeared in public were changed to 'There's Alice' as she was spotted by the crowd.

Alice and Feo Sturt joined the king's group of 'special ladies' who were to fill a reserved box at the abbey ceremony. It was dubbed 'the King's Loose-Box' by James Ludovic Lindsay, 26th Earl of Crawford and 9th of Balcarres who acted as a deputy marshal at the coronation.

Inside the abbey just before eleven o'clock was heard the thud of cannon from Hyde Park announcing that the king and queen had left Buckingham Palace. Preceded by the carriages of the Prince of Wales and other royalty, came the sovereign's escort of Royal Horse Guards, and the panoply of the monarch's medieval attendants, the Royal Bargemaster and the Watermen, the Yeomen of the Guard, the carriages of the royal household and the armed forces.

At length the golden and crystal coach, drawn by matched cream horses from Hanover, and carrying the new king and queen, came into view to draw up at the abbey's west door at half-past eleven. Alexandra entered first down the blue-carpeted nave escorted by the Bishops of Oxford and Norwich, her rich, heavy, violet ermine-edged train carried by eight pages, and accompanied by her ladies in white and gold. Those assembled were already hushed by the occasion, but the queen in her dress of golden Indian gauze stunned all to silence. With the king's regalia preceding him, King Edward entered escorted by the Bishops of Bath, Winchester and Durham, and Alice Keppel got her first glimpse of her royal lover. Her relief would be evident as she saw his firmness of gait. Looking well, he inclined his head to the right to acknowledge the cries of 'Vivat Rex Eduardus' from the boys of Westminster School.

In the chancel sat the royal princesses and above them the ladies of the 'Loose Box'. It was 'the one discordant note in the abbey', wrote Louisa, Countess of Antrim, lady-in-waiting to Queen Alexandra, in her diary. It 'did rather put my teeth on edge,' she added; there was 'La Favorita [Alice] of course in the best place, Mrs Ronnie Greville, Lady Sarah Wilson, Feo Sturt, Mrs Arthur Paget & that ilk'.[10] The 'ilk' included the king's former mistresses

Lady Warwick and Lillie Langtry with Sarah Bernhardt, Jennie Churchill, Leonie Jerome, Countess Torby, Lady Albemarle (Alice's mother-in-law) and Princess Daisy of Pless. Next to Alice sat Baroness Olga Alberta de Meyer, the king's reputed daughter by the Duchess di Caracciolo. Alice and his friends were relieved that the king opted for the shorter coronation service on medical advice.

The chief clergyman conducting the coronation service was the aged, almost blind Frederick Temple, Archbishop of Canterbury. His trembling hands had to be steadied by the king at the moment of crowning and the venerable cleric stumbled as he tried to rise after kneeling before his monarch. The service ended when the Archbishop of York crowned Queen Alexandra. The royal carriages were rattling back to Buckingham Palace by three thirty and Alice was to agree with Lord Rosebery that the whole had had 'the character of a family festival'.[11]

During the festivities that evening Alice and the ladies of the *haut monde* discussed the anecdotes of the day and were secretly pleased at the downfall of Louise, the imperious Duchess of Manchester. The fact that the haughty woman was German-born added spite to the retelling. So as to be near to the royal party as they left the abbey, the duchess had pushed her way from her place to the line of Grenadier Guards which had been drawn across the choir to prevent a mass exodus. The irate duchess began verbally to abuse the officer in charge, made to push her way through the line and slipped on the stairs. 'She fell heavily forward', remembered the Clerk of the Council, Sir Almeric William Fitzroy in his *Memoirs* (1925):

and rolled over on her back at the feet of Sir Michael Hicks-Beach, who was just leaving his stall; her coronet fell off and struck the stalls at some distance from the spot. The Chancellor of the Exchequer was too paralysed by the suddenness of the apparition to offer any assistance; but willing hands, directed by the indefatigable Soveral, at last restored the illustrious lady to her legs.

Once the coronation was over the king and queen attended various investitures and a review at Spithead, and set off for a cruise of the west coast of Scotland, via the Isle of Man. There were also visits to the Sutherlands at Dunrobin Castle on 6 September before a train journey to Balmoral where the king saw his coronation on a cinematographic film. Then there was a call at Whittingham, East Lothian, home of his new Prime Minister Arthur James Balfour, with Alice and George in attendance from Duntreath. At last it was the king's birthday on 9 November and a visit from the Kaiser to Sandringham.

Before Christmas 1902 the king and queen went to stay with the 4th Earl of Howe at Gopsall, and Lady de Grey saw what a boon it was to have Alice sitting next to the king at dinner. She herself, for the fourth time during the visit, sat next to the king. As the dinner progressed she whispered to Sir Frederick Ponsonby: 'For Heaven's sake suggest a topic for me to discuss with the king . . .' Ponsonby replied: 'Give away your relations and friends and repeat any secrets about them.' An anxious Lady de Grey replied: 'But I did that the first night!' Alice never had such problems.[12]

The coronation year was rounded off for Alice and George Keppel with a trip to Egypt. At the Savoy Hotel, Cairo, they met Winston Churchill, who in a letter home to his mother noted that Alice was 'very good company'.[13]

CHAPTER 9

INDISPENSABLE DUO

When the South African War ended in May 1902, the king insisted to Agnes and Fanny Keyser that the hospital they had founded should not close. They had successfully nursed 275 officers, with medical and surgical care being given free by eminent physicians and surgeons. In time officers were to be charged a nominal sum for their care (rising to 5 shillings [25p] per day); in the evenings the Keysers' butler poured the officers drinks' before dinner. The king averred, during one of his private tête-à-têtes with Agnes at 17 Grosvenor Crescent, that there was a great need for a peacetime haven for such officers serving the Empire. To strengthen the hospital's reputation he gave it his name and henceforth it was known as 'King Edward VII's Hospital for Officers: Sister Agnes Founder'. The king became its first patron and the Prince of Wales agreed to be the hospital's president.[1] Edward VII was to be a regular visitor to the hospital, paying a call on the officers who were being cared for there, after his dalliance with Sister Agnes in her private accommodation.

Like Alice Keppel, Agnes Keyser was becoming an indispensable part of the king's life. He enjoyed being bullied by Agnes concerning his health (paying no practical attention the while) and her disapproval of his heavy smoking provoked his guttural laughter. Yet no one could soothe him half so well as Agnes, as he recovered from his Corona y Coronas cigar-induced coughing fits in which he went a deep shade of purple.

By 1903 Agnes expressed her fears to her royal admirer about the hospital's financial future. She had endowed the foundation with her own funds and a trust was formed supported by Keyser securities; but Agnes and Fanny could not go on funding the project indefinitely. What was to be done? The king advised that a public appeal should be launched with subscriptions of say £100 per annum for five years. The king would help and Agnes sat down and wrote a list of twenty-four possible subscribers. Most of them were the king's friends and acquaintances and the list read like a page from the Court Gazette.

The king and the Prince of Wales topped the list, followed by such as Donald Alexander Smith, 1st Baron Strathcona and Mount Royal, the Scots-born Canadian financier who had raised 'Strathcona's Horse' in the South African War. Then was included the inventor of surgical appliances (as well as the designs to decorate the Albert Hall) Sir Ernest de la Rue, Sir Ernest Cassel, Sir Sigmund Neumann, the Bavarian-born banker, Edward Levy-Lawson, 1st Baron Burnham, principal proprietor of London's first penny paper, the *Daily Telegraph*, and Baron Ernest Samuel Palmer, director of Huntley & Palmers, the bakers. Keyser friends the financiers Sir Herbert Bulkley Mackworth Praed, Alfred Charles de Rothschild and Henry Louis Bischoffsheim rounded off the list, with South African War veteran Major Frederick Gordon, MP, Sir Sydney Hedley Waterlow, and a few philanthropists such as the erstwhile cockney bookie George Herring.

Thus in the short term the hospital's future was assured. In 1904 Agnes and Fanny's foundation moved to 9 Grosvenor Gardens to expand the permanent accommodation to twelve sick officers. The king approved of a new honorary medical and surgical staff under his personal surgeons Sir Frederick Treves and Sir Thomas Smith as consultants, and the hospital was recognised by the War Office. The king opened the freshly equipped hospital at its new address on 23 April 1904. The foundation was to work closely with the Officers' Convalescent Home at Osborne House; Edward had given Queen Victoria's Isle of Wight home to the nation in 1901, and the main wing designed by the Prince Consort housed the convalescent facilities.

While all this went on, Alice Keppel was securing her own

'foundation'. By 1903, as the Austro-Hungarian ambassador to the Court of St James's, Count Albert Mensdorff, recounts, Alice built up her own entourage, with her own 'lady-in-waiting' in Lady Sarah Wilson, whom she had met very early during visits with her royal lover to country houses. Lady Sarah was to feature in Alice's life in an important way during the First World War.

In his diary Mensdorff shows how Alice was something of a social embarrassment when Queen Alexandra was present. In one entry Mensdorff expresses relief that Alice did not attend a particular function he was concerned with, so he didn't have to present her. If he hadn't Alice would have made a fuss, and if he had the queen would have been icy. Others, too, found the king's latest mistress a trial. William Waldorf commented: 'when Mrs George Keppel had sunk to the life of a public strumpet, I no longer invited her to my house [Cliveden]'.[2]

It is Mensdorff, too, who gives proof positive of a new role that Alice had developed: that of go-between with the king. As his reign proceeded the king abandoned the custom of receiving his ministers in audience. Instead he talked to them at social gatherings or through 'people he knew well and trusted, such as Admiral Lord Fisher, Sir Charles Hardinge, Cassel, de Soveral, Knollys and Ponsonby . . . and Mrs Keppel'.[3] In turn ministers passed messages to the king through them. As a contemporary said: 'Alice evolved as the perfect amateur diplomat for the king; her circumspection and discretion came naturally to her and she was completely loyal to the king . . . she was a consummate liaison officer.'[4]

An example of Alice's diplomatic role occurred in 1907. In December of that year Kaiser Wilhelm II paid a visit to Highcliffe Castle, the home of (later Major-General) Edward James Stuart-Wortley. The king was not present on that occasion but Alice and a party came over to dine with the Kaiser from Lord and Lady Alington's house at Crichel Down, after the German Emperor had had an afternoon's shooting. With some audacity, but on seemingly royal orders, Alice was placed next to the Kaiser at dinner. Truth to tell, the Kaiser publicly deplored his uncle's relationship with

Alice,[5] and the Kaiserin Augusta Victoria would have nothing to do with her whatsoever.[6] But on this occasion His Imperial Majesty was pleasant to her. Writing in his diary under the date 7 December 1907, Mensdorff wrote: 'It was amusing to see how, at table, in disregard of all rules of precedence, the *Favorita* [Alice] was seated next to the Kaiser, so she might have the opportunity of talking to him. I would like to know what sort of report she sent back to Sandringham.'

Again Mensdorff knew that he could get personal opinions directly to the king through Alice. His diary records that during the Balkan crisis (wherein during January 1908 the Austrian government had announced plans to build a railway through what was to be Yugoslavia to Salonika thus 'threatening' Great Power influence) the king visited West Dean Park, West Sussex, the home of courtier William Dodge James, with a large party including Alice. The king was refusing to talk to Mensdorff about the Balkan crisis, as punishment for not keeping him abreast of Austrian intentions, but the ambassador felt that the Austrian opinion ought to be heard in royal circles, so he deliberately brought up the topic in conversation with Alice. Mensdorff wrote:

H.M. declined to exchange a single word with me about politics. Instead, I discussed the crisis briefly with Reggie (Lord) Lister [in reality the diplomat the Hon. Sir Reginald Lister], Favorita also brought it up and I talked a little with her about it. That little, however, was already too much, for when I got back [to London] I found Hardinge [Sir Charles Hardinge, later 1st Baron Hardinge of Penshurst, Assistant Under-Secretary for Foreign Affairs] rather annoyed that, at West Dean, 'you had talked . . . as if you were under the impression that we had prevented at Constantinople that your direct negotiations should succeed'.[7]

In the event Sir Edward Grey [later Viscount, and Foreign Secretary] also admonished Mensdorff for talking with Alice about the controversial matter.

In truth Hardinge had no qualms about Alice being a courier. In a future private note he was to write:

> I would like here to pay a tribute to her wonderful discretion, and to the excellent influence which she always exercised upon the King. She never utilized her knowledge to her own advantage, or to that of her friends; and I never heard her repeat an unkind word of anybody. There were one or two occasions when the King was in disagreement with the Foreign Office and I was able, through her, to advise the King with a view to the policy of the Government being accepted. She was very loyal to the King and patriotic at the same time. It would have been difficult to find any other lady who would have filled the part of friend to King Edward with the same loyalty and discretion.[8]

Hardinge underestimates the number of times that Alice acted as go-between for the king with the Liberals; although she was not what was called 'one of the great Liberal hostesses', her associations with Prime Ministers Sir Henry Campbell-Bannerman and H.H. Asquith were of great assistance to the king. Again there would be those would disagree that Alice did not use her place to further herself or her friends. Besides her own family, she promoted the cause of the Hon. Mrs Greville. Through her influence the Greville's house of Polesden Lacey, Surrey, was placed on the 'royal circuit', with the king visiting for weekends, and Mrs Greville being a denizen of the 'Smart Set'.[9]

Alice's dealings with the major political figures of the day warrant more than just surface examination. Although it seems that she played no role in party politics, her position in royal circles brought her much more than any political party could. She had been brought up in a Tory household and she moved in the Tory society which was pleasing to her royal lover, but she had a secret disaffection for the Tories in the circle of the Marquis of Salisbury (Prime Minister 1895–1902) and that of his nephew A.J. Balfour (Prime Minister 1902–5), which looked down on her for her 'immorality'. For Alice, ever astute in choosing allies and friends, the main chance was within the Liberal circles of Sir Henry Campbell–Bannerman (Prime Minister 1905–8) and H.H. Asquith (Prime Minister 1908–15) and thence the Coalition prime ministership of David Lloyd George during 1916–22. Indeed the king's adverse views of Lloyd George were tempered by Alice, whose friendship Lloyd George was keen to cultivate when he was Asquith's Chancellor of the Exchequer.[10]

Even to those who knew her very well, Alice always disingenuously averred that she knew little about privy political affairs. This was clearly nonsense. She was a regular guest at Liberal houses and knew the Asquiths very well. In a letter to her, Asquith once thanked her for her 'wise counsels',[11] despite the fact that he had admitted to his love Beatrice Venetia Stanley, in a letter of 19 August 1914, that Alice was one of 'a pack of the women one cares for least'.[12]

On the day, 23 January 1901, he had given his first speech to the Privy Council on his accession to the throne, Alice's royal lover had made it quite clear that he was going to conduct his role in a way completely different from his mother's. He showed in his style that he preferred an informal association with his ministers and was much taken with the personal face-to-face chat. He completely trusted Alice and through her (and others, of course) he could make his personal opinions known. A message to Alice was enough to get a controversial subject dropped casually into conversation to gauge the effect, which was then reported back to the king. After a while his ministers got used to the king's style and would be more personally open with him as to their own opinions rather than offering Civil Service versions wrapped up in ministerial jargon. The fact that the king's style began to be appreciated as effective was due in part to Alice's expertise as discreet messenger. Consequently Alice was privy to a wider range of secrets than she ever admitted.

It annoyed Alice if anyone made public reference to her influence or drew attention to her immediate access to the highest in the land. She was particularly annoyed with Margot Asquith in her book *More Memories* for alluding to Alice's being the political confidante of the king. Through Margot Asquith's comments, said Alice, she 'got . . . into endless trouble with George V'. This was undoubtedly Alice over-reacting because when Margot Asquith's comments appeared in 1933, King George had been aware of the depth of Alice's relationship with his father for decades.[13]

George Keppel was also developing his important role, that of what the French call *mari complaisant*. He was not expected to accept royal invitations – except for shooting parties, and where Alice needed an escort when not with the king. He spent a great deal of time when in London at his clubs; he had been a member of the St James's since 1898, and although he was not to join the Turf, at 5 Carlton House Terrace, until 1917, wherein he was sponsored by William Mansfield, 2nd Lord Sandhurst, and seconded by Major General the Hon. Cecil Edward Bingham, he visited here and other clubs as a guest, and it was through club gossip that George's reputation was now forged.

Up to Alice's meeting with the Prince of Wales, George had been deemed a gentlemanly, polite – if rather dim-witted – army officer of aristocratic mien, who at times gave the impression of being a buffoon. In time he was to bask in the reflected glory of his wife's position, and his MVO (conferred by the king in 1908) was a personal pride; the honour was given, his contemporaries said, because 'he had laid down his wife for his King'. George never complained about Alice's infidelity – there were those who said that he positively encouraged it for the house parties, shooting trips and social kudos it brought – 'I do not mind what she does as long as she comes back to me in the end,' he is said to have once remarked.[14]

The year 1903 was a particularly busy one for the king. On 10 March there was a dance at Buckingham Palace for the king and Queen's wedding anniversary. Alice now always took care on these occasions to keep her hems in control. At the first ball at Windsor Castle that had been held for fifty years, Prince Adolphus of Teck

Agnes Keyser's parents. Right: Charles Keyser Snr (1813–92); a stockbroker, he was the founder of the Keyser wealth. (Mrs Michael Sperling) Below: Margaret Blore (1823–90), pictured with Agnes's identical twin sisters Nelly and Fanny, c. 1853. (Peter Keyser)

*Charles Edward Keyser
(1847–1929), financier,
philanthropist and
antiquarian. He was Agnes's
only brother. (Mrs Michael
Sperling)*

*Margaret Fanny Keyser
(c. 1850–1926). Agnes and
her sister founded the King
Edward VII's Hospital for
Officers at their private residence
at 17 Grosvenor Crescent, near
Hyde Park in London.
(Mrs Michael Sperling)*

Agnes Keyser (1852–1941), pictured at the family home, Warren House, Great Stanmore, Middlesex. (Mrs Michael Sperling)

Agnes Keyser as she was best known: 'Sister Agnes'. A portrait of Agnes painted by Maud Coleridge in 1906 was hung in the dining-room at 17 Grosvenor Crescent; it was destroyed in the bombing raid of 11 January 1941. (Peter Keyser)

*Alice Keppel's parents.
Admiral Sir William
Edmonstone (1810–88)
and Mary, Lady
Edmonstone
(1827–1902). (Sir
Archibald Edmonstone)*

Colzium House, Kilsyth. Alice Keppel spent part of her childhood here before the family moved to Duntreath. (Cumbernauld and Kilsyth District Museums)

Duntreath Castle, Stirlingshire, c. 1900. This was the main residence of the Edmonstone family. (Sir Archibald Edmonstone)

Alice Keppel from the album of Leonie Blanche, Lady Leslie (d. 1943). Alice played bridge with Lady Leslie the day before Edward VII died. (The Estate of Leonie, Lady Leslie)

The Hon. George Keppel (1865–1947), pictured in 1906. He is dressed in the usual style for Edwardian gentlemen making 'afternoon calls'. (The Estate of Sonia Rosemary Cubitt)

The Albemarle family at Quidenham, Norfolk, 1891. William Coutts Keppel (1832–94), 7th Earl of Albemarle, is third from the left in the back row; on his right is his wife Sophia. Alice Edmonstone (front, left) married George Keppel (front, right) at St Paul's, Knightsbridge. George's brothers Derek and Arnold, Viscount Bury, are at either end of the back row. (The Estate of Sonia Rosemary Cubitt)

Violet Keppel (1894–1972), pictured in the early 1920s. (The Estate of Sonia Rosemary Cubitt)

Ernest William Beckett (1856–1917), 2nd Baron Grimthorpe and Tory MP for Whitby from 1885 to 1905. Beckett was reputed to be Violet Keppel's biological father. In 1908 he went to live at Ravello in Italy, where he was visited by Alice. (Leeds Leisure Services)

Sonia Keppel, aged three, pictured in 1903. She was dressed up as her great-uncle Admiral Sir Henry Keppel for a fancy-dress party. (The Estate of Sonia Rosemary Cubitt)

Sonia Keppel, the Hon. Mrs Ronald Cubitt OBE, photographed by Cecil Beaton. She was the younger daughter of George and Alice Keppel, although many believed she was the biological daughter of Edward VII. (The Estate of Cecil Beaton)

Sonia and Alice Keppel at St Moritz in 1920. They stayed at the Palace Hotel and Sonia took part in the bobsleigh derby. (The Estate of Sonia Rosemary Cubitt)

W.S. Stuart's portrait of Edward VII, c. 1901. He is dressed as he would have been when visiting Alice and Agnes. (STARALP)

The Hon. Mrs George Keppel by G.F. Zincke, 1903. (National Portrait Gallery)

Alice Keppel by F. Jenkins, after a portrait by Ellis William Roberts, c. 1903. (National Portrait Gallery)

Sir Ernest Cassel (1852–1921), financial adviser to Edward VII and Alice Keppel. (STARALP)

*Lady Sarah Wilson
(1865–1929), dubbed Alice
Keppel's lady-in-waiting.
During the First World War
she ran a field hospital at
Etaples, assisted by Alice.
(STARALP)*

*Luis Augusto Pinto, Marquis de Soveral
(d. 1922). The Portuguese Minister in
London, he was known as the 'Blue
Monkey' because of his blue-black hair. He
was one of the most influential members of
Edward VII's court. (caricature by Sir Leslie
Ward, 'Spy' and artist for* Vanity Fair)

A popular postcard study of Edward VII with his nephew Kaiser Wilhelm II. The Kaiser disapproved of his uncle's relationship with Alice Keppel. (STARALP)

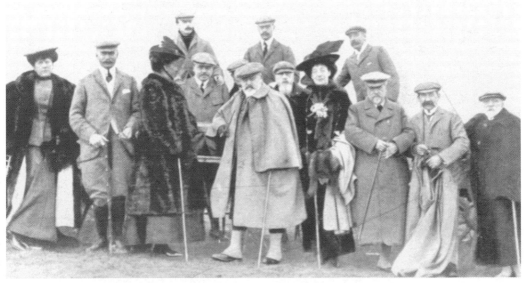

Edward VII and a party at Chatsworth, c. 1907. Left to right: Alice Keppel; the Prince of Pless; the Countess of Gosford (rumoured to be the mistress of Baron Nathaniel Rothschild); Edward VII; Lady Desborough; Earl de Grey; Sir Felix Simon; and Arthur Abraham Sassoon. (STARALP)

Edward VII visited Alice Keppel's childhood home, Duntreath Castle, in September 1909. Back row, left to right: George Keppel; Mrs Leopold de Rothschild; Leopold de Rothschild; Lord Elphinstone; Sir Archibald Edmonstone; William George Edmonstone; Alice Keppel; Col. Hon. Harry Legge; Sir Henry Stonor; Col. Sir Arthur Davidson. Front row: Mrs Ronald Greville; Lady Sarah Wilson; Lady Stradbroke; Edward VII; Ida, Lady Edmonstone; Violet Keppel. On the grass: Archibald Charles Edmonstone; Sonia Rosemary Keppel; Edward St John Edmonstone. (Sir Archibald Edmonstone)

In F. Matania's drawing, Alice Keppel is walking discreetly behind Edward VII as he takes a stroll from the Hotel du Palais, Biarritz, during his last visit to the resort in April 1910. He is walking with the Marquis de Soveral (on his left) and his Equerry, Sir Derek Keppel. (STARALP)

A mourning Queen Alexandra places a rose in the hands of her sovereign and husband, minutes after his death at 11.45 p.m. on 6 May 1910, at Buckingham Palace. Alice Keppel, hysterical with grief, had made a tremendous scene at the dying king's bedside before she was led away by Princess Victoria. (STARALP)

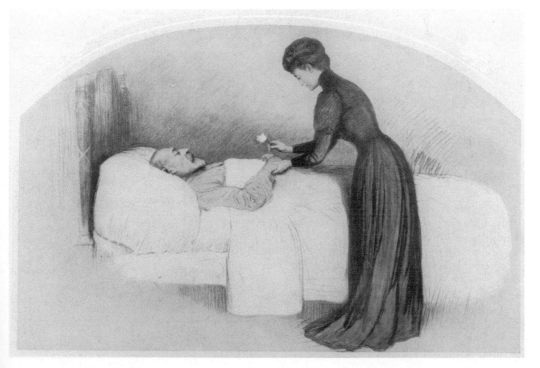

Precious objects from Alice Keppel's collection. Top: Alice Keppel's medals: 1914 Star; British War Medal; Victory Medal; Coronation Medal, 1902; Jubilee Medal, 1935. Centre, left: silver and enamel Vesta case, Birmingham, 1901, decorated with UK and Commonwealth flags. Alice Keppel was a dedicated smoker when it was fashionable for women not to smoke. Edward VII smoked some twenty cigarettes a day, plus a dozen large cigars. He popularised smoking throughout society. Centre, right: George III silver nutmeg grater, 1811, a gift from Alice Keppel's close friend Mrs Walker Heneage of Coker Court, West Coker, Dorset. Bottom: a set of Maundy money, 1916. (Sothebys)

Jewellery and trinkets from Alice Keppel's collection. Top left: a gold, green enamel and rose diamond New Year's novelty gift for 1 January 1908. Alice welcomed in the New Year that year at Sandringham. Top right: royal silver, gold and diamond presentation cigarette case, Ludwig Politzer, Vienna, c. 1910. Edward VII's cypher is set in diamonds. Bottom row, left to right: a pearl, emerald and diamond brooch with pearl tassels, c. 1900. Many such pieces were gifts from Edward VII; a gold, enamel and hardstone patch box by Fabergé; a pearl-set enamel heart pendant, c. 1895; an acorn-shaped 'Grandel' tiepin with stag-tooth mount, in gold, enamel and emeralds, Austrian, c. 1895; a jadeite and diamond hatpin, surmounted by a Buddhist lion, by Cartier, c. 1890. It was not unusual for Edward VII to buy gifts simultaneously for his wife and mistress from Cartier and Fabergé. (Sothebys)

and his niece Princess Victoria fell on their backs when the prince's spurs caught in Alice's long dress. Between 30 March and the end of July there were royal visits to Lisbon, Copenhagen, Gibraltar, Malta, Scotland and Ireland.

On 25 March Alice took over the lease of 30 Portman Square for a period of nineteen years, at £160 per annum; this included stabling at the rear in Berkeley Mews. From 1900 to 1903 they had been the tenants of the previous lessee Colonel T. Grant.[15]

During 12 August the king left for Marienbad, now Marianske Lazne, Czechoslovakia, a place that he was to visit regularly through the rest of his life. Alice was never to accompany him to the Bohemian spa town. Contemporaries explained that whereas Biarritz was usually 'free' from Europe's royalty, Marienbad was full of Prussian and Austrian courtiers who would have been delighted to gossip that the king of Great Britain was parading the boulevards with his mistress. So the king and Alice could not conduct their 'married life' in the same way as at Biarritz.

The French fishing port and coastal resort of Biarritz, five miles south-west of Bayonne, became fashionable after Emperor Napoleon III visited it in the 1850s. After Edward became king he regularly left England at the beginning of March for a two-month holiday. He aimed to spend a week in Paris, savouring his incognito walks along the boulevards, and then spend three weeks at Biarritz. This was usually followed by a month's cruise in the *Victoria and Albert*. He would then return at the beginning of May for the commencement of the Season. Three of the king's cars were despatched in advance to Biarritz in the charge of his chief driver Charles W. Stamper. The king stayed at the Hôtel du Palais with a small suite, and Alice and her daughters were ostensibly the guests of Sir Ernest Cassel and his sister at the Villa Eugénie.

Cared for by their nanny and governess, Violet and Sonia Keppel accompanied Alice and her maid to Victoria station. A royal courier met them at their reserved carriage on the boat train which took them to a special suite on the ferry for Calais. Once in France they were met by the *chef-du-gare*, who treated Alice with the due courtesy the French give to royal mistresses, and guided them unchecked through customs to another private carriage on the night sleeper for Biarritz.

France with the king was always a hectic holiday with daily excursions to watch pelota at Anglet or the races at La Barre. And there was the food; even a hasty royal lunch would include such items as plovers' eggs, fish and a meat dish washed down with champagne. And off they all went again when the king had downed his balloon of Napoleon brandy and smoked his Corona.

The Villa Eugénie, leased by Sir Ernest Cassel, had been an imperial residence during the time of Emperor Napoleon III. It had been designed for the Empress Eugénie in 1855 by Auguste Deodat Couvrechef, and had a decorative watchtower on the cliff. The Keppel children were housed in the wing which had been occupied by the Prince Imperial. As Queen Alexandra and George Keppel never went to Biarritz, Alice could assume the part of Queen *représentante* and play wife to her lover.

At Biarritz the king could relax from royal duties; there were usually no visiting fellow-royalty or diplomats to try his patience and he could enjoy what amounted to married life with Alice. At twelve-fifteen sharp the king and Alice would emerge from the king's hotel suite to stroll arm-in-arm along the promenade, accompanied by Caesar. They would return for lunch *à deux* in the king's suite and appear again in due course for the afternoon's jaunt.

As the king enjoyed impromptu picnics, Alice, the children and everyone else had to be ready at a moment's notice. A procession of cars took the royal party to their picnic site, where all were served lunch or tea by liveried footmen. Sonia noted that the king liked to picnic – despite the dust – by the edge of the road and was readily recognised. So a picnic soon became a public spectacle, which seemed to delight the king.[16] The Biarritz holiday lasted for about three weeks and then there was a visit to Paris for the Keppels, again as guests of Sir Ernest Cassel at rue du Cirque. This pattern of events was repeated for a decade or so.

The year 1903 was rounded off with a state visit to Britain in

November of the new King of Italy, Victor Emmanuel III, and Queen Helen and there were more 'Mrs George house parties'. One included a trip to Castle Rising, near King's Lynn, north-west Norfolk, the home of the king's Master of the Household, Horace Brand Townsend-Farquhar (later Earl).

Although Alice's diary continued to reflect the pattern of the court, from royal marriages and state visits to Queen Alexandra's absences and the sovereign's various junkets, as her daughters grew older Alice spent more time with them. Both Violet and Sonia were to attend Miss Helen Woolf's school in South Audley Street at separate times, and it was at Miss Woolf's that Violet was to meet Victoria Mary, 'Vita', Sackville-West (1892–1962) for the first time in 1904.[17] Their friendship was to develop in 1918 into a full-blown lesbian affair that gave Alice a great deal of social embarrassment.

Vita was the daughter of Lionel Sackville-West, 3rd Lord Sackville, and his cousin and wife Victoria. She was born at Knole, near Sevenoaks, Kent, the setting for her *The Edwardians* (1930) in which she was to feature Alice Keppel as a disguised character. Violet and Vita's friendship developed from their first meeting, with Violet making the running. They met again at a tea party – at Violet's instigation given by Alice's friend Ellen Constance, the Countess Kilmorey. From that point Violet paid increasing court to Vita as her sexuality grew stronger.[18]

In the meantime precocious Violet was to be allowed to go to Paris in 1905 with the Keppel girls' new French governess Hélène Claissac and Aunt Jessie (Winnington-Ingram). France was to play a permanent role in Violet's life, and Alice was to fund various trips; Alice, of course, was in France regularly herself to obtain her gowns from M. Jean Worth. Trips to Europe were now permanent features of the Keppel women's lives, with Violet and Alice in Spain in 1906. George Keppel, meanwhile, went his own way.

For the next fourteen years or so Violet and Vita were to be in and out of each other's lives. In 1908 Violet accompanied Vita and Lady Sackville to Italy, visiting Pisa, Milan and Florence. Before they left, Violet declared her love for Vita and in Florence gave her a ring in token of her devotion.[19] In 1908 Vita also accompanied Violet to Duntreath. This was the year that Sir Archibald Edmonstone, now a groom-in-waiting to the king through his sister's influence, accompanied the king's party to Russia aboard the *Victoria and Albert*.

Edward VII was to visit Alice's childhood home of Duntreath eight months before his death. It was the time of the usual autumn trip to Balmoral, and he was fulfilling a promise to Alice that he would return to her beloved Duntreath. Alice had worked closely with the king's secretary on the trip and had suggested that a halt be constructed up the line from Blanefield Station – and on the south elevation of the estate near the house – to make it easier for the king to alight. With the help of Shanks the stationmaster this had been accomplished.

The king arrived at a flower-bedecked Blanefield Station at five p.m. on Saturday, 11 September 1909. Sir Archibald Edmonstone and the Lord Lieutenant of Stirlingshire, Beresford Malise Ronald Douglas Graham, 5th Duke of Montrose, met the royal party. Mrs Ronald Greville, Lady Sarah Wilson and Alice had travelled with the king on the royal train and the king was attended by Colonel the Hon. (later Sir) Henry Legge, 'Harry', as equerry.

The royal party was transferred to a motorcade for the short distance from the wooden-platformed halt Alice had had constructed and the king was welcomed at Duntreath by his host and hostess. That evening a dinner was held at the castle attended by the royal entourage which now included Sidney Herbert, 16th Lord Elphinstone of Carberry Tower, Edinburgh, and a current favourite Mrs Marie de Rothschild (wife of the popular 'figure on the turf' Leopold Rothschild).

The next day an estimated crowd of five thousand turned up at Strathblane to watch the king arrive at church. The afternoon was spent at Buchanan Castle, the seat of the Duke of Montrose. The king left the next day after lunch and was accompanied to the station by Alice and George, Violet and assorted Edmonstones.[20]

During his first evening at Duntreath the king and Alice walked by themselves in the garden of the castle – the path is still pointed out as the 'King's Walk'. As she held his arm she would be aware of more than just his increasingly stumbling gait and his deteriorating health. The king was deeply despondent about the future. The escalating German build-up of naval armaments in the early 1900s had caused the Foreign Office to make known to him that a visit to Germany was desirable to try to raise the level of understanding between the two countries. So despite Edward's reluctance to visit in view of his nephew the Kaiser's growing dislike of him, he had consented to see his nephew on his journey to Marienbad. Thus the two sovereigns had met one August morning at Friedrickshof castle, but the king later commented to Charles Hardinge that no understanding had been reached about the naval escalation.

The international atmosphere got no better and during February 1909 Edward had journeyed to Berlin again for an official state visit. It was now plain to those who witnessed his stumbling speech at the banquet preceding the court ball that the king was gravely ill. Breaking his usual practice, Edward read through a prepared text, regularly punctuated with coughing spasms. As he sat later hunched through the court ball in the uncomfortable dress uniform of the Stolp Hussars, those around whispered that he was not long for this world.

On 10 February the king lunched at the British Embassy, on the day he was to visit the German *Rathaus*, and endlessly smoked his mammoth cigars. As he sat in conversation with his old friend the former Daisy Cornwallis-West, now Princess of Pless, he was gripped by one of his severe choking fits. As he struggled to breathe, the king turned puce with his bronchitic coughing and passed out. The Princess of Pless struggled to open the neck of his tight Prussian uniform, and Queen Alexandra and Charles Hardinge hurried over to assist. Sir James Reid, the king's physician, was summoned and the room was emptied of guests. Edward recovered after a few minutes to resume the assembly.

Alarmed over increasing German naval strength, the British

Parliament passed a new naval appropriations bill on 12 March 1909, and the inevitability of war came that much closer. Germany now sent Russia a diplomatic message requesting recognition of the Austro-Hungarian annexation of Bosnia and Herzegovina and a cessation of support for Serbia in the controversy. Wishing to avoid war the Russian Foreign Minister Alexander Izvolski agreed, placing the United Kingdom in an embarrassing position. From Armenia to Turkey and from Bulgaria to Crete, the spirit of belligerence seethed. Country upon country began to connive at the aspirations of others, even Italy agreeing to support Russian goals in the Dardanelles while the Russians agreed not to interfere with Italian aspirations in Tripoli. In London, Edward VII began to fear for his nation.

CHAPTER 10

THE ROYAL CURTAIN FALLS

Back in London from their state visit to Germany, the king's annual journey to Biarritz was planned with Alice, with a stop off at Paris, where the royal party visited the Théâtre des Variétés. While at Biarritz on this occasion they made an excursion to Pau to watch the American aviator Wilbur Wright fly his aeroplane.

For several weeks the monarch had been busy preparing for the coming General Election, for on 30 November 1909, the House of Lords had rejected the Liberals' 'People's Budget' prepared by Chancellor David Lloyd George, requiring the government to resign and the king to dissolve Parliament.

At 17 Grosvenor Crescent, Agnes Keyser anxiously noted that the king's health was deteriorating; he had more frequent bouts of coughing as they talked, and a bad kink left him gasping for breath for a quarter of an hour. Agnes could see he was becoming increasingly depressed about the future, and he was talking more and more about bad omens. And an event at Sandringham at New Year 1910 did not improve his state of mind.

Edward VII was extremely superstitious. Alice noted that he had a dread of crossed knives, which he deemed would bring bad fortune; quarrels, he would growl, were imminent if a knife was laid across a fork. Again a medal pinned incorrectly would bring forth from him a bellow of disapproval, not only because he was a stickler for correct protocol, but because he considered it an evil omen. His valets and footmen were forbidden to turn his mattress on a Friday lest it bring bad luck for a week. Neither would he sit down at table if there was a company of thirteen. On one occasion Lady Londesborough remembered Alice composing him at a table of thirteen by pointing out that one of the women present was pregnant.[1]

Alice Keppel was soon to find out that the king's pockets usually contained a mascot or two. When Sir Luke Fildes, who was commanded to prepare a drawing of the king on his deathbed, entered the dead King's chamber he was surprised to see the number of charms and talismans above the bedhead. The king's daughter, Princess Victoria, enlightened Fildes that, 'The old dear used to think they brought him luck'.[2]

It seems that Alice was able to add a Scottish superstition or two to the king's memory store. David Lindsay, 27th Earl of Crawford and 10th of Balcarres, mentioned how the king had a particular superstition about asparagus, the source of which was likely to be Alice: an odd number of sticks of asparagus on your plate is bad luck; to avoid disaster another one must be taken immediately from the serving dish.[3]

On that New Year's Eve as 1909 gave way to 1910, the royal family indulged in the Scottish and North Country ritual of 'first-footing'. This was the ritual of visiting friends, neighbours (and strangers) in the early hours of New Year's Morning, the first-foot strictly meaning the first person – other than a member of the household – to cross the threshold after midnight. The appearance of the first-foot was thought to indicate the quality of luck in the household for the ensuing year. Thus Scottish superstition decreed that a dark-haired person (and never red-haired), without blemish (such as cross-eyes), and bearing a gift of a piece of coal (a symbol of heat and light) and shortbread or an oatcake (to represent plentiful food for a year) was a good first-foot. First-footing had been a feature of Queen Victoria's court at Balmoral, and just before midnight 1910 the king shooed his guests out of Sandringham so that he could be the first to enter his house in the New Year. Before the king could cross the threshold, one of his grandchildren ran ahead and pushed the door open. The king was noticeably disturbed. Glancing solemnly at the child he commented in his German growl: 'We shall have some ver-r-ry bad luck this year.'[4]

In the first week of January the king and queen left for a week at Lord Iveagh's home at Elveden Hall with Alice and George, and a range of familiar faces. The party left on 8 January and the king made a visit to Brighton with his secretary Frederick Ponsonby and Sir Seymour Fortescue as his equerry, to stay with Arthur Sassoon at 8 Kings Gardens, Hove, for the period of the General Election.

The king was most depressed by the electioneering, wherein the Lords' rejection of the budget was being hailed by the Liberals as 'wrecking the Constitution'. Edward feared that the monarchy would be dragged into unpleasant controversy. The Liberals lost many seats at the election of 14 January, but were able to form a ministry with the help of the Irish and Labour members.

There was a touching scene one day when the king was driven to Worthing on an outing from Sassoon's house. His chauffeur parked for a while on the seafront and a huge crowd assembled around the car. The king fell asleep and the crowd became silent, just looking at the king with great sympathy.

Like Agnes's, Alice's anxiety about the king's health was growing steadily. Whenever they met he was seized with one of his violent coughing fits. She encouraged him to be away from smoky London as much as possible, but he refused to bypass his duty. But after his official dinner at Buckingham Palace on 26 February he felt able to leave duty and crossed to Calais on 7 March for Biarritz and a holiday with Alice. The queen, by the by, was extremely angry that her sick husband was going off with Alice.[5] First the king stopped off at Paris so that he could see Edmond Rostand's new play *Chantecler* at the Théâtre de la Porte-Saint-Martin. The theatre was sweltering and as he left the king was kept waiting for his car to arrive and he caught a chill; it developed into bronchitis as they travelled south.

The king's physician Sir James Reid and Alice monitored the monarch's condition with some alarm. He rallied, however, and to their dismay would not cut down on the work on his red boxes of state papers. The king filled his first few days, after he had been met at Biarritz by the mayor, M. Forsand, and Bellairs, the British Consul, with his usual round of motor trips, walks and visits from friends, including Queen Amélie of Portugal. It was to be the longest period during their affair that the king and Alice spent together. Alice wrote to de Soveral: 'the king's cold is so bad that he can't dine out, but he wants us all to dine with him at 8.15 at the Palais, SO BE THERE . . . I am quite worried *entre nous* and have sent for [Nurse Fletcher]'[6]

On this holiday the weather turned bad and the king was unable to continue the strolls which seemed to do him so much good. Instead Alice walked with him up and down the corridor of the Hôtel du Paris. Every day there were messages from London to disturb his mind. Somehow the king seemed to wish to cram as much as possible into his programme, and Sir James Reid had let him leave his rooms. As the weather cleared he went to the Basque mountain village of Sare to watch pelota. And on 20 April he drove with Alice and his party to the Hôtel de France at Pau for some sightseeing, including a visit to Lourdes. Meanwhile the queen was aboard the RY *Alexandra* with her daughter Princess Victoria, cruising the Mediterranean. She telegraphed the king to join her and get away from that 'horrid Biarritz' (her code-name for Alice); the king stayed put.

At length the royal party left Biarritz. Sir Sydney Lee was to write later that as the king left he stepped out onto his private verandah and gazing into the Atlantic sighed a sad 'I shall be sorry to leave Biarritz . . . perhaps for good'.[7]

The king arrived in London on 27 April and was off to the opera the evening of his return. Queen Alexandra was still cruising the Mediterranean. Various audiences followed in rapid succession and the king dealt with national and foreign affairs. On 30 April he spent a few days at Sandringham with Sir Dighton Probyn and Ponsonby to review various works that were being undertaken. On the Sunday he did not take his usual walk to church but went by barouche. His bronchial condition deteriorated, but the king made no concessions with his full diary. As April gave way to May the king's breathing difficulties did not respond to treatment. He dined with Agnes Keyser at 17 Grosvenor Crescent, and she was appalled at his condition and packed him off home early. When he had left she pencilled a note to Sir James Reid requesting that he go to the king as soon as possible.

On 3 May the king dined with Alice at Buckingham Palace, but was too tired to play bridge. Alice's agitation at the king's worsening condition became more marked and courtiers noted the increased number of times she was in and out of the palace to see him. During their consultations of 4 May the king's doctors diagnosed that he had severe bronchitis and on 5 May the first public bulletin was issued regarding the monarch's worsening health.[8] The Prince of Wales telegraphed his mother to return home as a matter of urgency.

In his last illness Edward VII was attended by his physicians Sir James Reid, Sir Francis Laking and the consultant throat specialist Dr St Clair Thomson. In his journal Sir James Reid noted that he kept Alice informed of the king's condition.

On 4 May Alice and Mrs William James had gone to Buckingham Palace to play bridge in the Chinese Drawing-Room. Alice had begged the king not to smoke that evening, but he waved aside her remonstrations and puffed away at one of his large cigars, although of late they were not giving him the pleasure they always had. Already that day he had had a violent coughing fit. He had ridiculed the suggestion that he should rest: 'No, I shall not give in – I shall work to the end. Of what use is it to be alive if one cannot work?'[9]

The king's condition was obviously worsening but he insisted on getting up each day to fulfil his royal duties, and on 6 May he received his old friend Sir Ernest Cassel in audience. That day too he had a winner at Kempton Park, but his pleasure over that was short-lived. As the day developed the king fainted twice and he gradually sank into a coma. Before he passed into a final comatose state Queen Alexandra gave instructions that any close friends he wished to see should be allowed to visit the king. Out of this invitation Alice Keppel was to build a curious story, her version of which she was to assert for the rest of her life.

Many of Edward VII's biographers have repeated Alice's assertions that she was 'summoned' by Queen Alexandra to say goodbye to the dying king. The truth of the matter was quite different and fully attested by the royal courtier Reginald Brett, 2nd Viscount Esher, and the king's doctor Sir Francis Laking, the latter via the unpublished diary of Wilfrid Scawen Blunt.

During the last few days of the king's life, Alice was frantic. She knew that her lover was dying and asked to be with him. The queen had not sent for her, although, according to Sir Francis Laking, Alice had been a constant visitor to Buckingham Palace before the queen came back from the Mediterranean. Alice played what she thought was her trump card – she sent the queen the letter that the king had sent her at the time of his appendix operation in 1902 which had said that if he was dying he was certain that the queen would allow Alice to come to him. The letter, and a further wish of the king's that Alice be invited, persuaded the queen to allow Knollys to contact Alice.

In due time Alice was to tell her friends of the scenario in the king's death chamber. When she arrived at Buckingham Palace, said Alice, she remembered in her emotional state to curtsey to the queen and Princess Victoria. The king then called her over to sit beside him. He stroked her hand and told her to dry her tears. Then he called to the queen who was standing by the window, to come over and kiss Alice. This, according to Alice, the queen did and she sat with the royal lovers by the bed.

The king, said Alice, then slumped back into one of his phases of unconsciousness and Alice left with the queen sobbing on her arm and promising that the royal family would care for her.

When Sir Francis Laking later heard Alice's version of the scenario he dismissed it as arrant nonsense. And Wilfrid Scawen Blunt was to attest, on Laking's authority, that the queen had taken hold of Laking's arm when the king slid into unconsciousness with the order: 'Get that woman [Alice] away.'

What really happened at the bedside was somewhat different. Lord Esher said: 'Mrs Keppel has lied about the whole affair ever since, and describes quite falsely, her reception by the queen.' Esher added in his journal:

> The queen did *not* kiss her, or say that the Royal Family would 'look after her'. The queen shook hands, and said something to the effect, 'I am sure you always had a good influence over him', and walked to the window. The nurses remained close to the king, who did not recognise Mrs K. and kept falling forward in his chair. Then she [Alice] left the room with Princess Victoria, almost shrieking, and before the pages and footmen in the passage, kept repeating, 'I never did any harm, there was nothing wrong between us,' and then, 'What is to become of me?' Princess Victoria tried to quiet her, but she then fell into a wild fit of hysterics, and had to be carried into Freddy's [Sir Frederick Ponsonby's] room where she remained for some hours. Altogether it was a painful and rather theatrical exhibition, and ought never to have happened.[10]

Sir James Reid's comments in his journal confirmed what Esher had said about the king's state when Alice visited him; Reid said: 'at 5 [o'clock the king] barely recognised [Alice]'.[11] And Wilfrid Scawen Blunt added this to the story: when the king was dead Queen Alexandra 'in a terrible state of despair' confided her feelings to Sir Francis Laking about the king and Mrs Keppel:

> years ago, when I was so angry about Lady Warwick, and the King expostulated with me and said I should get him into the divorce court, I told him once for all that he might have all the women he wished, and I would not say a word; and I have done everything since that he desired me to do about them. He was the whole of my life and, now he is dead, nothing matters.[12]

The king had sat up until eleven o'clock on 6 May, and was then lifted into bed. He died at 11.45 p.m. and Knollys telephoned Alice before the crowds outside Buckingham Palace knew anything.

Alice was greatly distraught at her lover's death, but was astute enough to know that when the king was dead she would be swamped with publicity, so on the day before the king died the Keppels had left 30 Portman Square to stay with their friends Mr and Mrs Arthur James (née Venetia Cavendish-Bentinck) at their house in Grafton Street, to the south of London's Oxford Street. Sonia and Violet were taken there after daylight on the day the king died. Gossips said, of course, that the Keppels had fled to avoid creditors; this was another piece of nonsense for Alice Keppel was a millionairess in modern terms when some London families were bringing up children on less than 10 shillings a week.

Prostrate with grief, for a short while Alice went through a character change. Gone was her cheery nature to be replaced by a black depression. The children were at first kept away from their mother's room by Mrs Arthur James, but when they were able to visit her in bed Sonia remembered: 'she turned and looked at us blankly, and without recognition, and rather resentfully, as though we were unwelcome intruders.'[13] Indeed ten-year-old Sonia Keppel left one of the most keen but simplest questions ever to be uttered at the passing of a monarch. She asked her father: 'Why does it matter so much, Kingy dying?' 'Poor little girl!' he replied. 'It must have been frightening for you [her mother's shattered emotions and the gloomy scene at 30 Portman Square.] . . . Nothing will ever be quite the same again. Because Kingy was such a wonderful man.'[14]

Once she had regained her composure Alice made efforts to save her public face and safeguard her position in Society. She went to Marlborough House to sign publicly the book of condolences opened for the late king. In deference to Queen Alexandra's feelings, the new King George and Queen Mary gave orders that 'she should not be allowed to [sign]'.[15] Stunned by the snub, Alice made sure that her version of what had happened at the king's deathbed was circulated in Society and 'made up the story' that Laking, Esher and Blunt so readily disputed.

It was important to Alice that Society, at all levels, received the right impression of her activities. She made sure that all the people who would be of use to her in the future 'were on her side'.[16] She even wrote to Elizabeth Knollys (the wife of the late king's private secretary) explaining that although she was asking friends to her house to chat about past times with the king, this did not mean she was giving dinner parties (i.e., during the period of court mourning). Her letter closed: 'How people can do anything I do not know, for life with all its joys have [sic] come to a full stop, at least for me.'[17]

The Knollys family were very much at the centre of arrangements following the king's death and Alice wrote to Queen Alexandra's woman of the bedchamber Charlotte Knollys, with the request that she be allowed to look after the king's dog Caesar. Although the queen referred to it as 'that horrid dog' (it was as free a spirit as Alice), Alice's request was refused. A more severe rebuff, in a growing series of snubs that Alice was not used to in royal circles, came from the Kaiser.

Wilhelm II knew the Albemarles well; a collection of Keppels were present for instance on 9 August 1895 when the Earl of Albemarle sailed his yawl *Morgiana* at Cowes, and had invited them for tea aboard the SM yacht *Hohenzollern*.[18] He had met Alice too, and greatly disapproved of her; this time he need not care about his uncle's feelings so when Alice requested an audience with him on his arrival for the king's funeral he curtly refused it.

Agnes Keyser's mourning was to be discreet, Alice Keppel's depressive and demonstrative. Leading up to the state ceremonial on 20 May there was a three-day lying-in-state at Westminster Hall, before interment at St George's Chapel, Windsor. Keppels were to play a prominent part in the funeral cortège. The Norfolk Yeomanry were represented, but George Keppel was not invited. The presence of the late king's mistress's husband would have been too embarrassing to his relatives, his cousin Rear-Admiral Sir Colin Keppel, commander of the Royal Yacht *Victoria and Albert*, and his brothers the Earl of Albemarle and Derek Keppel, who were official mourners. Alice, however, was allowed to say a final goodbye.

The queen had refused to have the king's cadaver moved immediately from his bedroom to the Throne Room. She assumed an ultra-proprietorial stance.[19] At first the queen was adamant that Alice should not be allowed anywhere near her dead husband. Her advisors persuaded her to change her mind; the courtiers were afraid that, having made a scene at Buckingham Palace, Alice would throw a public tantrum at Westminster or Windsor. Very well, agreed the queen, but Alice's presence would have to be chaperoned. On Tuesday, 17 May, after the doors had closed to the public at 10 p.m., Alice, in her full widow's mourning, was met at Westminster Hall by Sir Schomberg McDonnell, who with Ponsonby had been in charge of the lying-in-state. She was led to where the king's coffin lay on its purple-draped catafalque flanked by gentlemen-at-arms, Grenadier Guards officers and Yeomen of the Guard. After her final curtsey to her royal lover's remains Alice was escorted back to her closed carriage. Decorum had been satisfied.[20]

From Marlborough House, the new king's private secretary Sir Arthur Bigge wrote to the Duke of Norfolk that it was the monarch's wish that Agnes and Fanny Keyser were to be allocated seats for the funeral service at St George's Chapel, Windsor.[21]

CHAPTER 11

'ROYAL WIDOWHOOD' AND WAR

Agnes Keyser coped with mourning her great royal loss by busying herself with her hospital activities. On his accession King George V assumed his father's role as patron of the hospital and its work continued as before to the outbreak of the First World War. Records show that from its opening until the outbreak of hostilities around fifteen hundred officers had been cared for by Agnes's staff.[1]

No widow felt more the pangs of bereavement than Alice Keppel. She could not have mourned her dead lover more if she had been married to him the forty-seven years he had been wed to Queen Alexandra. Trying to hurt, one of her Society 'friends' reported to Alice what the queen had said to one of the Seymour family in reflection on Edward VII's past mistresses: 'After all, he always loved me the best.'[2] In her heart Alice felt that she knew differently and it made her devastation more intense in swings from hysteria to melancholy.

At length Alice decided what she must do – a new start was called for; along the way she would exploit those who had toadied her when her lover was alive, but first she must get away from Society for a while. In November 1910 she announced that she was taking her girls to Ceylon; 'In my opinion no young lady's education is complete without a smattering of Tamil,' she opined.

Alice, George and Alice's maid-companion Louise Draper were to spend a few days in Italy, where Violet, Sonia, their governess Hélène Claissac and their nanny were to join them in Naples. Alice had assembled a party of friends and relatives to sail via Algiers and the Red Sea to Ceylon. Archie and Ida Edmonstone, Alice's nephew and niece-in-law, Ronnie and Eva Graham Murray, and Walter 'Wattie' Montgomery – a kind of factotum Alice had adopted for the expedition – joined the Keppels. As was the custom among minions when she was abroad, Alice was fussed over by the ship's company who saw the Keppel party off safely at Colombo for their first night at Galle Face Hotel.[3]

The hotel was just to be a stopping-off place en route, via Kandy, for Sir Thomas Lipton's tea plantations at Nuwara Eliya and his bungalow of Dumbatenne, which he had lent to Alice for their three-month stay. Their three-car convoy caused a stir of interest among the Sinhalese unused to automobiles, and an old woman carrying fruit caused a minor fracas by failing to remove herself quickly enough from the path of one of the cars. Alice was able to placate the woman's vociferous relatives and the party proceeded.

Sir Thomas Lipton had first invested in Ceylon in 1890 and his plantation was well established by 1910. The Keppel party were generously equipped, from his stores at the bungalow, for big game hunting and went on a few days' safari without the Edmonstones and Sonia. Their exertions added nothing to Sir Thomas's collection as the only trophy was a well-peppered crocodile – which everyone in the party claimed to have killed; its carcass was too holed even to cure. The intrepid hunters were to receive their best view of big game at a circus in Colombo.[4]

Before she left London, Alice had made arrangements for Violet and Sonia to travel to Germany, while the rest of the party continued on an eastward journey. So, after three months in Ceylon the Keppel girls returned to London to prepare to sail for Hamburg. They were put under the care of Colonel Vincent Edwin Henry Corbett, the Minister for Bavaria and Württemberg. He had married Mabel Sturt, daughter of the Keppels' friends and neighbours Lord and Lady Alington of 38 Portman Square. The girls lodged at the Pension Glocker at Munich with their governess and nanny and each day they attended German classes in a school run by an Alsatian teacher called Herr Savaéte.[5] Violet and Sonia were also to attend the Slade School of Art for a while.[6] In the meantime Alice's party travelled to China, with Alice collecting a variety of Chinese *objets d'art* which were to have pride of place in her homes thereafter.

On their return to London, Alice continued her exploitation of the social scene and built up her round of houses to visit. At Whitsuntide 1911, for instance, they joined the Asquiths, Balfours and Churchills, at Hackwood House, near Basingstoke, Hampshire, as guests of George Nathaniel Curzon, Marquis Curzon. 'They played croquet and tennis on the lawns by day. The tables groaned with good food and wine in the evening, and then they talked, or played charades, or watched firework displays in the park. And they flirted and intrigued.'[7]

George Keppel took monthly trips to Munich to see the girls. Violet made great progress with her flair for languages, and both wove an expansive web of friends through the Corbetts. Yet, during a visit Alice declared that Violet was getting 'too German'. Alice's talent for networking 'useful people' was to become second nature to the Keppel girls. They stayed in Germany for a year and were brought back to England by their father. On meeting Alice again Sonia was shocked to see her hair had turned pure white from grief at the king's death.[8]

The Keppels now settled into a routine much changed by the death of the king. There were still trips to France and Spain for the girls and Alice, and Sonia went to Switzerland with her mother. George was to join them later at St Moritz for a few days. On George's return to London, Alice, Sonia and a party of friends, including the spinster Baroness Margaret 'Daisy' de Brienen, went bobsleighing. On a particular fast corner their bobsleigh overturned and Alice and Sonia sustained minor injuries. Alice was to bear the small facial scar for the rest of her life.

Home was now at 16 Grosvenor Street, off Grosvenor Square, undoubtedly the focal point of the 100 acre Grosvenor Estate in Mayfair, which, with the exception of Lincoln's Inn Fields, was the largest of the capital's squares. Grosvenor Street had been built in about 1720–34 and immediately attracted people of rank. No. 16 was one of the largest in the Grosvenor Estate and was built by architect Thomas Ripley; Baron Walpole, son of the English statesman Sir Robert Walpole, Earl of Orford was its first occupant.

Alice's neighbours included her old friends Sir James Reid, the king's physician, Lords Avebury and Henry Cavendish-Bentinck and Lady Edward Spencer-Churchill. The environs were not unknown to previous royal mistresses as George I's concubine, Ehrengard Melusina, Baroness von Schulenberg, Duchess of Kendal, had lived in Grosvenor Square. Alice had taken the lease on 16 Grosvenor Street in 1909 and renewed the lease for sixty-three years at a rent of £500 per annum from the estates of her friend the 2nd Duke of Westminster.[9]

The upper floors of the house had been set out and rented as flats before Alice took it over. Each member of the family now had her or his own 'apartment'. Violet, in her usual flamboyant way, had hers as a 'studio' in which she entertained her friends 'in the style of a *demi-mondaine*' without the sex.[10] George had his own suite of rooms – quite apart from Alice's and on a different floor – which he furnished with the less magnificent furniture from Portman Square. It was set out almost as a bachelor apartment and housed his collection of photographs of pretty women with the wasp-waists and voluminous bosoms of the era.[11] George was known in Society as 'something of an old flirt' and was to be seen regularly at the Ritz and other places taking tea with a variety of young female friends; no one ever suggested that the meetings were anything but platonic.[12]

Alice's boudoir and the public rooms at 16 Grosvenor Street were set out in some opulence. Those in the know gossiped that they recognised furniture from the royal collection; indeed two porcelain pagodas were identified as having come from the Regency Brighton Pavilion. Several other pieces were an accumulation of 'presents' from people who had wished to curry favour with Edward VII through Alice.[13] During the late 1890s the lower floors of the house had been a piano shop and in this sumptuously decorated area Alice set out the pieces from her China trip and her fine collection of glassware.

The house was to be the scene of the most glittering dinner parties in London, where the famous met to gossip and promote their egos, careers, flirtations and (adulterous) relationships. Around her birthday on 6 June 1913, Alice held a special coming-out ball at the house for Violet, whereat the garden was covered with a tent and the myriad guests sat at individual tables. It was all too much for the young teenage Sonia who fled to the house in Curzon Street of the octogenarian Elizabeth, Lady Williamson; Lady Williamson was the mother of one of Alice's admirers, Sir Hedworth Williamson.[14]

Violet had grown into something of a beauty and was fast getting a reputation as a flirt. Friends noted that Violet, however, had a fixation about chastity and that male sexuality seemed to be abhorrent to her. But, as Sonia pointed out, Violet gave short shrift to young men, preferring the company of older men like her mother's friend the Liberal MP and Secretary of State for War, Richard Burdon Haldane, Viscount Haldane, and the writer George Edward Moore, a denizen of the Bloomsbury Group. It was a part of Violet's attention-seeking; older men had the maturity for flattering conversation. In due time Violet was to absorb the precepts of the Bloomsbury home of Virginia Woolf and her sister Vanessa Bell, who pursued 'the pleasures of human intercourse and the enjoyment of beautiful objects'. The critic Raymond Mortimer was to be another of Violet's links with the Bloomsbury Group.

Since Violet's birth, Alice had kept up her friendship with the child's putative father Ernest Beckett. During 1913 the Keppels were holidaying at Beckett's villa at Ravello. George was just as accepting of his wife's affair with Beckett as he had been about her dalliance with the king. After all, some said, it brought in a wherewithal that saved him, for the most part, from having to seek regular employment.

In July 1913 the Keppels went to visit the Sackvilles at Knole, and Violet rekindled her friendship with Vita Sackville-West, although a peripatetic correspondence had continued over the years. There was as yet no expression of the physical love between them, and shortly after on 4 August Vita became engaged to Harold Nicolson. They were married on 1 October and eleven months later on 6 August 1914 Vita gave birth to Benedict Lionel (Ben).

At this stage there seems to have been little sign of Violet's underlying homosexuality. Despite liking much older men she did indulge in flings with men of her own age. There was, for instance, the Hon. Julian Grenfell. Julian Grenfell was the son of Liberal MP William Henry Grenfell and his wife Ethel, the former Lady Desborough. The Grenfells were key members of the Liberal coterie in which Alice moved and the Keppel girls were invited to their home of Taplow Court, near Maidenhead, Buckinghamshire. Sonia records that Julian pursued Violet 'alternately with poetry and pugilism'.[15] One of Violet's favourite places at 16 Grosvenor Street in which to take her romantic pleasures was a housemaid's walk-in cupboard. There she and Julian were discovered; the encounter was probably non-sexual – but Alice was furious. Julian had to ask his mother to 'straighten things out' with Alice. Julian joined the First Royal Dragoons in the First World War; he received severe head wounds at Ypres and died in hospital at Boulogne on 26 May 1915.

This was a time too when the Keppels began to see more of the strange Sitwell 'triumvirate' of (later Dame) Edith Louisa Sitwell, Sir Francis Osbert Sitwell and Sacheverell Sitwell. The Sitwells were to remain lifelong friends of the Keppel girls and despite their fundamental sexual predilections Violet and Osbert were deemed by Society to have had a short 'engagement'.[16] This engagement was, in reality, another of Violet's flights of imagination. When she announced the event to her parents – who had been pressing her to think of getting married – Osbert knew nothing about it. He was to be embarrassed by the whole thing particularly as down the years Violet referred to him as 'my ex-fiancé'.[17] They were to remain friends, however, until Osbert's death. Sir George Sitwell of

Renishaw Hall, Derbyshire, and his wife Lady Ida once consulted Alice about what they were to do with their 'graceless' daughter Edith. With a neat touch of self-parody, Alice replied: 'George and Ida, always remember that you never know what a young girl may become.' And writing in 1931, Edith said of Alice, 'She has always been so kind to me, for no reason, just out of sheer niceness.'[18] This was not entirely true. Sir Edward Marsh recalled Society gossip in 1925 noting that Alice had had a 'set to' with Edith, rebuking her for not living with her parents. Edith Sitwell had opined that 'she could write better if she lived alone'. To which Alice commented: 'And do you prefer poetry to human love?' With a jibe at Alice's past, Edith had replied: 'Yes, as a profession.'[19]

There had been another 'engagement' for Violet with Lord Gerald Wellesley, the future 7th Duke of Wellington, but he married Dorothy Ashton, 'Dottie', stepdaughter of the Earl of Scarborough, in the year of his supposed engagement to Violet. It is likely that were there any such agreement, this was Violet's reaction to Vita Sackville-West's rumoured engagement to Harold Nicolson . . . a whole variety of names were mentioned to Alice at Mrs Arthur Sassoon's ball in June 1913.

Duntreath was not left out of the Keppels' annual itinerary and Alice would regularly drive over from the castle to Ayr races to indulge her interest in horse-racing which had been developed by the king. During the autumn races at Ayr in 1913 Alice's party met up with a group who had been sailing up Scotland's west coast from Lloyd George's Welsh home. One of the party was the young Clementine Hozier, granddaughter of the Earl of Airlie; she had married Winston Churchill in 1908, when he was Liberal Colonial Under-Secretary. Clementine remembered Alice 'looking very prosperous', but she had given Clementine several tips that had proved losers.[20]

Clementine Churchill was to add some comments about the Keppels a few months later. During Easter 1914, Alice was at Madrid with Violet as guests of Sir Ernest Cassel. Clementine, another of the guests, was to tell of a visit to a bullfight in Seville;

the event was not to the Keppels' liking and Clementine noted that Alice and Violet were 'ashy grey and dreadfully upset' with the violence and gore of the occasion.[21] Sir Ernest encouraged Alice and Clementine to make their way home via Paris and stay on in the French capital for a while as his guests. This they did and Clementine reports being amused in a horrified sort of way at Alice's suggestion that she could do Winston's career no end of good if she took a rich and influential lover. Alice offered her services in 'such a search'; indeed, Clementine received a strong impression that Alice would believe her selfish if she did not help Winston in this way.[22]

Alice's busy social life had been conducted against a background of growing anxiety in Society. Those who thought at all in terms other than of their own pleasure, monitored the growing tension in Europe with alarm. With sang-froid the Keppels kept up a succession of trips to Europe. During 1913 Alice and George agreed to be paying guests at Clingendaal House, near The Hague, the home of Baroness Daisy de Brienen, and they spent time there from July to September with Violet and Sonia; they returned in July 1914. While the girls were there, the house was to be a magnet for friends and suitors, young men who would be slaughtered in the months ahead. Dinner parties were held for a continual procession of visitors. Alice always kept open house and Society was willing to flock to her generous table. There was a good mixture of nobility and commonalty with a few old royal court friends like Sir Frederick 'Fritz' and Lady Ponsonby. George arranged an itinerary of visits to galleries and museums all over Holland, there was bathing at Scheveningen and a wander round the royal summer residence of Queen Wilhelmina, 'The House in the Wood'.

One of the party during that last July–August of peacetime was Elizabeth Asquith (Princess Antoine Bibesco), the daughter of Margot Asquith, the second wife of Prime Minister H.H. Asquith. Margot Asquith had none of the qualms in allowing her daughter to be Alice's guest that Hugh Walpole's parents had felt. Of her, Margot Asquith was to write:

Alice Keppel is a woman of almost historical interest, not only from her friendship with King Edward, but from her happy personality, and her knowledge of society and the men of the day. She is a plucky woman of fashion; human, adventurous, and gay, who in spite of doing what she likes all her life, has never made an enemy. Her native wits cover a certain lack of culture, but her desire to please has never diminished her sincerity.[23]

The Keppels were at Clingendaal when war was declared on 4 August 1914, and they and their guests made a dash for the night boat to Newhaven. Violet maintained that the following morning they breakfasted at 10 Downing Street – although she said there was no sign of the Prime Minister – and felt much at the forefront of the terrible events that were unfolding to destroy the Society of which Alice Keppel had been a jewel.[24]

The declaration of war between Britain and Germany had been handed to the German ambassador, HSH Karl Max, Prince von Lichnowsky at 11.05 p.m., five minutes after the expiry of the ultimatum that took the country to war in order to protect Belgian neutrality. Few among Alice's circle were to appreciate the immensity of the carnage or the bitter nature of the conflict that stretched four years ahead. It was all rather distant; it took a long time to sink in in the drawing-rooms of Society. And even when it did there were few with an inkling that the safe, privileged and comfortable world they had known was to vanish for ever.

Alice had been privy for months, through her Liberal party connections, to the gossip in the corridors of power, concerning the tension in central Europe, particularly following the assassination on 28 June at Sarajevo of the heir-apparent to the crowns of Austro-Hungary, Archduke Franz Ferdinand, by the Bosnian revolutionary Gavrilo Princip. Many were more worried by the possibility of civil war in Ireland since the Liberals had promised the Irish nationalists a Home Rule that they could not wholly deliver immediately. Society, however, continued its round of town and country-house visitations, garden parties and flower-shows. Some hostesses even had a large table in a corner of their drawing-rooms set aside for displays of war-games; lead soldiers having been bought, or removed from the nursery, to depict the front.

Society even attended the church services which were preliminaries to soldiers going to France, and Alice said her special goodbyes to her nephews and to her husband. Edmonstone nephews William George and Archibald Charles had enrolled in the Coldstream Guards and the 9th Lancers respectively; and of the Albemarle nephews, Walter was to join the Scots Guards, Rupert the Coldstream Guards and Arnold the Rifle Brigade. William was to fall at the Somme during 1916 and Arnold was killed in 1917. George Keppel saw service in the 10th (Service) Battalion of the Royal Fusiliers and as Lieutenant-Colonel commanding the 2/4 East Lancashire Regiment and the 2/5 Highland Light Infantry in Ireland. George's transfer to Ireland saved him from certain death as the 10th Royal Fusilier Battalion was almost totally destroyed in the battle of Pozières in 1916 at the beginning of the Somme offensive.

For Agnes Keyser the First World War was to bring a great increase in the work and expansion of her hospital. Now many of Agnes's and Alice's mutual friends were opening up their homes for the hospital's overflow of sick and wounded officers. Agnes had succeeded in negotiating the use of several houses in London's Belgravia which belonged to such as Mrs Rupert Beckett, Sir Walpole Greenwell, Lady Maxwell, Mr Pandelli Ralli and Mrs Clarence Watney.[25] An added cachet was given to all these owners by visits to their properties by King George and Queen Mary to see the patients. A fleet of special ambulances was also organised to meet hospital trains and ships to bring the wounded officers to the hospital.

From October 1914 the British Red Cross and the Order of St John of Jerusalem combined to form the Joint War Committee to carry out their wartime relief and fund-raising work with the maximum economy and efficiency, under the protection of the Red Cross's name and emblem. Among the Joint War Committee personnel were Agnes and Fanny Keyser's nieces Dorothy, Muriel

Agnes and Sybil Violet who combined War Committee work with that of the hospital.

Many country houses were also procured as convalescent homes for Agnes's patients; Lady Wernher of Luton Hoo and Princess Helena, Duchess of Albany, at Claremont, Esher, were ready hostesses and Sonia Keppel's godmother Mrs Ronald Greville had also opened Polesden Lacey. Meanwhile Alice's friends like Edith Maud, Lady Hulse of Breamore House, Hampshire, and Henrietta, Lady Beresford-Peirse of Bedale House, North Yorkshire, were getting involved in such back-up war services as the Red Cross.

Alice decided to help the effort directly. Her entry was to be through her 'lady-in-waiting' of the old days, Lady Sarah Wilson (1865–1929), formerly Sarah Isabella Augusta Spencer-Churchill, one of the daughters of the 7th Duke of Marlborough, and Winston Churchill's aunt. Lady Sarah had married, in 1891, Lieutenant-Colonel Gordon Chesney Wilson of the Royal Horse Guards and she had been active in the South African War, becoming a prisoner of the Boers.[26] Colonel Wilson was killed in 1914 and Lady Sarah intensified her war work in response.

Many Society women like the Keppels' friend Millicent, Dowager Duchess of Sutherland were opening and running hospitals in France; the duchess organised ambulance units, was captured by the Germans and released, and ran a Red Cross hospital at Calais. So Lady Sarah decided to do this too, and selected the area of Etaples, the pre-war painters' haven on the estuary of the Canche, Boulogne-sur-Mer, where Millicent Sutherland's sister, Lady Angela Forbes – mistress of another Keppel friend Hugo, 10th Earl of Wemyss – already ran canteens. Etaples was to be a great centre for base hospitals.

Lady Sarah Wilson and Alice Keppel were to work at No. 7 Red Cross Hospital (Allied Forces Base Hospital). It had originally opened with 200 beds at the Hotel Christol at Boulogne on 23 October 1914 but was closed on 11 January 1915. Seven months later on 10 August it reopened at Etaples but was closed again on 30 November. During these periods the hospital treated over two thousand patients. It was subsequently transferred to Palermo.

Unlike other Society women of the Keyser-Keppel orbit, like the daughters of the Duke of Rutland, Lady Helen Manners who trained as an anaesthetist and Lady Diana Manners who took courses at Guy's Hospital, Alice took on no medical duties, her work being clerical. Back at Duntreath, Archie Edmonstone was increasingly worried about Alice's to-ing and fro-ing to wartime France. He wrote to Winston Churchill (First Lord of the Admiralty) to enquire if it was safe for Alice to return from Dieppe, because of the risk from German submarines. Churchill replied: 'I think the risk may be accepted.'[27]

Violet and Sonia Keppel, like other young women, gained much from the widening horizons brought by war; the old rules of chaperonage were almost swept away. The girls spent time at Melbury House, Lord and Lady Ilchester's house they had known from childhood. The house and policies, like many aristocratic estates, had become almost self-sufficient in terms of provender in the early days of the war as submarine action made food imports uncertain. So life was bearable for those who had influence.

At New Year 1915, Sonia and Violet returned to London, with Sonia taking up her studies again at Miss Woolf's and Violet war work collecting money for war charities and working at a soldiers' canteen in Grosvenor Gardens. On one occasion she sold shawls with Vita Sackville-West. Violet had pleaded with Alice to let her help at the Red Cross hospital in France, but Alice believed her to be too 'unstable'. Violet was soon sacked from the soldiers' canteen for making a 'cup of cocoa' for a visiting general out of knife-cleaning powder.[28]

Alice spent more time in London now her duties at Etaples had lessened, although she spent early February 1915 in Paris.[29] She supervised her own Grosvenor Street household against the zeppelin air raids. Where she could she continued to send the girls to friends' houses in the country and to Quidenham. The dinner parties at 16 Grosvenor Street continued. On 7 May the Keppels entertained Sir Leander Starr Jameson, the famous leader of the 1895 'Jameson Raid' of the South African War.[30] Domestically too, there had been changes; the Keppels' butler Rolfe had married Mrs Stacey the cook (who had replaced Mrs Wright), and Alice's maid-companion Miss Draper had married George's valet Bridger. Alice employed a new maid-companion in Miss Williams who was to remain with her for the rest of her life.

Two days before Prime Minister Asquith formed a Coalition government with the Conservatives Alice dined with Asquith at the house of Liberal Colonial Secretary, Lewis, Viscount Harcourt.[31] She had heard there that the Coalition would force out the Keppels' friend Winston Churchill, First Lord of the Admiralty, whose Gallipoli campaign was shaping up as a disaster. As a goodwill gesture Alice offered a designer gown to Clementine Churchill, but was rebuffed.[32]

During the summer of 1915, Alice opened her house for luncheons for visiting politicians, war correspondents, diplomats, her friends Asquith and Churchill and such serving officers as Major-General Sir John Cowans, Quartermaster-General of the Forces. Alice's circle was the best informed in London concerning the progress of the war. Queen Mary greatly disapproved of Alice's luncheons at a time when she and the king were advocating austerity in housekeeping.[33] Alice thought too of the young people of her ken and took parties of boys and girls to the music hall for light relief.[34] Sonia was now allowed to help with war work; for a time she worked on the land at Buckhurst Park, near East Grinstead, Surrey, home of the Benson family cousins. She also helped at a canteen run by May, Countess of Limerick, for soldiers at London Bridge.[35]

George kept returning home from leave looking increasingly older. Alice arranged for theatre trips and dinner parties to cheer him up but he increasingly enjoyed his own company, a trait that he was to keep up for the rest of his life. Christmas that year was spent with the Alingtons at Crichel, a house in gloom at the serious wounding of son Gerard Sturt.

By 9 February 1916 the Military Service Bill, calling for the conscription of all eligible men, passed the House of Commons to come into force as legislation, and Alice's dinner table became more populated with men in uniform. There was talk of the disaffection between those who worked in munitions and those serving at the front. Many young men needed at home for their skills in munitions manufacture were branded 'cowards' by those with family in the front lines, and women would stop such men in mufti in the street and give them white feathers as a mark of their supposed baseness.

It was a period too of worker strikes on the Clyde and armed rebellion in Dublin, resulting in the execution of Sir Roger David Casement, a former British consular official who in April 1916 was arrested on landing in Ireland from a German submarine to head a Sinn Fein rebellion. For a while before his execution Casement was a prisoner in the charge of Alice's brother-in-law Major-General Henry Pipton at the Tower of London.

During April, too, Alice was unwell and went to convalesce at Sir Ernest Cassel's house at Branksome Dene, Bournemouth. Clementine Churchill was to remember her visit and told her husband Winston about walks she had had with Alice on the beach. Clementine's encounters with Alice always seemed to result in a fountain of advice; Clementine remembered, 'she tires me by long political discussions about you.'[36]

Zeppelin air raids became more common over London and Britain's east coast. Despite her outward show of nonchalance, Violet was afraid of the air raids and invited herself to the Sackville-Wests at Knole. During her visits Lady Sackville was somewhat concerned at the way Violet prattled about the shady life at 16 Grosvenor Street; she confided to a friend, 'Violet certainly has some very immoral ideas.'[37]

Sonia spent more time at Buckhurst Park and celebrated her sixteenth birthday on 31 May with a party at 16 Grosvenor Street. The party was broken up when news was announced that a great sea battle was raging at Jutland. It was to result in a victory by old naval friends of the Keppels and Edmonstones, Admiral (later Earl) John Rushworth Jellicoe and Admiral (later Earl) David Beatty, over the German Imperial High Seas Fleet supremo Admiral Reinhard Scheer. Their success resulted in Britain's retaining control over the sea although Jellicoe was criticised for not totally disabling the German fleet. Alice had felt that to party at that time was not diplomatic and against the spirit of her father's career, so she called for the National Anthem to be played and the dispersal of Sonia's guests.[38]

Because of the threats of further air attacks on London, Alice took every opportunity for the family to be out of London. During August, Alice, George and the girls stayed at Watlington Park, in the Chiltern Hills of Oxfordshire. The house then belonged to Arthur Henry Renshaw and his wife Lady Winifred Renshaw, who had been Keppel neighbours at Portman Square. From time to time, on behalf of the Liberal government, Alice undertook dinner parties and weekends to entertain senior diplomats. A Watlington weekend was arranged to entertain Jonkheer Dr R. de Marees van Swinderen, Queen Wilhelmina of the Netherlands's Minister in London. Osbert Sitwell recalled visiting Alice and George at this time along with a house party of Vita and Harold Nicolson, the usual 'Keppel crowd' of Lord Ilchester, Lady Lilian Wemyss, Baroness de Brienen and a collection of young Guards officers. Although the weather was terrible the party enjoyed tennis, bridge and the Keppel favourite of 'hide and seek' from room to room.[39]

There was a trip for the Keppels, too, to Trent Park, Hertfordshire, which was being leased by the Curzons from Philip Sassoon. Grace Curzon, the 2nd Marchioness Curzon, noted in her memoirs how they had enjoyed the company of 'Dear Alice always gay and charming'.[40]

George Keppel took up his new post in Ireland and found a house for family visits at Connemara. Alice and the girls joined him almost at once and were served by their butler Rolfe and the new Swiss cook Perriatt. (Both dwelt in a tent in the garden during these Irish visits.) The Keppels were joined by Archie and Ida

Edmonstone and on 16 September 1916 they received a telegram from the War Office to say that their son William Edmonstone had been killed. Alice was as distraught as her brother at the news.

Sonia was now despatched to Scotland to stay for a while with 'Cousin Freddie' – C-in-C Rosyth, Admiral Sir Frederick Tower Hamilton – who had married Admiral Sir Henry Keppel's daughter Maria. It was an exciting time to be in Rosyth, a cockpit of action in the war. The town of Rosyth, abutting the Firth of Forth, was then still new, having been created by the Admiralty in 1903 as a centre for a naval base capable of taking Dreadnought-class ships. All around was land reclaimed from the Forth and high above the seaside resort castle of Mary Queen of Scots stood Admiralty House, where Sonia was to stay. Below were the vessels *Lion*, *Barham*, *Tiger*, and *Indefatigable* whose action at Jutland had broken up Sonia's party.

Someone at Rosyth had forgotten to send Freddie's staff car to collect Sonia and her nanny at a darkened Dunfermline station. They were obliged to hitch a lift from porter Johnnie McPhail's farm-cart. A lack of womenfolk in the mess was to make Sonia an 'enchantress' among the naval officers gathered at Rosyth, but she had fallen in love with McPhail. He was to write to her with an oblique proposal of marriage some time later, but Alice insisted that the letter be shredded into the waste-paper basket with a 'You know you don't really want to be a porter's wife . . .'.[41]

Food was short now, and Alice ordered that all the provisions at Grosvenor Street be pooled for sharing between family and staff. A strain on the store cupboard was almost immediate following her decision. Because of the supposed public perception of Prime Minister Asquith's bungling of things he resigned his position. On 7 December 1916, Lloyd George, who had quit Asquith's government because he believed that the war was not being conducted properly, became Prime Minister of a coalition government. Asquith and his family now moved into 16 Grosvenor Street from 10 Downing Street for a while.

The year 1917 was to be one of air raids, food shortages, fuel deficiencies and street blackouts. Edward Keppel, Alice and George's nephew, was now old enough to join the 2nd Battalion Rifle Brigade and went off to fight in France. The course of the war was talked about daily at Grosvenor Street at Alice's luncheons and dinners, but one conversational subject kept recurring.

The name of the royal house to which Alice's lover had belonged was entered in the history books as the House of Saxe-Coburg-Gotha, and had been inherited as such by George, Prince of Wales, as George V in 1910. As the war developed, the 'German aspects' of his court were continually criticised at dinner tables, in the London clubs, in the press and at public rallies. There was a call for the names of the Kaiser and his family to be expurgated from the lists of honorary commands of British regiments, and for their chivalric banners of the Order of the Garter to be removed from St George's Chapel, Windsor.

George V, who never liked any change in anything he looked upon as a tradition, was reluctant to follow the advice of his ministers on the subject, but the order was given for the expunging to be done. Asquith had told Alice of his surprise at the king's attitude to his German cousins; the king even averred that his cousin Prince Albert of Schleswig-Holstein was not actually supporting the German war effort by acting as commandant of a British prisoner-of-war camp near Berlin. The new premier, Lloyd George, made no secret of the fact that he considered George V to be completely German. Alice demurred, although her lover had been 'German to his fingertips'.[42]

The writer H.G. Wells voiced the opinion, which underlined a growing public feeling, that George V's court was 'alien and uninspiring'. The king's retort was reported at Alice's soirees: 'I may be uninspiring, but I'll be damned if I'm an alien.' So on 19 June 1917, the British royal family renounced its German nomenclature to adopt the name Windsor.

In Europe the Bavarian aristocrat Count Albrecht von Montegles summed up the feeling in continental royal and imperial circles: 'The true royal tradition died on that day in 1917 when, for a mere war, King George V changed his name.' And even for the patriotic Alice Keppel, it seemed that yet another filament in her lamp of memory to her royal lover had been dimmed. In July 1917 the Keppel household, moreover, was plunged into mourning once again on the death at the Third Battle of Ypres of Edward Keppel.

When Violet had become eighteen in 1912, Alice had considered her official coming-out into Society to be inappropriate; it was too soon after the king's death to publicise the Keppel name, and anyway her own mourning was not finished. But when Sonia achieved that age, Alice decided that she should come out after New Year 1918, incidentally quite against the 'injunctions' of the opinionated Margot Asquith.[43] However, Alice decided that she would not launch Sonia on Society herself but arrange for a series of proxy chaperones. So she enlisted the assistance of her friend Elinor, Lady Kinloch, to introduce Sonia officially to Society at a dinner party at Eaton Place. Thereafter Sonia would be chaperoned by Mary, Viscountess Harcourt and Edith, Lady Jessel.

During 16–20 April 1918 the House of Commons passed a new Military Service Bill that now made it possible for males up to the age of fifty-five to be conscripted and for the legislation to be extended to Ireland. The Irish nationalist MPs decided unanimously to oppose conscription of Irish males.

In Ireland George Keppel was undertaking another training programme, this time of a composite battalion of the Highland Light Infantry, against a scenario of increased Sinn Fein opposition in the south. So there were to be no more Keppel holidays in Connemara. For his war service George was to receive the usual campaign medals. Alice, too, was honoured. She received the 1914 Star, the British War Medal and the Victory Medal; these she wore mounted on a bar (rather than on a bow which was usual for women).

Sonia now obtained a job as a parlour-maid to a Russian hospital for officers in South Audley Street, but still had time for jaunts. A memorable one was to Sir Hedworth Williamson's Appley Hall, Ryde, Isle of Wight, where she was enrolled in a concert party to entertain wounded soldiers.[44]

Violet could never stick very long at anything; in reality she hated much to do with hospitals and charity work bored her. Her existence was becoming more and more vacillating and she embarked on a new 'affair'. Lady Cynthia Asquith was to note:

> Beb [her husband Herbert Asquith] and I dined with the Asquiths. I sat between the PM and Mr Meiklejohn . . . Violet Keppel was there and did some brilliant imitations, she has considerable 'pig-charm'. There is an 'affair' between her and Cis [her brother-in-law Cyril], and Beb and I felt *de trop* as everyone else played bridge and we were left alone with them.[45]

By now the Germans were in general retreat and on 11 November 1918 an armistice was signed at five in the morning in a railroad car in the forest of Compiègne, north of Paris. Hostilities formally ended at eleven in the morning. The Keppels joined the crowds outside Buckingham Palace to cheer the king and queen, but round the corner was a personal war for Alice.

CHAPTER 12

THE TROUBLE WITH VIOLET

In the years following the First World War Alice Keppel's main preoccupations were to get Sonia safely married, and to rein in Violet's excessive behaviour which might have an adverse effect on Sonia's prospects. 'There were many who disliked Violet Trefusis for what she had done to the Nicolsons. She had, of course, treated her husband Denys with cynical evil.' Thus Marion Purves had written to her father on Friday, 11 August 1936, after the farewell broadcast to the Empire by abdicating King Edward VIII. That afternoon they had talked of Alice *vis-à-vis* the monarch and Wallis Simpson.[1] The heartache such family friends had felt for Alice and George had its roots in a cab in Hyde Park some twenty-six years previously.

In 1918 Violet Keppel was twenty-two and had developed the eccentricities, whimsicalities and downright circuitries of her nature that were to entertain, appal and dismay all who knew her. '[Violet was] a law unto herself, perhaps the most selfish woman I have known, so selfish and inconsiderate that she became a joke,' Harold Acton was to say.[2] Violet's whole being was full of romance, fanaticism, wicked jealousies, galloping high spirits and social indiscretions. If she did not like the way in which her life was going, she invented a new role, and lived it as if it were real. Sibyl Colefax, a great Society hostess between the two world wars, probably summed up what most people thought about Violet: she was 'good company', but 'a really wicked creature'.[3]

Violet's flair for the learning of languages made her a keen internationalist, with a deep and abiding love for France, a country she had been introduced to as a child through the 'Mrs George jaunts' with Edward VII. Her ear for language made her a superb mimic. Being a Francophile also gave her one other thing in common with the selfishly pursued love of her life, Vita Sackville-West.

Vita had developed a friendship with Violet in 1904 when she was twelve and Violet was ten; they had met at a friend's tea party and soon after Violet persuaded Alice to invite Vita to tea at Portman Square. Violet sealed their friendship with a proprietary kiss. Daily meetings at Miss Helen Woolf's school in South Audley Street, just east of Park Lane, London, had developed into regular visits to the Keppels. Violet in her extreme precocity was far ahead of gawky Vita in maturity, but their shared childhood lives in big houses and high society, and romantic tastes in reading from Edmond Rostand – originator of *Cyrano de Bergerac* – to Sir Walter Scott led them down similar paths of interest.

Violet and Vita's friendship was cultivated through an imaginative correspondence in French and English, and by the time they met up in Florence their futures were destined to be intertwined. The girls had been sharing private lessons in Italian with Signorina Castelli before Violet's usual trip to Florence with the family in 1908. They parted with Violet's usual effusion of affection and the first love-lorn utterance of 'darling', with an inflection that put it above the sense of social cliché.

By May 1908 Vita was in Florence too, at the Villa Pestellini, and Violet's passion for her intensified. She gave Vita a lava ring – which she had cheekily extracted as a child, by her own admission, from the Bond Street store of the art dealer Sir [later Baron] Joseph Duveen while on a visit with Alice; Violet averred that the ring had belonged to a fifteenth-century incumbent of the chief magistracy of Venice, the Doge, and Vita was to keep it for the rest of her life.[4]

Before Violet had set off for Ceylon with her parents in 1910, Vita had joined their family house-party at Duntreath. It was not

Vita's first trip to Duntreath; she had been there before a Florence jaunt in 1908. At Duntreath Violet played childish court to Vita, decorating her room with tuberoses as a romantic bower; and she inveigled her way into spending the night in Vita's room. Vita noted that that was the first time she had passed the night hours alone with anyone, remarking on the innocence of the event.[5]

At Duntreath Violet had tried to persuade Vita to join the party for Ceylon. A final goodbye as they drove round Hyde Park before Violet departed had ended in a passionate kiss from Violet which had left Vita agitated.[6] It was not a schoolgirlish crush; Violet was sixteen, going on thirty-two, and had, as her sister Sonia remarked, always been an adult. Letters to Vita followed from Ceylon with Violet insisting that Vita did not marry in her absence. On Violet's return, and before she set off for Germany, she spent some time with Vita at the Sackville home of Château Malet, Monte Carlo, where Vita was given rubies from Ceylon.

The Keppels were to be regular visitors to the Sackvilles' estate at Knole. At New Year 1913, Violet and Vita played in a 'Persian Play' in the Great Hall at Knole, Vita as a young dusky-skinned caliph and Violet as a slave. It was an extension of their dual roles in life. Violet regularly sought out Vita when everyone had gone to bed, to express her love; though in the daytime she was an incorrigible flirt with men of all ages.

Among the other pupils at Miss Woolf's school had been Rosamund Grosvenor (b. 1888), the daughter of the 2nd Duke of Westminster's relative Algernon Grosvenor. Rosamund had regularly shared lessons with Vita at Knole, and at an early age Vita loved her more than she ever did Violet. Rosamund's infatuation with Vita was to last for some time, with Vita being introduced to physical love-making with Rosamund. Violet and Rosamund were deeply jealous of each other.

In tandem with all this was Vita's relationship with the Foreign Office diplomat Harold Nicolson, the son of Sir Arthur Nicolson, the 1st Lord Carnock, erstwhile British Ambassador at St Petersburg and currently Permanent Under-Secretary of State at the Foreign Office. They had first met on 20 June 1910 at a dinner party, the year of Vita's coming-out. Vita was immediately smitten by him and invited Harold to Knole a few days later. It was the beginning of a courtship, although Nicolson also had homosexual inclinations. They became engaged but Vita did not tell Violet who read about it in the papers and was lividly jealous; she wrote Vita a series of sarcastic letters.[7]

Vita and Harold were married by the Bishop of Rochester in the chapel at Knole on 1 October 1913. Violet did not attend the wedding, but gave Vita a diamond and amethyst ring. Vita's first child, Benedict Lionel (Ben), was born on 6 August 1914. Violet had disappeared from the scene for a while, but 'at her own sarcastic request', became Ben's godmother.[8] A third son, Nigel, was born on 19 January 1917, after a second son had been born dead in 1915.

On 13 April 1918, Violet invited herself down to Long Barn, a cottage near Knole, which had been bought in 1915 and rebuilt and enlarged by Vita and Harold. Five days later Violet and Vita's friendship developed into a full-blown homosexual affair.[9] By 20 April Violet and Vita went off to Polperro, Cornwall, to stay at 'The Cobbles', a fisherman's cottage belonging to Violet's childhood friend Hugh Walpole. Violet gave Vita a deep sense of romance, risk and adventurous excitement that Harold could not offer her, and in Cornwall Violet wove around Vita her special kind of enchantment that would almost lead to the destruction of Vita's marriage.

Vita began to write her novel *Challenge* (published by George H. Doron in the USA in 1924, but suppressed by Vita in the UK) on 14 May 1918. The plot is the love between Julian (Vita) and Eve (Violet) set in Greece; Violet collaborated in writing part of the book. Violet was also to appear as the boy-girl 'Sasha' in Virginia Woolf's book *Orlando* (1928).

Violet and Vita saw each other regularly and went off together as often as they could. Sometimes they stayed at the Keppel home at 16 Grosvenor Street, when Alice and George were absent, and throughout Violet made it clear to Vita that she was the great passion of her life. For some time Vita had been affecting men's clothes with a favourite outfit of wide hat, heavy jacket and jodhpurs; she began to wear this attire on their walks around London. They would walk and talk and sit in the parks like young lovers. Those who saw them remarked on the lovesick devotion Violet seemed to subject Vita to and when they were in company together Violet never took her eyes off Vita. They began to call each other by 'love names': Vita was 'Mitya' and Violet 'Lushka'.

Harold Nicolson was deeply upset by the affair. Whenever he was ill or out of sorts, Vita did act the devoted wife to Violet's jealous disgust and anger. Harold could see a deliberate pattern forming in Violet's actions; by the use of ridicule she was trying to undermine Vita and Harold's relationship. When they were apart Violet bombarded Vita with thick love letters. Violet was soon to use her techniques in another direction.

Among Violet's men friends, Major Denys Robert Trefusis, four years her senior, began to show a growing interest in her. Violet told Vita that she liked Denys because he reminded her of Vita.

Denys Trefusis had been born at Bickmaster, Somerset on 30 March 1890, the youngest of the four children of the Hon. John Schomberg Trefusis and his wife Eva 'Mitty' Louisa Bontein. Denys Trefusis was the grandson of the 19th Baron Clinton and had been educated at Charterhouse. At his own instigation he had left school and had gone directly to Russia to be a tutor to the children of an aristocratic family; consequently he was a fluent Russian speaker. He was an accomplished horseman and a fine sportsman and his dashingness appealed to Violet's fantasies.

After sojourning in Russia from 1910, Denys Trefusis joined the Royal Horse Guards at the outbreak of the First World War and spent the war in France and Flanders with the British Expeditionary Force. Denys had something of an elusive individuality that gave him the air of being a free spirit. In this he became a challenge to Violet, who in all things had to master people and situations, even though the mastery was only in her own mind. So she set about making Denys fall in love with her. Her technique was the same with most people she decided to dominate. She would soften them up with witty letters, then bombard them with her complete attention on meeting and finally smother them in charm.

Violet now fully intended to marry Denys Trefusis. Her mother's example and Society itself had shown Violet that Edwardian married life was a woman's token of independence and sexual freedom. She and Vita both as married women would have greater freedom to continue their affair. But she had to claim Vita as her own first and get her away from Harold.

As Violet's love for Vita ran its course Alice Keppel was becoming more and more agitated. People were gossiping freely about Violet's sexual preferences and Alice was determined to get Violet married off to Denys. After all, she told Marion Purves bluntly, when Violet was introduced to a man's 'natural attentions' she would forget the 'romantic nonsense' with Vita.[10] Not wishing to leave Violet to her own devices in London, Alice insisted on her daughter accompanying her on the Keppel circuit of social rounds to stay at such places as the Cassels' house at Branksome Dene, Bournemouth, and Sir Hedworth Williamson's house of Appley Hall, Ryde, Isle of Wight. On Sunday, 26 October 1918, Denys Trefusis made the first of his proposals of marriage to Violet; she dissembled a refusal to her mother's dismay and Alice's nagging of Violet intensified.

On 26 November 1918 Vita and Violet went to France and were to stay until 15 March 1919. By early 1919 Harold was to be on the British Staff at the Paris Peace Conference. At first Vita had been reluctant to go, and Violet, a consummate attention-seeker, had threatened suicide. At Paris they stayed for ten days at 30 rue Montpelier, Palais-Royal, a *pied-à-terre* loaned to them by the 'fashionable homosexual' Edward Knoblock. At Paris they dined with Denys, then with his regiment in Belgium, and then went off via the Hôtel Beau Rivage, Saint-Raphael, to the Hôtel Bristol at Monte Carlo. Alice fumed that she did not know of their exact whereabouts.

At Monte Carlo they gambled and lost a lot, Vita pawning her jewels to pay their hotel bill. They read, wrote and socialised – dancing together to raised lorgnettes – while Violet was severally clinging, hysterical, passionately loving and suicidal. Harold, much depressed by Vita's absence, although he was enjoying a new affair with Victor Cunard, nephew of Alice's sister-Society hostess, Emerald, Lady Cunard, rented a flat in Paris in order to encourage her to return. Vita broke a promise to return and remained with Violet. By this time London Society – and the reciprocal network in Monte Carlo – was buzzing with their escapade.

Alice's social diary was as full as ever, and she tried to shut her ears to the gossip about her errant daughter. On 29 November at a dinner party held by General Sir Archibald Hunter, who had served with Kitchener and had been Governor of Gibraltar, she had parried questions about Violet and Vita's whereabouts by detailing her dismay at her car's faulty starter-motor. She was to be cut to the quick, however, by Vita's mother Lady Sackville – who was just as in the dark about Vita's activities – saying in public that Violet was a 'sexual pervert'. Alice fulminated that Lady Sackville had had a 'protector' for years in Sir John Murray Scott and was hardly free from stain herself. Yet Violet must be married without delay. Her 'no' to Denys was backdated as a 'yes'. When Violet returned to England, Alice announced her daughter's engagement to Denys on 26 March 1919. Society folk who knew the Keppels described it as a 'bizarre' match. Violet's true intentions were not to live a full, sexual married life with Denys; she planned to elope with Vita a day before the wedding.

Violet increased the emotional pressure on Vita to abscond, and Vita wrote to Harold, then in France, that she might join him soon, as to be around if Violet actually married might drive her to create a scandal at the ceremony. Vita indeed left for France two days before Violet's wedding.

It was to be perhaps the most curious wedding of many a Season; all who knew Violet thought she would call it off at the last minute, and if it did go ahead few believed, least of all Alice who insisted that it take place, that it would last. Alice's attitude was that once she had got Violet safely married, she would have an ally in Denys to make Violet be less of a public embarrassment. Denys was more than keen to be married to Violet, but two of the conditions he had accepted were severe: Violet was to continue her affair with Vita uninterrupted, and she would never sleep with Denys in a sexual sense.

Despite these outwardly impossible conditions a marriage was agreed. Alice with her usual panache was to make it a Society wedding to remember. Her guest list was almost pure Debrett and she held a luncheon before the wedding, followed by a rehearsal at the church, to make sure that her instructions were fully understood by all. Violet and Denys's wedding presents were sumptuous. The king and queen sent Violet a brooch with the royal cipher; George gave a gold-fitted dressing-case and writing-case; Alice gave her daughter a pearl and diamond bandeau and a pearl necklace; and from Duntreath came George I silver candlesticks. The staff clubbed together for a silver inkstand.

The wedding took place on Monday, 16 June 1919 at fashionable St George's Church, Hanover Square, and beneath the fine reredos of the Last Supper, Violet and Denys plighted their curious troth before the Dean of the Royal Chapels, Canon Edgar Sheppard, and Prebendary Francis Thicknesse, a Keppel neighbour in Gloucester Street. For those not invited, papers like *The Times* gave the roster of guests such as old Keppel friends Lord and Lady Savile, Lady Desborough (who escorted Alice), the Duchess of Beaufort and her daughter Lady Diana Somerset. *The Sketch* of 25 June was to supply a range of pictures of the happy couple with their bridesmaids Sonia, Joan Poynder, Olive Paget and Myrtle Farquharson, and child attendants Crispian Keppel, Cecilia Keppel, Phyllida Walford and David McKenna. Eventually Violet arrived with her father – who had made most of the arrangements for the wedding: Alice had thought it better to mount guard on Violet lest she bolted – and the bride received a bouquet in military colours from the guard of honour from Denys's regiment. Violet wore old Valenciennes over chiffon, and a train of gold brocade with a raised pattern of velvet flowers. She gave her best dissembling public performance to date.

As the congregation waited for the Keppels to arrive, and before Dame Nellie Melba gave forth with Gounod's 'Ave Maria', there was much speculation during the rendering of Purcell's 'Trumpet Voluntary' about the strange couple. Although friends insisted that he was in love with Violet, others whispered that Denys was impotent; it seemed to be fitting, averred the most catty, that Denys be son-in-law to George Keppel, who had been cuckolded for more than a decade.

Violet and Denys began their rumbustious honeymoon in Paris staying at the Ritz, Alice's funding giving them all the luxuries they might need. After her royal lover's death, Alice's wealth had increased rapidly through wise investment. Violet never tired of telling Vita that by this time her mother was worth £20,000 a year.[11] But the opulent surroundings in Paris did nothing to brighten the strange scenario that was being played out. Violet and Denys rowed about her continual watching out of their room window for Vita, who was also in Paris and had begun to dog their steps. Where they dined, so did Vita at a table nearby. At length Vita prised Violet, who had jettisoned her wedding ring, away from Denys and took her to the small hotel where she was staying, to make love. A miserable Denys hovered between them throughout the Paris trip, his rows with Violet escalating.

As the German signing of the Peace Treaty of Versailles on 28 June 1919 came and went, Violet was bombarding Vita with telegrams as she and Denys travelled south from Paris on their nightmare *voyage de noces*. When they returned to England, Violet and Denys took Possingworth Manor, Blackboys, near Uckfield, Sussex, some twenty miles from Vita's Long Barn. Alice and Sonia visited occasionally to assess the Trefusis household atmosphere.[12] One particular occasion (30 July 1919) Vita was there too and wrote to her husband how she loathed Alice who had undermined her spirit.[13] Denys resigned his commission but became acting

Major of the Regular Army Reserve of Officers of the Royal Horse Guards. Business took him to London, and when he was away Vita made regular visits to Possingworth Manor. Violet longed for divorce.

Violet continued pressuring Vita to run away with her, and Vita agreed that they should go abroad; after all it would be good to escape the growing Society gossip. Despite the opposition of Alice, Denys, the Sackvilles and the Trefusises, they left on 19 October and made a leisurely journey to Monte Carlo. Violet and Vita behaved as a married couple might, impervious to the letters of reproach from their husbands.

Vita rejoined Harold, however, in Paris on 18 December. But back in London Vita and Violet met up again and by January 1920 they were planning a real elopement. Violet became increasingly indiscreet as the affair developed. She had confided some of her passion for Vita to the equally fanciful Margaret 'Pat' Dansey, who lived with her uncle Lord Fitzhardinge at his Gloucester castle of Berkeley, where Violet had been a guest. For once in her life Alice was really angry with Violet; adultery her set would connive at, but not blatant homosexuality. When Violet threatened to go off and live with Vita, Alice agreed to bow to the inevitable but *insisted* – as only she could with a firm hand on the purse strings – that Violet wait until Sonia was safely married. A scandal, she emphasised, would blight Sonia's chances.[14]

Alice was doing what she could to advance Sonia in Society. Because of the closeness of the king's death to the event, and her high profile in the defunct Edwardian court, Alice had never contemplated having Violet presented at court. Now the war was over, things were different and Sonia was groomed by Alice to be a 'deb'.

Society was changing fast following the armistice. Although there was a conspiracy of silence in Society about the horrors of battle – Siegfried Lorraine Sassoon's *Memoirs of an Infantry Officer*, for instance, did not appear until 1930 – it was developing a cynical distancing of itself from what was brewing abroad. There was a new flippancy and sophistication in the air, and the influence of cocktails, jazz, nightclubs, gramophones and sex across the classes – all influenced by America – was taken up by the upper classes as an analgesic to blot out the traumatic memories of war.

Ever able to adapt to the fashions of the day, Alice assessed the latest trends of the Season following the armistice. Dancing was now *de rigueur* at all the major parties as was rushing about in cars. Alice had bought Violet and Sonia a Studebaker (although Violet had refused to drive it) to facilitate attendance at country-house parties. Thus London Society and country Society merged more than they had done. At first after the war England's old country houses were still run on the same lines as before with large staffs indoors and out. But this was to change slowly as the Second World War approached, with many of the landed families Alice had known selling their large estates. Indeed by the 1920s over a hundred houses that Alice had visited with the Prince of Wales (and later as king) and his entourage were demolished and a thousand of the families who had hob-nobbed with her and her royal lover had vanished from Burke's famous directory *Landed Gentry*.

Violet and Sonia were to be young people of this age of transition as the emphasis changed from the country-house weekend Alice had known to the new sophisticated London scene; one of the major reasons for this was the squeezing of the old landed families by death duties and the new money being made in the City. And Sonia, in particular, was to be one of the young women of the nightclub age, who combined visits to 'Norfolk House *and* the Blue Lantern'.

The Season of May, June and July belonged to the stunningly dressed debutantes for whose ranks Alice was grooming Sonia. For those three months houses of the prominent in Mayfair, Bloomsbury and Belgravia had awnings outside stretching from front door to kerb where drew up the transport of 'debs' and their bored, well-bred and eligible escorts. Following the opening up of the Season parties came racing at Ascot, but where carriages had rattled the roads in Alice's day there was a tailback of cars. Then after the races at Goodwood there began the Smart Set's official holiday season, somewhat ironical as most of the prosperous were permanently on holiday. And after the race parties at Goodwood came the post-Season exodus to Euston Station for those who were making for the grouse moors of Scotland, or to Victoria Station for those who were bound for the south of France.

No one knew Society better than Alice Keppel and how it could be manipulated and exploited. Armed with her assessment of how Society trends were going she set about launching Sonia into its midst.

The concept of the debutante was as old as the beginning of Queen Victoria's reign, and Sonia's entry into Society by this exalted route was less of an ordeal than for some girls. Her mother had built up a very wide network of friends and acquaintances, so at gatherings leading up to the court presentation Sonia was among familiar faces. Presentation at court, wherein daughters of the great and good lined up to curtsey to the king and queen, while dressed in fabulously expensive evening dresses topped off with Prince of Wales feathers, was a key role in a girl's coming-out into Society and a ritual that had to be endured for the right doors to open.

Alice elected to present Sonia herself at one of Their Majesties' summer courts in 1919. It was to be Alice's first main court function since her royal 'widowhood' as sovereign's mistress, and it was Sonia's first visit to Buckingham Palace. A further launching of Sonia took place at that year's Ascot with her being included in a house party at Lady Lowther's rented house at Maidenhead; Lady Lowther was the widow of a former British ambassador and had been recruited by Alice to her roster of matchmakers for Sonia. Lady Lowther interpreted her brief very widely and included introducing Sonia at Maidenhead to the brother-in-law of Prince Feliz F. Yussoupov, murderer of Gregory Rasputin; Grand Duke Dimitri Pavlovich was hardly a suitable husband for Sonia, and she had eyes elsewhere, but the presence of exiled Russian Imperial Royalty indicated to the circuit that Alice still dominated after her 'widowhood'.

During the spring of 1920 Sonia Keppel became engaged to Roland Calvert Cubitt, 'Rolie', whom the war had made the eldest surviving son of the 2nd Baron Ashcombe. He was an officer in the Coldstream Guards. They had become unofficially engaged in 1918 as his parents thought them too young to contemplate matrimony; Alice backed them up. Indeed her mother had said to her: 'It isn't that I don't like Rolie. I think he's very nice. But if you marry him, you'll marry into a world you've never known, and I'm not at all sure that you'll like it.'[15] Sonia indeed entered the stiffly formal world of Lord Ashcombe at Denbies, near Dorking, Surrey, determined in her own mind to marry Roland Cubitt despite the continuing matchmaking of 'Alice's roster'.

While Violet and Vita were playing their love-games, George and Alice took Sonia to the Palace Hotel, St Moritz for three weeks. Just before they were due back, Denys telegraphed to say that Violet was suspected of having an appendicitis – a code, it seems, to Alice concerning Violet's intentions – and Alice and George returned home; Sonia went on, with Alice's maid Williams, to Lady Nunburnholme's villa at Nice, accompanied part of the way by Alice's old friends the Duke of Alba and the Duke and Duchess of Santona.

Sonia and Roland now decided to marry at the Guards Chapel, and Alice took the prime role in the arrangements for Sonia's wedding. When Lord Ashcombe arrived at 16 Grosvenor Street to discuss the couple's financial wedding settlements, he was more than surprised to be greeted and interviewed alone by Alice who was to drive a hard bargain. As he reflected on the large amount of money he had agreed to settle on his son, he added that he hoped that the marriage would be a long-lasting one. Whereupon Alice commented: 'My dear Lord Ashcombe, neither you nor I can legislate for eternity.'[16]

During 3–8 February 1920, Violet and Vita went off to the Saracen's Head Hotel, Lincoln. Society gossiped that Vita had taken Violet away because Denys was threatening to shoot her. There they plotted their elopement. Harold was involved in diplomatic business and Denys was soon spurned by Violet when the two women returned to London. Singly Vita and Violet crossed to France, but Denys had met Vita on the quay at Dover and insisted on crossing the Channel with her. He was unable to persuade them to give up their plan of elopement and he left them before their journey to Amiens. Alice had known that Denys would not succeed and sent George in pursuit, after she had pulled strings with Scotland Yard, it seems, to watch which port they were to leave from. There was a heated and abusive argument at Amiens with George, who stayed on at the Hôtel du Rhin, on Alice's instructions, to monitor progress. Vita and Violet continued their programme of sightseeing unconcerned.

On 14 February, backed by Lady Sackville and Alice Keppel, although the two dames were acting separately, Denys and Harold flew to Amiens. The two husbands successfully broke up the absconding pair and returned to Paris, Denys and Violet to the Ritz, and Harold and Vita to the Alexandre III.

Violet and Denys now set out for Toulon to a prearranged meeting with Alice. Almost at every village a hysterical Violet insisted on stopping to telegraph Vita. At length they met up with Alice, who with her famous charm at full blast offered to give Violet an annual allowance of £600 should she patch up her marriage with Denys; she did not insist that Violet give up Vita entirely. But to Society the marriage must look 'normal'. Violet was unmoved.

Denys now threatened to apply for an annulment of the marriage. The Keppels were appalled, and Alice threatened never to speak to Violet again unless she co-operated and regularised her marriage, in a public sense. A cooling-off period was suggested and Violet stayed for a while with Alice in Monte Carlo.

Yet by 20 March Violet had joined Vita at Avignon. On returning to London, Violet found that her parents would hardly speak to her. Indeed Violet was finding it hard to come to terms with their attitude. Once she had been the centre of their universe as the clever, beautiful child-prodigy, now she was almost a pariah.

She was barred from 16 Grosvenor Street and was allowed to visit only by invitation. For Alice, Violet was totally ruined in Society and she and Denys would have no other option but to pursue a 'rural existence'. Denys, in response to Alice's pressure, took the Manor House at Sonning-on-Thames where Violet fumed and vegetated.

Violet's passion for Vita continued unabated, but there were signs of Vita's reciprocated feelings waning. It was a gradual cooling, for in January 1921 Vita was with Violet at Hyères for six weeks. By now Violet's hold over Vita had become more sinister as she was playing the suicide card regularly. There was talk now of Violet's marriage really being annulled by Denys. He discussed it with Alice, who confirmed that if he did not press for an annulment she would fund them if they lived permanently abroad. Alice took Violet for a while to Duntreath and Clingendaal to consider her position.

The strain of her hurt and the Society humiliation she perceived Violet had brought on her caused the normally placid Alice to erupt. She became forthrightly rude to Violet in company and so much so in the family that their travelling companion Vie, Lady de Trafford (wife of the foxhunting enthusiast Sir Humphrey de Trafford) was constrained to remonstrate, as did George. Denys, who was languishing in a hut in the gardens of Clingendaal with suspected tuberculosis, treated Violet with icy silence.

Talk of a Trefusis divorce, of course, had horrified Vita. The scandal would greatly affect the Sackville-Wests' place in Society if her affair with Violet was made universal public knowledge. In any case she had no wish to have to admit in public that she was homosexual.

Alice kept up a perpetual state of high dudgeon with Violet; what she feared most was a Keppel replay of the Radclyffe-Hall scenario. Society had been scandalised by the lesbian love affairs of the poet and novelist Marguerite – *soi-disant* 'John' – Antonia Radclyffe-Hall. She was to win notoriety with her largely autobiographical novel *The Well of Loneliness* for which she was prosecuted under the Obscene Publications Act of 1857. Recognised in Society, whether right or wrong, as a promiscuous bohemian Marguerite Radclyffe-Hall had been conducting a tumultuous affair with Mabel Veronica Batten, when she fell in love with Una, Lady Troubridge, the second wife of the Keppel acquaintance Admiral Sir Ernest Charles Troubridge, then head of the British Naval Mission to Serbia. On Mabel Batten's death in 1916, Marguerite Radclyffe-Hall and Una Troubridge set up house together as 'husband and wife'; Alice realised that this was what Violet intended to do with Vita.

Una Troubridge was to go through a messy divorce with Admiral Sir Ernest citing Marguerite Radclyffe-Hall as co-respondent; Alice cringed at the thought of Denys doing the same. That would be bad enough, but to have Violet as one of the young starlets of the 'lesbian scene' of Italy and Paris, where many British lesbian women had fled to avoid the odium of Society, made Alice nauseous. Ironically, though, Radclyffe-Hall and Una Troubridge were to merge with the lesbian literati of Europe including Sidonie Gabrielle Colette who was later to become a friend and correspondent of Violet.

Back in London, with Denys and Violet at Sonning, Alice was greatly distressed by the death on 29 June 1921 at 8 Westbourne Street of her old friend Jennie, Lady Randolph Churchill. The news brought back memories of her lover's sparkling court and the twinkle the beautiful Jennie had brought to the sovereign's eye. Alice wrote to Jennie's son Winston, now Colonial Secretary, to express condolences.[17]

Violet, when she was not a virtual prisoner at 16 Grosvenor Street – a precaution taken when Denys was away – was having her mail censored by Alice and was forced to follow in her mother's wake to Holland, Rome and Florence. At length some kind of peace was agreed with Denys and in the autumn of 1921 Violet moved to Paris – London was out of bounds to her in Alice's eyes – with Denys to a flat in the rue Fourcroy, and thence to the rue Laurent Pinchat. Denys had secured a job in finance and they were quickly absorbed into the Russo-French chic society and Violet channelled her talents into being a key personage in Parisian life.

Alice celebrated a family reconciliation in 1922 with a grand luncheon party in Paris. Violet now used as a platform the inner circle of the Franco-American lesbian Winnaretta Singer, Princesse Edmond de Polignac, in whose salon at 57 avenue Henri-Martin, Violet built up a rich and powerful network of friends. For a while Violet was closely chaperoned by Alice until she was confident that her once-adored daughter would not cause further public scandal in her mother's orbit.

Although Winnaretta de Polignac was the centre of a flamboyant circle of rampant lesbians, there is no suggestion that Violet was anything but faithful to Vita. Denys himself was having affairs. One which caused a great row with a jealous Violet was with Madame Ludmila Rubassof, a mannequin for Chanel.

In 1923 Violet and Denys purchased a house at Auteuil, in the rue de Ranelagh, and Violet developed her own salon of the good and the great, entertaining her old friends the Sitwells and a wide range of literati from Rebecca West to Cyril Connolly. During the Christmas of 1923 they cruised the Nile with Alice and George aboard Winnaretta de Polignac's yacht. It was a time of great interest in ancient Egyptian civilisations among the smart set of Europe, for in the previous year Howard Carter and Lord Carnarvon had discovered the relatively untouched tomb of the young king Tutankhamen in the Valley of the Kings at Luxor.

During the winter of 1921–2 Violet had met the French writer Marcel Proust, another of the de Polignac circle, at the home of Walter Berry. During conversation Proust had talked to Violet of a delightful village called Saint-Loup de Naud, with its fine Romanesque church, some fifty miles from Paris. She was not to visit the village until 1927, but there she fell in love with a medieval *tour* adjacent to the eleventh-century abbey and parkland; her enthusiasm for it was such that Alice bought it for her. Violet was to use the *tour* in her own novel *Hunt the Slipper* (1937).

In the spring of 1927 Denys and Violet made their only visit to the United States in the company of the Princesse de Polignac, Alice and George. Violet and the princess called on the Republican President, John Calvin Coolidge, at the White House, before continuing their journey to Florida and Cuba. On 2 September 1929 the long-ailing Denys Trefusis died of tuberculosis in the American Hospital at Neuilly. Friends were not surprised that the self-obsessed Violet had virtually ignored Denys during his final illness. Death had made divorce no longer necessary.

Years back, once she had helped to regularise Violet's marriage as much as she could in the eyes of Society, Alice had turned her attention to the interest in international affairs that she had had when her royal lover was alive. On 12 October 1922 she wrote to the diplomat Sir Horace Rumbold congratulating him for his part in the Chanak Crisis of the Anglo-Turkish confrontation of September 1922. Rumbold was senior Allied High Commissioner at Constantinople and Alice fulsomely praised him and Major-General Sir Charles Harington for managing the difficult situation with Mustafa Kemal Ataturk, the Turkish general and statesman who was to be President of Turkey during 1923–38. She reported that at her dinner table both Winston Churchill and Lloyd George had been stirred by Rumbold's sterling efforts.[18]

The letter underlined how Alice retained her high profile in the 1920s as a Society hostess. At this time, too, she was beginning to form thoughts that she could win greater social dominance in a more international scene.

CHAPTER 13

AN ENDING AT
BUCKLAND HOUSE

During 1919 Agnes Keyser acquired the lease of 16 Grosvenor Crescent for use as her private residence. Shortly before, on 31 October 1918, the Duke of Westminster's solicitor, George F. Hatfield, had confirmed that Agnes could lease and use 17 Grosvenor Crescent as a hospital. In June 1919 Agnes and Fanny Keyser moved into No. 16 and the hospital took up its old quarters at No. 17. On 12 June the hospital was reopened by King George V and Queen Mary.[1]

By 1920 funds for the hospital were strained once more and Agnes circulated an appeal, this time asking all units of the Armed Forces to subscribe. The hospital was now dealing with outpatients and had cared for some seven thousand admissions. On 19 May 1926 Agnes suffered a severe blow with the death of her sister Fanny after a series of strokes; within five years she was to lose her beloved brother Charles and her sister Marian Charlotte. Their deaths were to affect her greatly and caused her to reassess the future of the hospital.

Now in her late seventies Agnes agreed to the Hospital Trustees' suggestion that they apply for a Royal Charter of Incorporation to assure the future of the foundation. The legal niceties were facilitated by the old Keyser family friend Sir Bernard Halsey-Bircham and the hospital was so confirmed by Royal Charter on 21 August 1930 to be managed by a house committee with rules vested in a corporate body.

On the outbreak of the Second World War, the hospital was

evacuated to Lady Ludlow's house at Luton Hoo, yet, as the expected enemy air attacks on London did not materialise, the hospital was reopened at 17 Grosvenor Crescent during March 1940. On 11 January 1941 a bomb destroyed the interior of the house. Agnes Keyser was never to recover from the shock of seeing her life's work so shattered.[2]

From the death of her beloved friend King Edward VII, Agnes retained royal connections. King George V and Queen Mary saw her frequently in London, where she often walked with the king in the gardens of Buckingham Palace. During the First World War Agnes had secured permission to bring the wounded officers in her care to the garden. Agnes was to be a regular correspondent with the king and queen and she gave them regular reports of the hospital and 'my boys', mostly officers of the Household Cavalry and the Brigade of Guards. In her letter of 7 March 1920 she referred to King George as her 'Kindest & best Friend'.[3]

The diaries of King George V and Queen Mary confirm that Agnes Keyser was invited to stay at Abergeldie and dine at Balmoral for a few days each year between 1921 and 1935.[4] There she regularly joined the royal family on motor trips and picnics, cutting a rather eccentric figure striding over the heather in a bright mauve suit and an orange wig. Their Balmoral garden walks were a special delight for Agnes as the king described his plans for a new pansy garden and alpine feature that was to evolve as 'Queen Mary's Garden'. Queen Mary dispensed traditional Balmoral hospitality to a favourite group of guests every September. At this time Agnes joined such as Dr Cosmo Gordon Lang, Archbishop of Canterbury, King George's old tutor Canon John Neale Dalton, Count Albert Mensdorff and Viscount Esher.[5] Sir Harold Nicolson remembered: 'Sister Agnes could be relied upon to enliven the Balmoral conversation by repeating, not always with useful results, the talk of the town.'[6] Agnes's gossip was said to include titbits about the current indiscretions of the Prince of Wales; in this Agnes was deemed a part of 'an intelligence network said to include Princess Victoria [King George's unmarried sister]'.[7]

During King George's incapacity following a severe infection of the blood, Agnes was a regular visitor, and called on her old friend when he was convalescing in the spring of 1929 at Craigwell House, the home of the founder of the Dunlop Rubber Company, Sir Arthur du Cros, at Bognor (later Bognor Regis). As Alice Keppel had done, Agnes was not averse to using her friendship with the king to promote her relatives; in 1935 she urged the king to 'give Sir John Simon [Foreign Secretary] a little poke . . . to find a better place for my nephew Sir Rowland Sperling'.[8]

Because of declining health, her increased age and the threat of enemy bombing, Agnes Keyser left London to live at Buckland House, Faringdon, Oxfordshire (then in Berkshire), the home of Lady Amelia Fitzgerald, daughter of the old Keyser family friend H.L. Bischoffsheim. Lady Fitzgerald had married Sir Maurice Fitzgerald, 20th Knight of Kerry, in 1882; he became equerry to King Edward VII's brother Prince Arthur, Duke of Connaught. Buckland House had developed from a thirteenth-century manor owned by a succession of Chaucers, Brandons and Throckmortons. During 1755–9 John Woods built a new mansion for the Roman Catholic squire Sir Robert Throckmorton as a hunting lodge and holiday home, and the whole estate was bought by the Fitzgeralds in 1909 when it became the scene of lavish Edwardian house parties at which the Keysers were regular visitors.

Agnes Keyser died at Buckland House on 11 May 1941 of myocardial degeneration, attended at the last by one of her own nurses, the now retired Sister Lilian Thomas. Following the granting of probate to her nephew Sir Rowland Sperling and her nieces Muriel Agnes and Sybil Violet Keyser, Agnes's will was declared at a gross value of £68,272.[9] To the hospital she left the leasehold to her properties at 17 Grosvenor Crescent and 12 Wilton Crescent Mews, along with the sum of £25,000 and the residue of her estate.

As with Alice Keppel's will, Agnes Keyser's, after a wide range of small bequests to friends, relatives, former domestic staff and nurses, gave evidence of her royal connections. To Queen Mary she left two tables from her dining-room at 16 Grosvenor Crescent; to Princess Mary (the Princess Royal) she left her 'Elephant' cigarette lighter which King Edward VII had given her; and to Henry, Duke of Gloucester, she left the original picture 'The Three of Us' by Miss E.A. Drage. To Florence, Lady de la Rue, went the gold purse gifted to her by King George and Queen Mary and the gold cup given by Edward VII.

To the family lawyer friend Sir Bernard Halsey-Bircham went an engraving of the actress Sarah Siddons as well as a silver cigarette box given by King George and Queen Mary; Francis Garford Brenton received the autographed engraving of King Edward and his brother the Duke of Connaught given to her by the king at the height of their friendship.

Herein too were bequeathed mementoes of the conversations she had had with King Edward. At her rooms he had talked with her about his latest successes on the turf. She gave to Sir Harold Wernher the silver cigarette box bearing the picture of 'Persimmon': the horse had won the Derby in 1896. To Sir Harold also went the photograph of the king and 'Minoru'; in the last year of the king's life 'Minoru' won the Derby to rapturous public adulation as the king led the horse back to the unsaddling area. And there were those who recounted to Agnes with glee a story that the king had shown more recognition of his horses on his death-bed than he had of Alice Keppel. As he slipped in and out of a coma the Prince of Wales had informed his father that his horse 'Witch of the Air' had won the Spring Two-Year-Old Plate at Kempton Park. 'I am very glad', the king had remarked before he lapsed into his final coma.[10]

CHAPTER 14

'QUEEN OF FLORENCE';
'EMPRESS OF THE RITZ'

During the early 1920s, Alice and George Keppel were increasingly away from 16 Grosvenor Street, letting their house by the season. In 1921 it was taken by the widow of the American steel-magnate James Corrigan, Laura Mae Corrigan from Cleveland, Ohio. When agreeing terms, Mrs Corrigan surveyed Alice Keppel's magnificent collection of antique furniture and carpets with the disparaging, 'Why, they're not even new'. She dismissed Alice's fine Chippendale chairs as being spoiled by the covering of '*petits pois*'.[1] Yet with Alice Keppel came a platinum social cachet and Mrs Corrigan paid Alice an extra premium to leave behind her guest list.[2] In her drive for acceptance among London Society Laura Corrigan was assisted by Alice's butler Rolfe, who went with the lease: he encouraged Alice Keppel's friends to call.

Whereas Violet had been taken with France from childhood, Alice was more enamoured of Italy. In 1924 she assigned the lease of 16 Grosvenor Street to Captain Gerard Leigh – who had previously been her neighbour at No. 17 – and put forward plans to live permanently in Italy with the Tuscan city of Florence as the prime real-estate target.[3]

Queen Victoria had been the catalyst in the encouragement of wealthy Britons to seek out Florence, the capital of Tuscany, standing on the Arno river some 145 miles north-west of Rome. Here they were to indulge in the cultural refinement that had given Italy its language, its arts and its philosophy, for their health and recreation. As the *British Medical Journal* (1894) was to opine:

The preference which the Queen has shown for Florence as a place of spring residence, and the benefit which Her Majesty is understood to have derived from her sojourns there, will serve to increase the popularity of the beautiful Tuscan city, with the large and growing class who follow the wise custom of taking an early spring holiday.

Victoria made three visits to Florence, her royal coach tacked on to a transcontinental train, in 1889, 1893 and 1894. She travelled under the totally unconvincingly pseudonym of Madame la Comtesse de Balmoral. The queen had an entourage of some eighty people, including courtiers and Highland and Indian servants – whom the Florentines thought were princes – as well as her long-suffering companion, her youngest daughter Princess Beatrice, the soon-to-be widowed wife of Henry, Prince of Battenberg, and her private secretary Sir Henry Ponsonby who was her link with her ministers back home. For the 1889 and 1893 trips Victoria stayed at the Villa Palmieri, lent by Margaret, Countess of Crawford and Balcarres, who caused the villa to be redecorated and a new water supply and telephone fitted for the queen's visit. For the 1894 jaunt Victoria stayed at the Villa Fabricotti, in the Via Vittorio Emmanuele.

The writer Iris Origo, granddaughter of the Irish peer Baron Desart of Desart Court, who married the Italian Marchese Antonio Origo in 1924, had spent much of her childhood at the Villa Medici on the southern slopes of the Fiesole Hill, above Florence. She was to paint an interesting pen portrait of the expatriate Florentine society into which Alice now merged. Just as she had been a skilled player of the Edwardian era, Alice was to be a central figure of Anglo–Florentine life in that long-gone expatriate Italy.

Iris Origo described the various 'colonies' of expats of several nations, who dwelt in and around Florence. The largest and most prosperous group were of British extraction. The focal points of Anglo–Florentine life, averred Iris Origo, were Vieusseux's Circulating Library, the Tennis Club at the Cascine, the Anglican

Holy Trinity Church in Via La Mormora, Maquay's Bank in the Via Tornabuoni, Miss Penrose's school and the Anglo-American stores in the Via Cavour.[4] But there was much, much more. Alice was to delight in the company of the Bright Young Things who congregated at the smart Doney's, noted for its chocolate and caviare, or Procacci's with its mouthwatering *panini*. Not much taken with matters intellectual – unless it was for her own advantage – Alice eschewed the British Institute (set up by Lina Waterfield in 1917), preferring the causerie of the Casa dei Bombolini in the Via del Corso. With its smartest shops, the Via Tornabuoni was the centre of Florentine gossip, and until she had established her position in Florence, she was to be seen gossiping at the jeweller Parenti's and patronising Gucci (then a small family leatherworkers) in the Via della Vigna.

The Anglo-Florentines transformed their homes, be they villas or palaces, into little bits of fashionable British Society. Osbert Sitwell, who was to visit the Keppels many times, noted that Alice's Tuscan home translated the splendour of her Grosvenor Street house to the hills over Florence.[5]

In 1925 Alice purchased from the Russian Countess Maria Zubow the Villa dell'Ombrellino, on the hill known as Bellosguardo ('beautiful view'). Funded by the money her royal lover had left for her through Ernest Cassel Alice was to make the Ombrellino, as everyone called it, the centre for the next fifteen years for the 'International Set' of writers, artists, diplomats, gamblers, upper-class ne'er-do-wells and dysfunctionals, and those whose only merit was their wealth and status in Society. With its glorious panoramas over Florence, the Ombrellino was set in the 1372 estate of Bartollo de Pace, and Violet averred that local tradition had it that it had been lived in by such as the Italian scientist Galileo Galilei (1564–1642).[6] In due time Alice was to landscape the spacious garden terraces, with their guardian groups of statues. Iris Origo remarked that Alice was one who introduced a bit of England into her garden. On one occasion Iris Origo observed Alice prodding her gardener with her parasol and uttering the words *Bisogna begonia* ('I must have begonias') repeatedly, then gesturing to where the begonias should be placed. 'The next time we called, the begonias were there – as luxuriant and trim as in the beds of Sandringham,' said Iris. It seems, too, that Alice never evinced a need to acquire any further words in Italian.[7]

At the Ombrellino the gardenias and azaleas, too, festooned terraces which rang to the laughter and witty conversation of Europe's most prominent, and sometimes most decadent, socialites. Here Alice's old friend Winston Churchill painted and there was hardly a week went by when the Keppels were in residence that European royalty were not guests, from Princess Helen of Greece and Denmark, second wife of the Hohenzollern King of Romania, Carol II, to Prince Paul of Yugoslavia who was to be Regent 1934–41. The exaltedness of her guest list made Alice 'Queen of Florence' visitors said, but when the Sitwells dined at Ombrellino in May 1930, Osbert was constrained to comment, 'She was [arrogantly] conscious of a role she had to play.'[8]

Alice remained a generous hostess dispensing hangover cures from Robert's British Pharmacy (the *Profumeria Inglese*) and Oxford marmalade from Signor Carlo and the best of everything her vast funds could buy. It was her custom to invite to Ombrellino any girls whose families she knew and heard about being 'finished' in Florence. Elizabeth Sutherland was a young teenager in Florence at Mrs L'Estrange's finishing school in the Via Fosco during 1937–8 and remembers being entertained to tea wherein Alice was 'jolly company'.[9]

Many saw the Ombrellino as an extension of Alice's personality and a unique blend of English taste and what were best in Florentine décor. Her grace and her vitality, even into her eighties, was played out against a setting that underlined the close links the city of the Medicis had always had with Anglo-Saxon society.

Alice included in her soirées members of the distinguished Florentine families, the Rucellai, the Rocasoli, the Serristori and the Guidi, most of whom spoke the grammatically correct English that betrayed the accents of their governesses' origins. Several, too, had English-born mothers who all became Alice's neighbours and acquaintances, such as Count Neri Capponi's mother, Elnyth Arbuthnot, and the mother of Baroness Constanza Ricasoli (née Romanelli).[10]

Alice came and went to the Ombrellino as the seasons changed and as polite Society migrated to various parts of the continent and London. A favourite destination for Alice was still Egypt, and in 1928 she was a guest at the British Residency at Cairo of Sir Edward Marsh, who worked for Chancellor of the Exchequer Winston Churchill at the Treasury. Marsh remembered Alice sparkling with anecdotes at the dinner table; one such amused him greatly. It appears that a friend of Alice's had had her portrait painted by the cubist pioneer Pablo Picasso. She had packed it and was attempting to take it in her luggage to France. Alice explained that at the Franco-Spanish frontier the friend had been told she could not enter. On asking indignantly why not she was told: 'How can we let you into France when you've got a plan of the fortifications of Madrid in your luggage?'[11]

At the Ombrellino George Keppel continued his separate life in his own suite of rooms, known as the 'Colonel's Wing'. He spent time compiling lists of useful notes about Florence for visitors exploring the local galleries, and taking tea with pretty young women. He called the girls his 'little cuties' and was to be seen regularly taking tea at Doney's on the Via Tornabuoni wearing his panama hat and two-toned footwear (dubbed 'co-respondent's shoes'), while persuading the girls to take a spin in his red Lancia sports car to the Ombrellino for a dip in the pool. The girls knew that he wanted them to pose nude for him while he took their picture. Kinta Beevor who spent her childhood in Tuscany and knew well the Florence of the 1930s recalled that George had a photographic studio in the city to which he tried to persuade the 'cuties' to go with him for photo sessions, noting with humour that the studio was 'rather under-used'.[12]

When Sir Henry 'Chips' Channon (1897–1955) visited 'super-luxurious' Ombrellino in 1935 he observed George's eye for young beauties and called him 'amorous old George'. Sir Harold Acton (1904–94), the historian and aesthete whose family home was at nearby La Pietra, was to describe George as 'every inch a colonel' with a strict primness when required. Acton remembered how shocked George was to discover that Acton's mother, the Chicago-born Hortense, was reading a book by Oscar Wilde (1854–1900). 'A frightful bounder', exploded George. 'It made me puke to look at him.'[13] George kept a certain insouciance when an indiscreet comment about Alice and King Edward VII was made in his presence. His reaction is unrecorded when on one occasion a deaf dowager sitting next to him at dinner said loudly: 'Kep-pel, Kep-pel, how strange you should have the same name as the king's mistress.'

Behind his back George Keppel was sniggered at by the Florentines as il vecchio cornuto ('the old cuckold'), and a gaffe by one of the amateur guides to a house party at Florence was the talk of dinner tables for weeks. Pointing out George at a café table with one of his 'little cuties', the guide remarked that he was L'ultimo amante della regina Victoria ('Queen Victoria's last lover').

Following his affair with the American-born Wallis Warfield Simpson, King Edward VIII abdicated the throne on 10 December 1936 to marry her. Ever since Edward VIII had first met Wallis Simpson – when he was Prince of Wales – through the introduction organised by Thelma, Lady Furness, in mid-January 1931 at Burrough Court, the Furnesses' house at Melton Mowbray, Leicestershire, Society had known a lot more than the general public about the royal affair. Marion Purves remarked that parallels were drawn between the Prince of Wales and Wallis, and his grandfather Edward VII and Alice.[14] A whole raft of 'Mrs Keppel' anecdotes were resuscitated to suit the gossip. One popular one oft told at Anglo-Florentine tables related how Alice and the king had retired to the monarch's cabin after lunch on the royal yacht. Steps were heard down the companionway: 'Pst, there's someone coming,' said the king. To which Alice was overheard by a passing crew-member to reply: 'Well, Sir, it is certainly not Your Majesty.'

Commenting on the Edward and Wallis affair, Alice said over dinner at the Ritz, averred the journalist Janet Flanner, in *Travel and Leisure* magazine: 'Things were done better in my day.' Of all the quotes of Alice herself, the most famous was: 'A royal mistress should curtsey first – then jump into bed.'

During visits to London in the 1930s, Alice kept up acquaintance with the family of Violet's putative father. On 27 July 1936 the diplomat and 'entertainingly scurrilous' Sir Robert Hamilton Bruce Lockhart (1887–1970), noted seeing her at Muriel Beckett's party. Muriel was the wife of the banker and *Yorkshire Post* chairman the Hon. Rupert Evelyn Beckett (1878–1955) – brother of Alice's former lover Lord Grimthorpe; Lockhart commented that Alice was looking 'rather formidable' and turning 'slightly coarse'.[15]

Following the death of her husband Denys in 1929, Violet continued her writing and in the summer of 1936 cruised to Scandinavia and visited Russia and Budapest. In her imaginative autobiography *Don't Look Round* Violet mentions falling in love with Horthy Estvan, the son of Admiral Nikolaus Horthy de Nagybanya, Regent of Hungary 1920–54.[16] Estvan was killed in an aeroplane crash in 1942 and many of Violet's friends dismissed the romantic encounter as one of her fantasies. During the spring of 1937, Violet also mentions in her autobiography, she had an interview with Benito Mussolini at the Palazzo Venezia in Rome; her record of the dialogue between them is somewhat unbelievable.[17] Her renting of the Eiffel Tower for a fancy dress ball to celebrate her forty-third birthday in the same year was more her style.

Alice and George Keppel's sybaritic and racy life in Florence was played out against a tempestuous Italian political scene. In the January of the year Alice bought the Ombrellino, Mussolini formed his Cabinet composed entirely of Fascists.

In the 1920s and 1930s he introduced some reforms that were intended to improve order and reduce unemployment. Yet the price of 'making the trains run on time' was total control over government and daily life, suppression of opposition, press censorship, prison camps and secret police. Still his conquest of Ethiopia in 1935–6 and his meeting with Hitler in 1938 in Florence 3–9 May 1938, to emphasise the Rome–Berlin Axis, caused not a ripple of alarm across the gin-and-tonics served at the Ombrellino. The bridge and baccarat parties continued and the champagne was still flowing when the Second World War broke out on 3 September 1939.

When German pressure caused the Italians to enter the war on 10 June 1940, the British Consulate in Florence did its best to repatriate all UK expatriates who wished to go. At the time Violet was in Paris ostensibly working for the Red Cross. She escaped from the French capital in the company of her friend Princesse Gilone de Chimay. She received a reply to her flurry of telegrams to her mother that Alice and George had closed up the Ombrellino and were at the Hôtel de Paris, Monte Carlo. At last Violet met up with her parents at Dax, near Bayonne, and all together they travelled to Saint-Jean-de-Luz to board a Royal Navy troopship for Britain.

Alice was soon in touch with her friends, and Nancy, Viscountess Astor – the first woman to take her seat in the House of Commons – regaled Society with news of Alice's arrival in Britain. Already in a letter to Philip Kerr, 11th Marquis of Lothian, on 2 July 1940 she had said that Alice had arrived at Plymouth 'looking like a disturbed blancmange'.[18]

In Italy Alice had been social 'Queen of Florence', now she was to be 'Empress of the Ritz'. Alice had patronised the Ritz from the early days of its opening by César Ritz in 1906. Regularly she had swept into the east entrance in Arlington Street with the king and had walked elegantly through the expectant crowds in the Circular Vestibule and the Grand Gallery to the monarch's favourite Marie Antoinette Room where Sir Ernest Cassel had been their regular host. Churchill, de Gaulle and Eisenhower were to meet in the same room.

So here Alice installed herself for the duration of the war in the

Keppel family suite overlooking Green Park with its views of Buckingham Palace where she had once been a prize jewel. During the Second World War, the Ritz was to be a fashionable watering-hole for those who were still rich and influential. The regulars at the Ritz – the basement bar being known as 'homosexual' in its clientele and the upper bar 'heterosexual' – were to be Alice's visitors throughout the rest of her life at the Ombrellino. Although rampantly heterosexual herself, and disapproving of Violet's public display of lesbian preferences, Alice did have a penchant for male homosexuals for their wit and eccentricities. One of the reasons why many did not approve of her parties in Florence was the presence of a large number of those of ambiguous sexuality.

Because of its steel frame the Ritz was deemed a 'safe shelter' from the German air raids, with floors six and seven closed as a hedge against bomb damage to lower floors. With the fall of France – the country had capitulated to Hitler's National Socialists on 22 June 1940 – there was a flood of European royalty aristocracy and politicians at the Ritz, with the Albanian royal family perhaps the most celebrated. King Zog, who had ruled Albania since 1928, was forced into exile with his half-American wife Queen Geraldine and their infant son Crown Prince Leka; they inhabited the Ritz's third floor for a while.

The Keppels lived a comfortable life at the Ritz under the care of manager Eduard Schwenter, and the chef M. Avigon who did wonders with a penny's-worth of meat per guest and a government ceiling of 5 shillings for a three-course lunch. Laura, Duchess of Marlborough remembered 'inter-table jealousy in the Restaurant' when guests complained if they believed that their fellows were getting larger portions.[19] Ever gregarious Alice was not against lunching at such pubs as the Blue Posts (opposite the Ritz) with Violet's friend the cookery writer Robin McDouall, when she found out that the food was better there.

Many people remembered Alice at the wartime Ritz and her being 'a game old bird ready for anything'. Anita Leslie recalled her uncle Seymour Leslie talking to Alice in the air-raid shelter at the

Ritz. 'An old lady, white-haired and *soignée*, she sat bolt upright, her back straight as when she poured tea for King Edward, and, as the Nazi bombs smashed London, over the face of Alice Keppel, that face which had never shown scorn to any human creature, there crept an expression of utter contempt.'[20] James Lees-Milne, the architectural writer, who used to stay with Violet at the Ombrellino, remembers seeing Alice 'wandering white-faced and like a ghost, always long cigarette holder in hand, along the corridors and in the dining room of the Ritz Hotel'.[21]

Sir Henry 'Chips' Channon met Alice several times during the war and he jotted down the encounters in his diary.[22] He saw an ageing Alice who kept her youthful spirit alive, but her conversation became a succession of inventions and deliberate lies, he noted, to give the impression that she was at the heart of things. She spoke of the war leaders as if she were an intimate friend, advising them on politics and strategy as she had done when her royal lover was alive. Almost every sentence began with 'Winston [Churchill] says . . .' or, 'Archie [Sir Archibald Sinclair, Secretary of State for Air and later Viscount Thurso] told me . . .'. She also drank too much and became loquacious; sometimes it led to confusion in her conversation and it was difficult to judge on which world war she was giving her opinions. She smoked too many of her favourite cigarettes from the Ramadan Tobacco Co. in Piccadilly and suffered much from the London fogs. A trip to Bournemouth and the Palace Court Hotel with her beloved brother Archie eased her lungs somewhat, yet the thought of the Ombrellino being pillaged depressed her and she became obsessively worried about money.

For a while Violet stayed with her parents at the Ritz and was much disliked by the staff. After dining with one of London's best-known Society hostesses Emerald – really Maud – Lady Cunard, Violet mislaid her luggage and had made a fuss with the Ritz porterage. One night porter was overheard (also by Violet) to say: 'Well, we've 'ad V1 [German flying bomb], we've 'ad V2, we've 'eard of VD, but in my opinion VT is the worst of the lot!'[23]

In 1941 Violet rented the Manor House at West Coker, Yeovil, Somerset, near to her old friend Dorothy Walker-Heneage, and there she kept open house for her parents, Scottish Edmonstones and any of her friends who cared to call. Whenever she was in residence at the Manor House Alice was made much fuss of by local folk but she missed the facilities of the Ritz and never settled to country living.

There were trips too for Violet to stay with her sister Sonia at Hall Place, West Meon, Hampshire with Alice and George, and forays to acquaintances over the south of England. On one occasion Alice visited Francis Underwood, Bishop of Bath and Wells, in his quaint moated palace. At one moment there seems to have been a lull in the conversation. Alice remembering her royal lover's dislike of conversational vacuums at table was always ready to stir causerie and asked the bishop about his favourite books. The clergyman replied that he liked nothing better than to be at ease on a sofa with 'my favourite Trollope'.[24] Alice repeated that remark at many a dinner table thereafter.

There were to be resumed meetings for Violet and Vita Sackville-West. For years Vita had actively avoided Violet, dreading that her friends might invite her and Harold to an engagement where Violet would also be a guest. Vita did agree to Violet's invitation to meet alone for lunch at the Red Lion Hotel, Pulborough, Sussex, on 15 December 1940. Subsequently she told Violet that she did not want to fall in love with her again or to disturb or complicate her life. One day, out of the blue, Violet telephoned Vita at Sissinghurst. Her call unsettled Vita, afraid that Violet would pressure her to recommence the affair. There was to be no resumption of their relationship; Violet called off a planned visit but did go on 12 May 1943. Vita found the call discomfiting and somewhat illusionary and was glad when Violet left. They were to meet again only sporadically until Vita's death. In 1948 Vita stayed with Violet at La Tour de Saint-Loup on her way home from Africa, and in June of the same year met her for tea at the Ritz, where she pronounced Violet desolate and wretched at her parents' deaths. In 1949 Violet and Vita were in Paris together, meeting as Vita made her way to lecture in Spain for the British Council. Again there was a trip to Saint-Loup and Violet made Vita the unexpected offer of St Loup in her will; Vita turned it down. In fact Violet was to use legacies as emotional weapons to her friends and relatives for some years and was to leave a succession of tortuous wills. In 1950 Vita lunched with Violet at the Ritz and they went off to the theatre to see *Gigi*. That year Violet was with Vita and Harold at the Ombrellino and had lunch with Harold Acton. They were to meet for the last time in 1953, and in 1957 Vita wrote Violet a sort of expiatory letter about their love affair.

Romantically Violet had not caused her mother further social anguish. Alice was not alarmed at Violet's relationship with Winnaretta de Polignac, or later with Betty Richards (Mrs William Batten); neither had created a public scandal that impinged on Alice. People did gossip about Violet and her various affairs with women and supposed flings with prominent men but no social damage was done. Violet was to do some broadcasting in London to occupied France for the BBC, and before she returned to France she accompanied Alice on what was to be her mother's last personal contact with British royal circles.

During the Second World War, Queen Mary spent some time at Badminton House, Gloucestershire, as a guest of her niece the Duchess of Beaufort – elder daughter of the queen's eldest brother 'Prince Dolly', the 2nd Duke of Teck (Lord Cambridge) – and there she received Alice and Violet. On the quiet Queen Mary had rather liked Alice Keppel but kept her feelings to herself as the king was still 'embarrassed' at his father's dalliance with 'Little Mrs George'. Nevertheless he had been persuaded to agree to send the wedding gift of a brooch to Violet, but since the queen had been displeased with Violet's 'disreputable behaviour', during the audience she totally ignored Violet. Yet as they were leaving and Violet curtseyed to the queen the self-obsessed Violet noted that the queen had mentioned her fine deportment.[25]

On the liberation of Paris on 25 August 1944 when General Leclerc's 4th Armoured Division forced General Choltitz to surrender, Violet prepared for a triumphant return and Alice began her plan to take up residence again at the Ombrellino.

The return was not going to be easy; the war had caused all kinds of financial problems and many of Alice's assets were still frozen. While she fussed about tax and currency restrictions she found time to dine with old friends and make a trip to Mount Stewart, Newtownards, County Down, to see the Marchioness of Londonderry and relive happier days. She longed to be meeting her friends again at Doney's and remarked to Harold Acton that if the Ombrellino proved inhabitable she would ask (Marchesa) Lulie Torrigiani to house them.[26] She was heartened, too, by hearing from Major Hamish Erskine, who had just returned from Florence, that the Ombrellino had been spared the ravages of war even down to her Chinese pagodas being intact. With a riposte that was pure Alice she noted that those had been the 'common pagodas'; the ones given to her by her royal lover had already been secreted elsewhere.[27]

Christmas of 1945 was spent at the Ritz and then Alice went to Violet's house at Saint-Loup in spring 1946. It was to be her last trip to France. For most of her life Violet had been a friend of Lady Diana Manners who had married Alfred Duff Cooper the same year that Violet had married Denys. Cooper was now British Ambassador to France and Alice lunched with him and Diana before a last visit to her old friends the de Beisteguis at their château at Groussay, near Paris.

Alice was now nearly eighty and her health was causing some concern, so she now spent a little time at the Hôtel Splendide Royal et Excelsior, Aix-les-Bains for the 'cure'. It was, as she knew herself, a waste of time for a London specialist had diagnosed cirrhosis of the liver and a poor long-term prognosis. Her increased drinking had not helped her condition. Alice knew that what she had was terminal but refused to give up her buoyant attitude to life although she was still worried about her cash flow. Yet when a friend asked her how she looked forward to being an octogenarian, she replied that eighty was a 'dull age'; yet ninety was 'rather chic. So I shall start counting from ninety.'[28]

By September 1946 Alice had surveyed what needed to be done at the Ombrellino and set in motion plans to refurbish her garden, obtain a new car, repair the house's water system and restore the whole property to its pre-war style. While the work was being done she went back to the Ritz. She also spent some time with Sonia at Hall Place where her worries were added to by the deterioration of Sonia's marriage. By spring 1947 she was back at the Ombrellino.

When the Second World War broke out and the Italians threw in their lot with the Germans, several of the older British residents of Florence refused to leave. After all, one told Alice, their home was no longer in Britain, they had become Anglo-Tuscans. Another to remain was Miss Gladys Elliott who recalled Alice Keppel very well. Speaking in 1994 the nonagenarian remarked:

> She was naturally kind and understanding and strange to say I personally received a proof of that kindness at Holy Trinity Church, at a service after the last war – when the Allies had left. I, as the last Church Warden . . . sat in the Consular Diplomatic Pew in the front row. It happened that Mrs Keppel and her party attended the service and came and sat in the front row on the opposite side of the aisle. When the service ended we all stood while the priest left the altar; when he had gone I remained standing to allow her to precede. To my great surprise she came over the aisle to me and putting her hand on my arm led me down the aisle with her, while she said so kindly – 'My dear, I hope they were not unkind to you' – for she knew we were amongst 'those who stayed behind'. Her words were such comfort, after having received various 'snubs' from those who did not understand [why I had stayed].[29]

When she was in residence at the Ombrellino, Alice Keppel

attended the Anglican services first at Holy Trinity, Florence, and then, when that church was given to the Waldensians, St Mark's. Alice's presence at Holy Trinity was a potential cause of some embarrassment to Canon Archibald Augustus Knollys, who had married his cousin the Hon. Constance Knollys (sister of Queen Alexandra's woman-of-the-bedchamber, the Hon. Charlotte Knollys). Knollys was chaplain of Holy Trinity during 1896–1931 and had known Alice in the old days as royal mistress and many in the congregation thought that he would snub her, after all Queen Alexandra was Knollys's daughter Alexandra's godmother. On the first occasion Alice and Knollys met after all those years, Alice thanked him for a 'beautiful service' and he greeted her with courtly charm. Gladys Elliott commented, however: 'He advised his young assistant chaplain not to accept any invitation to her parties, for they were also gaming parties and quite beyond his possibilities financially.'[30]

As 1947 developed, Alice's health deteriorated. She spent more and more time in bed. Violet and George read to her, fed her gossip and were in constant attention. She died on 11 September 1947 aged seventy-nine. Alice was laid to rest at the Protestant cemetery of I Allori, Florence.

George Keppel was bereft at Alice's passing. To relieve him of painful duties Alice's death was registered by the chaplain at St Mark's, Via Maggio, the Revd F.J. Bailey; the certificate was authenticated by the Consul, H.L. Greenleaves. George had loved Alice in his own way for the fifty-six years of their marriage, despite her cuckolding of him and the underlying social humiliation. The romantic idea of death from a broken heart, the fate of fictional lovers throughout history, is by no means limited to the realm of fantasy; and there were those who said that this was George Keppel's fate.

Violet and George went back to London after Alice's funeral and George developed pneumonia. While he lay ill in what was to be his death-bed at the Ritz, Violet carried on a bizarre conversation with writer Richard Buckle as she flitted in and out of the bedroom to see if her father was still alive. Only Violet could have discussed her ideas for a ballet in which the main character was the Loch Ness Monster as her father expired.[31]

George Keppel died on 22 November 1947 and was buried with Alice at I Allori. He was to be remembered as a kindly man, exquisitely mannered, and as the anonymous obituarist of *The Times* pointed out, his empathy with the young gave him a 'strange quality of agelessness'.[32]

'The English watched their last Edwardian bastion crumble, a fortress of good spirits, with an optimistic bent for intrigue and cynicism', wrote Jacques Dumaine, France's Chef de Protocole, of Alice's demise in Florence, as her executors began to dismantle the financial fortress she had put together with her royal lover's help. Alice Keppel's last will of 28 June 1941, and its two codicils, left in Great Britain alone an estate worth £177,637.[33] She also had an 'Italian will' for her Tuscan property and there were funds too to be gathered in North America, all based on the financial plan worked out for her by Sir Ernest Cassel.

Sonia and Violet received substantial financial provision and there were portions for her brother Archie Edmonstone, and an annuity of £100 to secure a comfortable retirement for her maid Ethel Williams. Violet was to have use of the Ombrellino for her lifetime whence it was to pass to Sonia and her heirs. The contents of the Ombrellino – Alice's lavish and expensive furnishings – were dispersed at Sonia's insistence and Violet had to refurnish the large villa; it was not until 1955 that she completed this memorial to her mother.

Violet now lived at the Ombrellino, La Tour de Saint-Loup par Longueville, Seine et Marne, and eventually in 1958 in a *pied-à-terre* at rue de Cherche-Midi, Paris, usually spending April–May and September–October in Florence. She became a prominent and eccentric member of the *gratin* (France's wealthy).

As she grew older Violet had little to do with her Keppel relatives and less with the Edmonstones of Duntreath. Violet and Sonia were not pleased that their cousin Sir Archibald had

Duntreath Castle reduced to a quarter of its former size in the 1950s. Violet's relationship with her sister Sonia developed into mutual indifference, although Violet did visit Sonia's well-run house in Hampshire. During August 1963 Violet made her last trip to Scotland with sojourns at Wemyss Castle, Fife, and Dalmeny House, West Lothian; Duntreath was not included. During this year, too, Violet broke her leg at Saint-Loup and developed a greater dependence on friends John Nova Phillips and Frank Trelawny Arthur Ashton-Gwatkin. As time passed Violet spent more time at the Ombrellino; every week she gave luncheon parties for her friends which were looked upon by some with great foreboding; Violet's mood was never predictable.

In 1966 Violet's thoughts turned to Scotland again, and during October of that year Florence and Edinburgh became twin cities, and Violet gave a lunch at the Ombrellino which the Lord Provost of Edinburgh, Sir Duncan Weatherstone, attended as well as Christopher Pirey-Gordon the British Consul-General. In the official pictures Violet posed with due hauteur draped in a scarf of Royal Stuart tartan.

Author Joan Haslip remembered Violet's last few painful and lonely boudoir-incarcerated months, as she slowly descended into incapacity.[34] She had developed a stomach infection around September 1971 which made it almost impossible for her to eat. She became emaciated. The end came for Violet on Wednesday, 1 March 1972. After a funeral service at Florence and cremation, Violet's ashes were buried at her final request in the vault of her parents at I Allori. There were memorial services in Paris and Florence.[35]

In her will of 26 April 1971, Violet apportioned her £18,665 cash estate in legacies to friends. With a last flourish of morbid romance she had requested that her heart be removed at death and placed 'in a casket in the Grange aux Dimes, Saint-Loup de Naud'. In the event a portion of her ashes were scattered at Saint-Loup. This property she left to John Phillips and the apartment at rue de Cherche-Midi was sold by her nurse (who fell heiress to it), to

Andy Warhol.[36] The Ombrellino was sold by Sonia and it underwent several subsequent commercial roles.

Sonia Rosemary Keppel had become Mrs Roland Calvert Cubitt in 1920. She was divorced in 1947, the year of her parents' death, shortly before her husband became the 3rd Baron Ashcombe (1899–1962). Most of Sonia's life was spent at her house at Hall Place, East Meon, near Petersfield, Hampshire, where she had gone to live around 1935, and at her home in Hyde Park Gardens, London, where she followed her mother's role as a fashionable hostess. As well as her autobiography, Sonia wrote a novel called *Sister of the Sun* (1932) which was reviewed as an 'unadmiring' assessment of Victorian and Edwardian society. She died on 2 August 1986.[37]

The passing of Alice Keppel and Agnes Keyser was a reminder that the last vestiges of the Edwardian era were fast slipping away. They had been part of a court that was the zenith of the Age of Royal Romance and the era when sexuality was an upper-class sport and adultery was an aristocratic art form. Their days were the age of the kept high-class courtesans, whose broughams, phaetons and landaus could be seen in London's Hyde Park, several emblazoned with the heraldry of their aristocratic lovers. Alice Keppel was the last of the royal courtesans of the old school, and both she and Agnes lived through the vogues of the Prince of Wales and the Marlborough House Set where sinning was done with style.

Alice and Agnes were to benefit from a personal royal patronage that is gone for ever and were confidantes at the time when the royal mistress had changed roles. In the past many of the great mistresses of European royalty had been women of the middle class made *grandes dames* with titles and estates to support them. In Alice's and Agnes's day, this role had reversed. Their sovereign entered their realm of privacy and discretion and enjoyed the 'homeliness' of their private houses.

What was different, too, was that Alice and Agnes were accepted as a good influence on Edward VII. Even though the power of the monarch was circumscribed at this time, the king's temper was uncertain and his patience very thin. His strongly held opinions on certain matters of foreign policy and domestic politics cholerically expressed could cause Cabinets to resign. Diplomatist Lord Hardinge was not the only one to express deep gratitude to Alice in bringing a certain official point of view to the king expressed in a way to head off his ire. And Agnes as a practical adviser and watchdog on his health helped ensure that his declining condition did not spark off erratic behaviour with his ministers.

The story of Alice Keppel and Agnes Keyser at the court of King Edward VII is one of unusual friendship and romance. It is likely that no other woman ever really understood his character and personality as they did. And no other woman could turn the often bored, aggressive, immature, impatient, selfish and rude monarch into the affectionate, genial, tolerant and witty sovereign his people came to love and respect. Without Alice and Agnes, Edward's declining years would have been intolerable.

NOTES

INTRODUCTION

1. The service, to which Queen Mary had sent a representative, was conducted by the Revd K.H. Thorneycroft, assisted by the Venerable C.E. Lambert, Archdeacon of Hampstead, and the Revd E.C.W. Rusted.
2. *The Times*. Obituary references: 13 September 1947 [4f]; 15 September [7e/7x]; 18 September [7b]; 20 September [6e].
3. Pless, Daisy, Princess of. *From My Private Diary*, John Murray, 1931, and in conversation.
4. Sitwell, Osbert. *Great Morning*, Vol. III of *Left Hand, Right Hand: An Autobiography*, Macmillan, 1948, pp. 217–18.
5. Brook-Shepherd, Gordon. *Uncle of Europe: The Social and Diplomatic Life of Edward VII*, Collins, 1975, p. 64.
6. Lees-Milne, James. *The Enigmatic Edwardian: The Life of Reginald, 2nd Viscount Esher*, Sidgwick & Jackson, 1986, p. 206.
7. Bell, Anne Oliver, (ed.). *The Diary of Virginia Woolf*, Hogarth Press, 1982, pp. 80–1.
8. Royal Archives, CC/7/32; CC/3/29; CC/7/68.
9. Alice, Princess, Countess of Athlone. *For My Grandchildren*, Evans, 1966, pp. 124–5.
10. Sitwell, Osbert. *Rat Week*, Michael Joseph, 1986, p. 37.
11. Lambert, Angela. *1939: The Last Season of Peace*, Weidenfeld & Nicolson, 1989, p. 165.
12. Sackville-West, Vita. *The Edwardians*, Hogarth Press, 1930, p. 204.
13. Purves Papers: unbound leaves, jottings, notes, letters collected by Marion Purves.
14. *The Times*, 15 May 1941 [7d].
15. *Historical Record, 1899–1986: King Edward VII's Hospital for Officers*, 1986, p. 6. This record was completed by Lieutenant-Colonel C.I. Shepherd from documents collated by Sir George Ogilvie.

CHAPTER 1

1. London Stock Exchange Records, Manuscripts Section, Guildhall Library, London, MS 17957/51 [vol. for 1852]. Robert Lubbock & Co. later merged with Coutts & Co.
2. Jullian, Philippe. *Edward and the Edwardians*, Sidgwick & Jackson, 1967, p. 13.

3. Magnus, Philip. *Edward VII*, John Murray, 1964, p. 21.

4. St Aubyn, Giles. *Edward VII: Prince and King*, Collins, 1979, pp. 50–3.

5. Hibbert, Christopher. *Edward VII: A Portrait*, Allen Lane, 1976, p. 85.

6. Royal Archives, Z/463/72.

7. Edmonstone of Duntreath, Sir Archibald. *Genealogical Account of the Family of Edmonstone of Duntreath*, 1875.

8. Smith, John G. *Parish of Strathblane*, Glasgow, 1884, p. 74.

9. *Complete Baronetage*, Vol. V, London, 1906, pp. 170–1.

10. *O'Byrne's Naval Biography*, 1861, p. 353.

11. McNair, Robert. *Doctor's Progress*, London, 1933, pp. 33–9.

12. Froude, J.A. *Rectorial Address*, [St Andrews], 1869.

13. Trefusis, Violet. *Don't Look Round*, Hutchinson, 1952, p. 24.

14. Keppel, Sonia. *Edwardian Daughter*, Hamish Hamilton, 1958. p. 24.

15. Trefusis, op. cit., p. 17.

16. Keppel, op. cit., p. 49.

17. Ibid.

18. West, Rebecca. *1900*, Weidenfeld & Nicolson, 1982. p. 151.

19. Keppel, op. cit., p. 49.

20. Ibid.

21. Ibid., p. 47.

22. Purves Papers.

23. Keppel, op. cit., p. 47.

24. Ibid., pp. 49–50. Majuba Hill, Transvaal: during the South African War it witnessed a Boer victory over the British.

25. Keppel, op. cit., p. 48.

26. Trefusis, op. cit., p. 21.

27. Ibid., p. 24.

CHAPTER 2

1. Obituaries: *The Times*, 24 May 1929; *Reading Mercury*, 25 May 1929.

2. Keppel, op. cit., p. 47.

3. Purves Papers; Trefusis, op. cit., pp. 25–7.

4. Cornwallis-West, George. *Edwardian Hey-Days*, Putnam, 1930, p. 5.

5. Airlie, Mabell, Countess of. *Thatched with Gold*, Hutchinson, 1962, p. 34.

6. Matriculation Records, Christ Church, Oxford.

7. Trefusis, op. cit., p. 27. Despite Archie Edmonstone's 'wincing', George Keppel made him a present of Purdey guns on marrying Alice.

8. J. Arthur Muir, building contractor, Blanefield, in correspondence with the author, 1993.

9. Trevelyan, G.M. *Grey of Fallodon*, London, 1943, p. 7.

10. Confirmed by Lady McGrigor, in conversation with the author; Trefusis, op. cit., p. 28.

11. Confirmed as above; ibid.

12. Ibid., p. 106.

13. Keppel, op. cit., p. 11.

14. Bonham-Carter, Violet. BBC Sound Archives, 24 May 1948.

15. Anita Leslie in conversation with the author.

16. Trefusis, op. cit., p. 16.

17. Tweedsmuir, Susan. *The Lilac and the Rose*, London, 1952, p. 109.

18. Airlie, op. cit., p. 40.

19. Balfour, Lady Frances. *Ne Obliviscaris*, London, 1930, p. 55.

CHAPTER 3

1. Purves Papers.
2. Trefusis, op. cit., p. 35.
3. Gibbs, Vicary. *The Complete Peerage*, St Catherine's Press, 1910, pp. 91–6.
4. Keppel, op. cit., p. 124.
5. Sandhurst Military Records.
6. Marriage Records, St Paul's Church, Knightsbridge, London, 1 June 1891, entry 75.
7. Trefusis, op. cit., p. 20; Purves Papers.
8. West, op. cit., p. 151.
9. Balsan, Consuelo Vanderbilt [Duchess of Marlborough]. *The Glitter and the Gold*, Heinemann, 1953, p. 120.
10. Obituary: *The Times*, 24 November 1947 [4g].
11. Balsan, op. cit., p. 120.
12. Purves Papers.
13. Marginalia: 'Quidenham Park Book', Albemarle Archives. Norwich Record Office.
14. Marriage records: *vide* note 6.
15. Keppel, op. cit., p. 4.
16. Purves Papers.
17. Dalton, B.J. 'Sir George Grey and the Keppel Affair', *Historical Studies* [Australia], 1974, 16[63], pp. 192–215.
18. Trefusis, op. cit., pp. 37–9.
19. Keppel, op. cit., p. 122.
20. *Daily Mirror*, 18 October 1909.
21. Keppel, op. cit., p. 123.
22. Quidenham Hall, and its immediate policies, were sold in 1948 by the Earl of Albemarle to the Carmelite Order and were developed as the nunnery of Our Lady of Mount Carmel. A list of George Keppel's 'bolt-holes' and the pattern of his solo visits to friends can be built up from the Albemarle Archives (*vide* note 13), p. 150–1.

CHAPTER 4

1. Data extracted from the records of Westminster City Libraries and those of Grosvenor Estate Holdings.
2. Purves Papers. Daisy, Princess of Pless (op. cit.) also has some inferences in this connection.
3. McLeod, Kirsty. *A Passion for Friendship: Sibyl Colefax and her Circle*, Michael Joseph, 1991, p. 22.
4. Balsan, op. cit., p. 74.
5. Purves Papers. Even among the Albemarles Violet was considered only 'an honorary Keppel' as John Phillips points out in 'The Last Edwardians', a catalogue prepared for an exhibition at The Boston Atheneum, 1985, p. 58.
6. Trefusis, op. cit., p. 16.
7. Ibid., p. 18.
8. Ibid., p. 38.
9. Ibid., pp. 28–31.
10. Hart-Davis, Rupert. *Hugh Walpole*, Macmillan, 1952, pp. 34–5.
11. Ibid., p. 35.
12. Ibid., p. 36.
13. Trefusis, op. cit., pp. 34–7.
14. *Balsan, Consuelo Vanderbilt. The Glitter and the Gold*, Heinemann, 1953, p. ???.
15. Keppel, op. cit., p. 30.
16. Ibid., p. 29.
17. Balsan, op. cit., p. 120.

CHAPTER 5

1. De Stoeckel, Baroness. *Not All Vanity*, John Murray, 1950, p. 67.
2. Leslie, Anita. *Edwardians in Love*, Hutchinson, 1972, pp. 229–30. It may be noted that Victoria, Lady Sackville-West, mother of Violet Keppel's lover Vita Sackville-West, averred that Alice met the Prince of Wales for the first time at the house of Georgina, Countess Howe, the daughter of the Duke of Marlborough, and wife of Richard Penn Curzon, 4th Earl Howe, who was lord-in-waiting to the Prince of Wales as king 1901–3, thence Queen Alexandra's chamberlain. The assertion is not substantiated elsewhere.
3. Murphy, Sophia. *The Duchess of Devonshire's Ball*, Sidgwick & Jackson, 1984. Guest List.
4. Purves Papers.
5. Keppel, op. cit., p. 28.
6. Candidates' Book, 1898. St James's Club Records, Greater London Record Office and History Library. Financial difficulties led the club to be merged with Boodles in 1975.
7. Purves Papers.
8. Asquith, Margot. *More Memories*, Cassell, 1933.
9. Bell, op. cit., pp. 80–1.
10. Sackville-West, op. cit.
11. Hibbert, *Edward VII*, p. 213.
12. Beddington, Mrs Claude. *All That I Have Met*, Cassell, 1929, p. 46.
13. Hutchins, Chris and Thompson, Peter. *Diana's Nightmare*, Simon & Schuster, 1993, p. 54.
14. Langtry, Lillie. *The Days I Knew*, Hutchinson, 1925, p. 46.
15. Balsan, op. cit., p. 120.
16. *The Life of Edith, Marchioness of Londonderry*, Sinclair-Stevenson, 1992, p. 105.
17. Purves Papers.
18. De Rothschild, Mrs James. *The Rothschilds at Waddesdon Manor*, London, 1979, pp. 60–4.
19. Brook-Shepherd, op. cit., pp. 143–5. Quoting a letter in the Soveral Papers.
20. Pless, op. cit.

CHAPTER 6

1. Both Agnes and Fanny Keyser were awarded the Royal Red Cross Medal on 9 August 1901; Agnes for her hospital's work, Fanny for her nursing services in South Africa. Awarded by the sovereign, the medal was instituted in 1883 and its badge forms a cross of gold with red enamel. Agnes was always proud to use its membership letters 'RRC' after her name. On her death she bequeathed this and her other honours to her hospital. Alice Keppel received the award of the British Red Cross Society (BRCS) for her voluntary work in France in the First World War.

   On 26 February 1901 Agnes Keyser was admitted to the Most Venerable Order of the Hospital of St John of Jerusalem as a Lady of Grace. The Order had been founded in the early twelfth century as a religious order in Jerusalem with the particular remit of caring for the sick. Henry VIII had dissolved the Order in 1540, but it had been revived in the early nineteenth century and its modern tradition led to the founding of the St John Ambulance Association in 1877. A royal charter was granted in 1888 to establish the British Order of St John as a British Order of Chivalry with the sovereign at its head.

2. *Historical Record, 1899–1986: King Edward VII's Hospital for Officers*, op. cit. NB: the Royal College of Nursing was founded in 1916, but neither Agnes nor Fanny Keyser became a member. The statutory registration of nurses was introduced in 1920.

3. Gray, Sheila. *The South African War 1899–1902: Service Records of British and Colonial Women*, Uniprint, 1993.

4. Wolferton is some eight miles north of King's Lynn off the A149. The station now houses a museum on the downside (arrival) platform. The waiting-room and lavatories have been preserved in their original style.

5. *Sandringham*, guidebook, Estate Office, Sandringham, 1991, p. 3.

6. Sandwich Papers.

7. Keppel, op. cit., p. 3.

8. Lamont-Brown, Raymond. *Royal Murder Mysteries*, Weidenfeld & Nicolson, 1990, p. 3.

9. *Kelly's Directory of Dorset*, 1898, p. 202. Devonshire House still exists as a part of a fine, low-windowed, early nineteenth-century terrace at the Esplanade's southern end, converted to hotels and guest houses.

10. The author is indebted to Mr John Phillips, Switzerland, for a sight of the original wording of the telegram.

11. Purves Papers.

12. Keppel, op. cit., p. 3.

13. Anne Edwards comments thus in *Matriarch: Queen Mary and the House of Windsor*, Hodder & Stoughton, 1984, p. 101: 'On the day of Sonia's birth, the road outside the Keppel house was smothered in straw to deaden the sounds of the traffic. After the child's birth, orchids, malmaisons and lilies – great beribboned baskets of them – were delivered by a coachman and attendant in the Prince of Wales's livery.'

14. Violet maintained for the whole of her life the self-delusion that she was of royal birth. Cecil Beaton remembered how, while watching with her friends the state funeral of Sir Winston Churchill in 1965, Violet punctuated the viewing with such comments as 'There's cousin Lilibet [the queen] . . .' and so on. Hugo Vickers, in correspondence with the author.

15. Stephenson, John (ed.). *A Royal Correspondence*, Macmillan, 1938. Van der Kiste, John. *Edward VII's Children*, Alan Sutton, 1989.

16. Sonia's comments were to cause some distress among the Sturts. Mary Anne Marten in correspondence with the author, 1993.

17. Keppel, op. cit., p. 22.
18. Rose, Kenneth. *Kings, Queens and Courtiers*, Weidenfeld & Nicolson, 1985, p. 138.
19. Purves Papers.
20. Keppel, op. cit., p. 15.
21. Nicolson, Nigel. *Portrait of a Marriage*, Weidenfeld & Nicolson, 1973, p. 27.
22. Purves Papers.
23. Pope-Hennessy, James. *Queen Mary*, Allen & Unwin, 1959, p. 361.
24. Blunt, Wilfrid Scawen 'Secret Diary', MS6, 28/3/1901. The original mss are held at the Fitzwilliam Museum, Cambridge.
25. Curzon, Mary. *Lady Curzon's India: Letters of a Vicereine*, ed. John Bradley, Weidenfeld & Nicolson, 1985, 11 September 1901. Wilson, Christopher. *A Greater Love: Charles and Camilla*, Headline, 1994, p. 18.
26. Hough, Richard. *Edward & Alexandra*, Hodder & Stoughton, 1992, p. 219.
27. Brook-Shepherd, op. cit., p. 140.
28. Mensdorff Papers.
29. Jullian, op. cit., p. 228.
30. Purves Papers.
31. Magnus, op. cit., p. 340.
32. De Stoeckel, op. cit., pp. 68–70.

CHAPTER 7

1. Blunt, Wilfrid Scawen. 'My Diaries 1881–1914', in holograph mss 1919–20.
2. Allfrey, Anthony. *Edward VII and his Jewish Court*, Weidenfeld & Nicolson, 1991, p. 193.
3. Ibid., p. 13.
4. Ibid., p. 268.
5. Keppel, op. cit., p. 201.
6. Sharpe, Henrietta. *A Solitary Woman*, Constable, 1981, p. 174.
7. Soveral Papers, quoted by Brook-Shepherd, op. cit., p. 139.
8. Sharpe, op. cit., p. 22.
9. Alice had considerable foreign funds in mining and transport. In South African stock she held shares in the British South Africa Co. and the Transvaal Diamond Mining Co. In marine stocks she held Royal Mail Steam Packet Co. shares. And in railway debentures and stock Cassel had advised her to invest in the Chicago–St Louis and New Orleans, the Baltimore and Ohio, the Illinois Central, and the Great Northern. She also held stock in the Cordoba Central and the Argentine Great Western railways. Executors' Inventory, probate application, William Easton & Sons, solicitors, March 1948.
10. Sotheby's, *Objets de Vitrine from the Collection of Mrs George Keppel*, catalogue, Geneva, 1989. Maundy Money is a gift distributed to 'the poor' by the reigning sovereign every year on the Thursday before Easter. It is a symbol of the former practice when the sovereign washed the feet of the poor as did Our Lord. The number of sets distributed is the same as the monarch's age; thus in 1916 fifty-one sets were distributed to men and fifty-one to women. Commemorative sets of Maundy

Money were distributed to dignitaries attending the particular service. In 1916 the Maundy Service took place at Westminster Abbey on 20 April in the presence of Queen Alexandra and the princesses Victoria and Beatrice.

11. Bainbridge, Henry C. *Peter Carl Fabergé*, Spring Books, 1949.
12. Jullian, op. cit., p. 205.
13. Papers of Sir Ernest Cassel, Broadlands, Hampshire.
14. Allfrey, op. cit., p. 247.
15. Purves Papers.

CHAPTER 8

1. Churchill Archives.
2. Alice, Princess, op. cit., p. 124.
3. Keppel, op. cit., pp. 22–3.
4. The visitors' book at Melbury shows annual visits by the Keppels, with Sonia remaining a regular guest long after her parents' deaths.
5. Curzon, Mary, op. cit., p. 130.
6. Keppel, op. cit., p. 33.
7. Correspondence between the author and Earl Howe, 1993.
8. Brett, Maurice. *Journals and Letters of Reginald Esher*, London, 1934; under 12 June 1910.
9. Purves Papers.
10. Antrim, Lady Louisa. *Louisa, Lady in Waiting*, ed. Elizabeth Longford, Jonathan Cape, 1979, p. 97.
11. Lee, Sir Sidney. *King Edward VII*, Vol. II, Macmillan, 1927, p. 106.
12. Ponsonby, Sir Frederick. *Recollections of Three Reigns*, Eyre & Spottiswoode, 1957, p. 152.

13. Gilbert, Martin. *Winston Churchill*, Vol. II, Heinemann, 1969, p. 175.

CHAPTER 9

1. *Historical Record King Edward VII's Hospital for Officers, 1899–1986*, op. cit.
2. Astor Papers: William Waldorf, 1st Viscount Astor to Amy Richardson, 11 January 1909.
3. Hibbert, Christopher. *The Court of St James's*, Weidenfeld & Nicolson, 1979, p. 56.
4. Purves Papers.
5. Bulow, Bernhard von. *Denkwurdigkeiten*, Vol. II, Berlin 1930–1, p. 189.
6. Ibid., Vol. I, p. 261; Vol. II, p. 248.
7. Mensdorff Papers.
8. Hardinge, Charles Hardinge, Baron. *Old Diplomacy*, John Murray, 1947.
9. Aslet, Charles. *The Lost Country Houses*, Yale University Press, 1982, p. 68.
10. Rowland, Peter. *Lloyd George*, Barrie & Jenkins, 1975, p. 207.
11. Jullian, Philippe and Phillips, John. *Violet Trefusis: Life and Letters*, Hamish Hamilton, 1976, p. 11.
12. Asquith, H.H. *Letters to Venetia Stanley*, Oxford University Press, 1982, Letter 125, p. 178.
13. Bennett, Daphne. *Margot: A life of the Countess of Asquith and Oxford*, Gollancz, 1984, p. 376.
14. Purves Papers.
15. Records: Portman Family Settled Estates.
16. Keppel, op. cit., p. 45.

17. Nicolson, op. cit., p. 74.
18. Trefusis, op. cit., p. 41. Nicolson, op. cit., p. 25.
19. Ibid., p. 27.
20. *Stirling Saturday Observer*, 11 September and 18 September 1909.

CHAPTER 10

1. Purves Papers. Magnus, op. cit., p. 338 also refers to the superstition, citing an occasion concerning the pregnant Princess Frederick-Charles of Hesse.
2. Fildes, L.V. *Luke Fildes*, Michael Joseph, 1968, pp. 191–2.
3. Vincent, John, (ed.). *The Crawford Papers*, Manchester University Press, 1984, 19 May 1936, p. 750.
4. Purves Papers.
5. Blunt Papers, ms 10, 13 May 1910.
6. Soveral Papers.
7. Lee, op. cit., Vol. II, p. 709.
8. Reid, Michaela. *Ask Sir James*, Hodder & Stoughton, 1987, pp. 440–3. Anita Leslie, correspondence with the author, 1984.
9. Redesdale, Lord. *King Edward VII*, London, 1915, pp. 32–3.
10. Lees-Milne, op. cit., p. 206. Writing to the author (1995), Sir Steven Runciman noted court gossip that the queen would not allow Alice Keppel to enter the king's bedroom until *after* he had died. Sir Steven's father (Sir Walter Runciman, a member of Asquith's Cabinet 1908) attested that the king and queen had quarrelled over his going to Biarritz with Alice when he was so ill. In high dudgeon the queen set off cruising to Corfu with her daughter Princess Victoria. When she was told of her husband's deterioration she was in Venice, not planning to return immediately. At length she was persuaded of the seriousness of the king's illness and returned just in time to see him alive.
11. Reid, op. cit., p. 241.
12. Blunt Papers (*vide* note 5).
13. Keppel, op. cit., p. 53. Sonia was very aware of the sombre change in their home at the king's death. She wrote: 'A pall of darkness hung over the house. Blinds were drawn, lights were dimmed, and black clothes appeared, even for me, with black ribbons threaded through my underclothes.'
14. Ibid., p. 54.
15. Blunt, (*vide* note 5).
16. Purves Papers.
17. Ibid.
18. Albemarle Archives, Norwich Record Office.
19. Reid, op. cit., p. 243.
20. Purves Papers.
21. Royal Archives, RA PP3/42/31.

CHAPTER 11

1. *Historical Record, 1899–1986, King Edward VII's Hospital for Officers*, op cit.
2. Battiscombe, Georgina. *Queen Alexandra*, Constable, 1969, p. 71.
3. Trefusis, op. cit., pp. 56–9; Keppel, op. cit., pp. 57–60.
4. Keppel, op. cit., pp. 62–3.
5. Trefusis, op. cit., p. 60.

6. Ibid., p. 75. Violet was enrolled during 1916–18, and Sonia from 1916. (Records Office, University College London).

7. Mosley, Leonard. *Curzon: The End of an Epoch*. Longman, 1960, p. 143.

8. Keppel, op. cit., p. 74.

9. Data extracted from records of Grosvenor Estate Holdings.

10. Purves Papers.

11. Keppel, op. cit., pp. 83–4.

12. Purves Papers.

13. Jullian, op. cit., p. 211.

14. Keppel, op. cit., p. 87.

15. Ibid., p. 115.

16. Correspondence between the author and Sir Reresby Sitwell.

17. Pearson, John. *Façades: Edith, Osbert and Sacheverell Sitwell*, John Murray, 1978, p. 77.

18. Ibid., p. 35.

19. Hassall, Christopher. *Edward Marsh: Patron of the Arts*, Longman, 1959, p. 539.

20. Letters: Clementine to Winston Churchill, 19 September 1913, Churchill Archives.

21. Ibid., 22 April 1914.

22. Soames, Mary. *Clementine Churchill*, Cassell, 1979, p. 97.

23. Asquith, Margot. *The Autobiography of Margot Asquith*, ed. Mark Bonham Carter, Eyre & Spottiswoode, 1962, p. 279.

24. Trefusis, op. cit., p. 72. This may have been a little romancing on Violet's part. Sonia – Keppel, op. cit., p. 103 – remembered that her father went to his club and she with Violet and Alice breakfasted at the Ritz.

25. See note 1.

26. Wilson, Lady Sarah. *South African Memories*, Arnold, 1909.

27. Letter, 3 February 1915, CHAR/1/111/34, Churchill Archives.

28. Sharpe, op. cit., p. 39.

29. H.H. Asquith. op. cit., Letter 312 to Venetia Stanley, 18 February 1915.

30. Ibid., Letter 420.

31. Ibid., Letter to Venetia Stanley.

32. Ibid., Letter 337.

33. Edwards, op. cit., p. 245.

34. Keppel, op. cit., pp. 119–21.

35. Ibid., p. 128.

36. Letters: Clementine to Winston Churchill, 4 April 1916, CHAR/1/118A/1123–4, Churchill Archives.

37. Purves Papers.

38. Keppel, op. cit., p. 133ff.

39. Sitwell, Osbert. *Laughter in the Next Room*, Vol. IV of *Left Hand, Right Hand: An Autobiography*, Macmillan, 1949, p. 109.

40. Curzon, Marchioness of. *Reminiscences*, Hutchinson, 1955, pp. 37 and 59.

41. Keppel, op. cit., pp. 142–3.

42. Purves Papers.

43. Keppel, op. cit., p. 155.

44. Ibid., p. 163.

45. Asquith, Lady Cynthia. *Diaries, 1915–18*, Hutchinson, 1968, p. 34.

CHAPTER 12

1. Purves Papers.

2. Harold Acton in conversation; his sentiments on Violet he repeated many times in many places to many people.

3. McLeod, op. cit., p. 115.
4. Trefusis, op. cit., pp. 18–19. On Vita's death on 2 June 1962, Harold Nicolson returned the ring to Violet.
5. Vita Sackville-West's autobiography within Nigel Nicolson's *Portrait of a Marriage*, op. cit., p. 28.
6. Ibid., p. 30.
7. Ibid., p. 39.
8. Ibid., p. 41.
9. Vita Sackville-West was to begin an account of her affair with Violet Keppel, the torment of it and her wish to expiate its pain, on 23 June 1920. After her death in 1962 that account was found in a locked Gladstone bag by her son Nigel Nicolson and formed the basis of his book *Portrait of a Marriage*.
10. Purves Papers; Sharpe, op. cit., p. 22.
11. Purves Papers.
12. Ibid.
13. Nicolson, Nigel. *Vita and Harold*, Weidenfeld & Nicolson, 1992, p. 97.
14. Purves Papers.
15. Keppel, op. cit., p. 183.
16. Ibid., p. 199.
17. CHAR/1/142/26, Churchill Archives.
18. Gilbert, Martin. *Sir Harold Rumbold*, Heinemann, 1973, p. 274.

CHAPTER 13

1. Grosvenor Estate Holdings.
2. *Historical Record, 1899–1986: King Edward VII's Hospital for Officers*, op cit.
3. Royal Archives, RA GV AA49/3.
4. Royal Archives, RA George V Diaries.
5. Rose, Kenneth. *King George V*, Weidenfeld & Nicolson, 1983, pp. 91–2.
6. Goodman, Jean, in collaboration with Sir Iain Moncrieffe of that Ilk, Bt. *Debrett's Royal Scotland*, Debrett/Webb & Bower, 1983, p. 200.
7. Rose, *George V*, p. 305.
8. Royal Archives, RA GV AA49/204.
9. Extracted by Bircham & Co., 8 August 1941, from the Principal Probate Registry.
10. Magnus, op. cit., p. 558.

CHAPTER 14

1. McLeod, op. cit., p. 86.
2. Brandon, Ruth. *The Dollar Princess*, Weidenfeld & Nicolson, 1980, p. 143.
3. Details from Grosvenor Estate Holdings archives.
4. Origo, Iris. *Images and Shadows*, John Murray, 1970, pp. 127–8.
5. Sitwell, Osbert. *Tales My Father Taught Me*, Hutchinson, 1960, p. 104.
6. Trefusis, Violet. Lecture for the Conferenza sulla Villa Ombrellino alla Soc. Leonardo Da Vinci, Florence, 24 May 1961.
7. Origo, op. cit., pp. 127–8.
8. Sitwell, Osbert. *Tales*, p. 119.
9. Elizabeth, Countess of Sutherland in correspondence with the author, 1994.
10. Nancy Pearson in correspondence, via Bishop Eric Devenport, to the author, 1994.

11. Hassall, op. cit., p. 539.
12. Beevor, Kinta. *A Tuscan Childhood*, Penguin 1995, pp. 147–8.
13. Acton, Harold. *More Memoirs of an Aesthete*, Methuen, 1970, p. 66.
14. Purves Papers.
15. Young, Kenneth (ed.). *The Diaries of Sir Robert Bruce Lockhart*, Vol. 1, *1915–38*, Macmillan, 1973, p. 350.
16. Trefusis, op. cit., pp. 132–3.
17. Ibid., pp. 124–30.
18. Sykes, Christopher. *Nancy: The Life of Lady Astor*, Collins, 1972, p. 421.
19. Montgomery-Massingberd, Hugh and Watkin, David. *The Ritz*, Aurum Press, 1989, p. 110.
20. Leslie, op. cit., p. 231.
21. James Lees-Milne in correspondence with the author, 1993.
22. James, Robert Rhodes (ed.). *Chips: The Diaries of Sir Henry Channon*, Weidenfeld & Nicolson, 1967, p. 264.
23. Montgomery-Massingberd and Watkin, op. cit., p. 117.
24. Trefusis, op. cit., p. 174.
25. Jullian and Phillips, op. cit., p. 108.
26. Acton, op. cit., p. 183.
27. Trefusis, op. cit., p. 183.
28. Brook-Shepherd, op. cit., p. 60.
29. Correspondence between the author and the Rt Revd R.J. Satterthwaite, 1994.
30. Ibid.
31. Montgomery-Massingberd and Watkin, op. cit., p. 125.
32. Obituaries: *The Times*, 24 November 1947 [4g]; 25 November [6f]; 3 December 1947 [7b].
33. Principal Probate Registry, extracted by William Easton & Sons, solicitors, 11 September 1947.
34. Correspondence between the author and Joan Haslip, 1994.
35. Obituaries, *The Times*, 2 March 1972 [16h]; 7 March 1972 [16g]; 9 March 1972 [16g].
36. Jullian and Phillips, op. cit., p. 138.
37. Obituaries, *Daily Telegraph*, 19 August 1986, p. 8.

BIBLIOGRAPHY

Acton, Harold. *More Memoirs of an Aesthete*, Methuen, 1970.

Airlie, Mabell, Countess of. *Thatched with Gold*, Hutchinson, 1962.

Alice, Princess, Countess of Athlone. *For My Grandchildren*, Evans, 1966.

Allfrey, Anthony. *Edward VII and his Jewish Court*, Weidenfeld & Nicolson, 1991.

Antrim, Lady Louisa. *Louisa, Lady in Waiting*, ed. Elizabeth Longford, Jonathan Cape, 1979.

Aronson, Theo. *The King in Love: Edward VII's Mistresses*, Guild, 1988.

Aslet, Charles. *The Lost Country Houses*, Yale University Press, 1982.

Asquith, Cynthia. *Diaries 1915–18*, Hutchinson, 1968.

Asquith, H.H. *Letters to Venetia Stanley*, Oxford University Press, 1982.

Asquith, Margot. *More Memories*, Cassell, 1933.

——. *The Autobiography of Margot Asquith*, ed. Mark Bonham-Carter, Eyre & Spottiswoode, 1962.

Bailey, John. *The Diary of Lady Frederick Cavendish*, John Murray, 1927.

Bainbridge, Henry C. *Peter Carl Fabergé*, Spring Books, 1949.

Balfour, Lady Frances. *Ne Obliviscaris*, London, 1930.

Balsan, Consuelo Vanderbilt. *The Glitter and the Gold*, Heinemann, 1953.

Battiscombe, Georgina. *Queen Alexandra*, Constable, 1969.

Beddington, Mrs Claude. *All That I Have Met*, Cassell, 1929.

Beevor, Kinta. *A Tuscan Childhood*, Penguin, 1995.

Bell, Anne Oliver (ed.). *The Diary of Virginia Woolf*, Hogarth Press, 1982.

Bennett, Daphne. *Margot: A Life of the Countess of Asquith and Oxford*, Gollancz, 1984.

Birkett, Jeremy and Richardson, John. *Lillie Langtry: Her Life in Words and Pictures*, Shuft, 1979.

Blythe, Henry. *The Pocket Venus: A Victorian Scandal*, Weidenfeld & Nicolson, 1966.

Brandon, Ruth. *The Dollar Princess*, Weidenfeld & Nicolson, 1980.

Brett, Maurice. *Journals and Letters of Reginald Esher*, London, 1934.

Brook-Shepherd, Gordon. *Uncle of Europe: The Social and Diplomatic Life of Edward VII*, Collins, 1975.

Brough, James. *The Prince and the Lily*, Hodder & Stoughton, 1975.

Bulow, Bernhard von. *Denkwurdigkeiten*, Berlin, 1930–1.

Channon, Sir Henry, see James, Robert Rhodes (ed.).

Coats, P. *Of Kings and Cabbages*, London, 1984.

Cornwallis-West, George. *Edwardian Hey-Days*, Putnam, 1930.

Cowles, Virginia. *Edward VII and His Circle*, Hamish Hamilton, 1958.

Curzon, Marchioness of. *Reminiscences*, Hutchinson, 1955.

Curzon, Mary. *Lady Curzon's India: Letters of a Vicereine*, ed. John Bradley, Weidenfeld & Nicolson, 1985.

De Rothschild, Mrs James. *The Rothschilds at Waddesdon Manor*, London, 1979.

De Stoeckel, Baroness. *Not All Vanity*, Murray, 1950.

Dempster, Nigel and Evans, Peter. *Behind Palace Doors*, Orion, 1993.

Draper, Alfred. *The Prince of Wales*, New English Library, 1975.

Edmonstone of Duntreath, Sir Archibald. *Genealogical Account of the Family of Edmonstone of Duntreath*, privately printed, 1875.

Edwards, Anne. *Matriarch: Queen Mary and the House of Windsor*, Hodder & Stoughton, 1984.

Fildes, L.V. *Luke Fildes*, Michael Joseph, 1968.

Fitzroy, Sir Almeric William, *Memoirs*, London, 1925.

Froude, J.A. *Rectorial Address*, St Andrews, 1869.

Gibbs, Vicary. *The Complete Peerage*, St Catherine's Press, 1910.

Gilbert, Martin. *Winston Churchill*, Heinemann, 1969.

——. *Sir Harold Rumbold*, Heinemann, 1973.

Glynn, Elinor. *Romantic Adventures*, Nicholson & Watson, 1936.

Goodman, Jean, in collaboration with Sir Iain Moncrieff of that Ilk, Bt. *Debrett's Royal Scotland*, Debrett/Webb & Bower, 1983.

Gray, Sheila. *The South African War 1899–1902: Service Records of British and Colonial Women*, Uniprint, 1993.

Guinness, J. and Guinness, C. *The House of Mitford*, Hutchinson, 1984.

Hardinge, Charles Hardinge, Baron. *Old Diplomacy*, John Murray, 1947.

Hardy, Alan. *The King's Mistresses*, Evans, 1980.

Hart-Davis, Rupert. *Hugh Walpole*, Macmillan, 1952.

Hassall, Christopher. *Edward Marsh: Patron of the Arts*, Longman, 1959.

Hibbert, Christopher. *Edward VII: A Portrait*, Allen Lane, 1976.

——. *The Court of St James's*, Weidenfeld & Nicolson, 1979.

Hough, Richard. *Edward & Alexandra*, Hodder & Stoughton, 1992.

Hutchins, Chris and Thompson, Peter. *Diana's Nightmare*, Simon & Schuster, 1993.

James, Robert Rhodes (ed.). *Chips: The Diaries of Sir Henry Channing*, Weidenfeld & Nicolson, 1967.

Jullian, Philippe. *Edward and the Edwardians*. Sidgwick & Jackson, 1967.

——. and Phillips, John. *Violet Trefusis: Life and Letters*, Hamish Hamilton, 1976.

Keppel, Sonia. *Edwardian Daughter*, Hamish Hamilton, 1958.

Kingsley, Rev. Charles. *Lectures to Ladies on Practical Subjects*, London, 1855.

Lambert, Angela. *Unquiet Souls: The Indian Summer of the British Aristocracy 1880–1918*, Weidenfeld & Nicolson, 1984.

——. *1939: The Last Season of Peace*, Weidenfeld & Nicolson, 1989.

Lamont-Brown, Raymond. *Royal Murder Mysteries*, Weidenfeld & Nicolson, 1990.

Lang, Theo. *My Darling Daisy*, Michael Joseph, 1966.

Langtry, Lillie. *The Days I Knew*, Hutchinson, 1925.

Lee, Sir Sydney. *King Edward VII*, Macmillan, 1927.

Lees-Milne, James. *The Enigmatic Edwardian: The Life of Reginald, 2nd Viscount Esher*, Sidgwick & Jackson, 1986.

Leslie, Anita. *Edwardians in Love*, Hutchinson, 1972.

——. *The Marlborough House Set*, Doubleday, 1972.

McLeod, Kirsty. *A Passion for Friendship: Sibyl Colefax and her Circle*, Michael Joseph, 1991.

McNair, Robert. *Doctor's Progress*, London, 1933.

Magnus (Magnus-Allcroft), Philip. *Edward VII*, John Murray, 1964.

Maurois, André. *Edouard VII et son temps*, Paris, 1932.

Montgomery-Massingberd, Hugh, and Watkin, David. *The Ritz*, Aurum Press, 1989.

Mosley, Leonard. *Curzon: The End of an Epoch*, Longman, 1960.

Murphy, Sophia. *The Duchess of Devonshire's Ball*, Sidgwick & Jackson, 1984.

Nicolson, Nigel. *Portrait of a Marriage*, Weidenfeld & Nicolson, 1973.

——. *Vita and Harold*, Weidenfeld & Nicolson, 1992.

Origo, Iris. *Images and Shadows*, John Murray, 1970.

Pearson, John. *Edward the Rake*, Weidenfeld & Nicolson, 1975.

——. *Façades: Edith, Osbert and Sacheverell Sitwell*, John Murray, 1978.

Pless, Daisy, Princess of. *From My Private Diary*, John Murray, 1931.

Ponsonby, Sir Frederick. *Recollections of Three Reigns*, Eyre & Spottiswoode, 1957.

Pope-Hennessy, James. *Queen May*, Allen & Unwin, 1959.

Quennell, Peter. *Customs and Characters: Contemporary Portraits*, Weidenfeld & Nicolson, 1982.

Redesdale, Lord. *King Edward VII*, London, 1915.

Reid, Michaela. *Ask Sir James*, Hodder & Stoughton, 1987.

Rose, Kenneth. *King George V*, Weidenfeld & Nicolson, 1983.

——. *Kings, Queens and Courtiers*, Weidenfeld & Nicolson, 1985.

Rowland, Peter. *Lloyd George*, Barrie & Jenkins, 1975.

Sackville-West, Vita. *The Edwardians*, Hogarth Press, 1930.

St Aubyn, Giles. *Edward VII: Prince and King*, Collins, 1979.

Sharpe, Henrietta. *A Solitary Woman*, Constable, 1981.

Sitwell, Osbert. *Great Morning*, Vol. III of *Left Hand, Right Hand: An Autobiography*, Macmillan, 1948.

——. *Laughter in the Next Room*, Vo. IV of *Left Hand, Right hand: An Autobiography*, Macmillan, 1949.

——. *Rat Week*, Michael Joseph, 1986.

Smith, John G. *Parish of Strathblane*, Glasgow, 1884.

Soames, Mary. *Clementine Churchill*, Cassell, 1979.

Souhami, Diana. *Mrs Keppel and Her Daughter*, HarperCollins, 1996.

Stephenson, John (ed.). *A Royal Correspondence*, Macmillan, 1938.

Sykes, Christopher. *Nancy: The Life of Lady Astor*, Collins, 1972.

Trefusis, Violet. *Don't Look Round*, Hutchinson, 1952.

Trevelyan, G.M. *Grey of Falloden*, London, 1943.

Tweedsmuir, Susan. *The Lilac and the Rose*, London, 1952.

Van der Kiste, J. *Edward VII's Children*, Sutton, 1989.

Vincent, John, ed. *The Crawford Papers*, Manchester University Press, 1984.

Warwick, Frances, Countess of. *Life's Ebb and Flow*, Hutchinson, 1929.

——. *Afterthoughts*, Cassell, 1931.

West, Rebecca. *1900*, Weidenfeld & Nicolson, 1982.

Wilson, Christopher. *A Greater Love: Charles and Camilla*, Headline, 1994.

Wilson, Lady Sarah. *South African Memories*, Arnold, 1909.

Young, Kenneth (ed.). *The Diaries of Sir Robert Bruce Lockhart*, Macmillan, 1973.

FAMILY PAPERS CONSULTED

Albemarle Papers; Blunt Papers; Cassel Papers; Churchill Papers; Crawford and Balcarres Letters and Papers; Du Cross Papers; Grosvenor Estate Holdings; Mensdorff Papers; Portland Family Settled Estates; Purves Papers; Royal Archives, Windsor; Sandwich Papers; Soveral Papers.

INDEX